Globalization and Labour Relations

Globalization and Labour Relations

Edited by
Peter Leisink
Associate Professor of Labour Studies,
Utrecht University, The Netherlands

Edward Elgar
Cheltenham, UK • Northampton, MA, USA

Published by
Edward Elgar Publishing Limited
Glensanda House
Montpellier Parade
Cheltenham
Glos GL50 1UA
UK

Edward Elgar Publishing, Inc.
6 Market Street
Northampton
Massachusetts 01060
USA

A catalogue record for this book
is available from the British Library

Library of Congress Cataloguing in Publication Data
Globalization and labour relations / edited by Peter Leisink.
   Includes index.
   1. Foreign trade and employment. 2. Industrial relations.
I. Leisink, Peter, 1952–
HD5710.7.G548 1999
331—dc21   99-13584
                                                       CIP

ISBN 1 85898 669 9

Printed and bound in Great Britain by
Biddles Ltd, Guildford and King's Lynn

Contents

List of Tables and Figures

List of Contributors

Leni Beukema is a Lecturer in Labour Studies at the Department of General Social Sciences, at Utrecht University, the Netherlands.

Harry Coenen is Professor of General Social Sciences and Labour Studies at Utrecht University, the Netherlands. He co-edited *Work and Citizenship in the New Europe* (Edward Elgar, 1993).

Paul Du Gay is Lecturer in Sociology at the Open University, UK. Recent publications include: *Consumption and Identity at Work* (Sage, 1996), *Questions of Cultural Identity* (edited with S. Hall, Sage, 1996) and *Production of Culture/Cultures of Production* (edited, Sage, 1997).

Stephen Heycock teaches in the Department of Industrial Technology at the University of Bradford, UK. He co-edited *The Re-design of Working Time: Promise or Threat?* (Sigma, 1989).

Paul Hirst is Professor of Social Theory at Birkbeck College, London, UK. He co-authored *Globalization in Question* (Polity Press, 1996) with Grahame Thompson.

Richard Hyman is Professor of Industrial Relations at the University of Warwick, UK. He is the author of many publications on industrial relations, including the co-edited volumes *Industrial Relations in the New Europe* (Blackwell, 1992) and *New Frontiers in European Industrial Relations* (Blackwell, 1994). He is also the editor of the *European Journal of Industrial Relations* (published by Sage).

Rob Lambert is the Co-ordinator of the Asian Business Program at the University of Western Australia. He edited *State and Labour in New Order Indonesia* (University of Western Australia Press, 1997). Rob Lambert is also the International Officer of the Western Australian Branch of the Australian Council of Trade Unions and the Co-ordinator of a major regional initiative of the new union movement in Australia, Asia and Southern Africa.

Peter Leisink is Associate Professor of Labour Studies at Utrecht University, the Netherlands. He co-edited *Work and Citizenship in the New Europe* (Edward Elgar, 1993) and *The Challenges to Trade Unions in Europe: Innovation or Adaptation* (Edward Elgar, 1996).

Jill Rubery is Professor of Comparative Employment Systems at the Manchester School of Management, UMIST, Manchester, UK. She is also co-ordinator for the EC Network on the Situation of Women in the Labour Market.

Grahame Thompson is Senior Lecturer in Economics at the Open University, UK. He co-authored *Globalization in Question* (Polity Press, 1996) with Paul Hirst.

Jacques Vilrokx is Professor of Industrial Relations at the Vrije Universiteit Brussel, Belgium. He co-edited *The Challenges to Trade Unions in Europe: Innovation or Adaptation* (Edward Elgar, 1996).

Foreword

The Netherlands School of Economic and Social Policy Research held an international conference on *Globalization and the New Inequality* at Utrecht University, the Netherlands, in November 1996. The conference was very successful in providing a state-of-the-art program of papers, and in drawing more than a hundred researchers from various parts of the world. The conference workshop on *Globalization and the Erosion of Organized Class Relationships* attracted much in- terest and the papers sparked off lively debates. This was a strong stimulus to undertake the work of preparing a book on *Globalization and Labour Relations*.

Conference proceedings frequently offer the good with the bad, but in this case the workshop papers were only the starting point of an intellectual project leading to this book. Some expert conference papers were revised to be included in the book. Paul Hirst and Grahame Thompson kindly gave permission to reproduce their article that originally appeared in *Soundings* Issue 4, 1996, as chapter 2 in this book. Most chapters were commissioned specifically to achieve a focused coverage of essential aspects of globalization and labour relations, combining theoretical and empirical issues, and concentrating on different actors and regions throughout the world. There is of course a danger in such an approach because the momentum of the workshop may be lost in the process. In this case the approach chosen proved advantageous, firstly, because it was possible to benefit from the framework of analysis which the conference had inspired, and secondly, because later events have had a significant impact on the analysis and appreciation of globalization and labour relations. To indicate just a few of them:
- the financial crisis in Asia and Russia and its impact on the Western economies influences current ideas on the role of the IMF and World Bank and the regulation of speculative capital;
- the popular protest in Indonesia against the Suharto regime has not reversed the financial and economic crisis but it has restored at least some basic democratic institutions including the right to organize;

– and the open conflict in Australia over a neo-liberal if not authoritarian restructuring of industrial relations has shown that the future of labour relations in an era of increasing global competition does not inevitably lead to further deregulation, polarization and increasing inequalities at the national and, hopefully, also at the global level.

We would like to thank Edward Elgar for the confidence he showed in the quality of our project and the extra time he granted to take account of these recent developments. We appreciate that the publishing sector continues to offer room for a publisher who puts quality over production deadlines. We would also like to thank Dymphna Evans for her understanding and support.

Unfortunately universities in the Netherlands have gone through many changes during the past decade, which have made academic research and teaching more difficult to combine. Therefore, I would like to thank the Labour and Social Participation research group for the freedom I enjoyed to work on this project. Organizational changes in the university have also had an impact on the working conditions of the secretarial staff. Nevertheless, Sabine Jansen was again ready to co-ordinate the entire production process of this book and completed her editorial task even after having moved to another position. We are very grateful to her for doing a dedicated and professional job. We would also like to thank Saskia Kinnegin-van Tessel who assisted in the final stage of the production, and Diederik van Werven who corrected the chapters written by non-native speakers.

In spite of all the support we had, this book may have its defects, for which we accept entire responsibility as a matter of course.

Peter Leisink

1. Introduction

Peter Leisink

National economies are becoming more closely integrated as firms spread their operations and assets across countries. This brings greater economic efficiencies and welfare, as well as more intense competition, greater need for adjustment and more demands on national and international policy. The current challenge for many countries in a situation of low economic growth and high unemployment is to ensure effective adjustment while minimising related international frictions, so that the potential welfare and efficiency gains from globalization are attained.

Organisation for Economic Co-operation and Development, OECD (1996, p. 9)

If labour market regulation were the principal cause of poor labour market performance, then the less regulated settings should show forth a more thoroughly positive than checkered performance. Since checkered it is, we should be suspicious that the problems facing the advanced or high-standard labour markets are just the standards themselves, and we might be right in thinking that the absence or weakness of standards may not solve the problem, but exchange one problem for another.

Campbell, International Labour Office (1998, p. 233)

Introduction

It may be that the flow of publications on globalization has resulted in a clarification of the meaning of the concept, but, as the quotations above illustrate, the difference of opinion about the real and potential effects as well as about the policies which governments and other actors had best pursue, is as big as ever. Thus the OECD promises greater efficiency and welfare as a result of globalization, provided countries ensure effective adjustment by promoting liberalization of trade and investment, by improving the business environment and infrastructure, and upgrading the skills and adaptability of the workforce. One of the measures for improving business competitiveness, which the OECD advises, is the lowering of production costs and prices by removing market imperfections in the supply of production factors including labour. (OECD 1996, p. 56) This represents the line of thought which, in his analysis of orthodox economic theory, Campbell criticizes as an approach that assumes that labour-market interventions largely interfere with and impede efficient adjustments and that all rules work to the detriment of economic growth and job creation. (Campbell 1998, p. 235) These assumptions are unsubstantiated, Campbell argues, discussing some empirical studies which show that high labour standards do not go hand-in-hand with poor economic performance. He concludes that labour standards and good economic performance are complements rather than substitutes.

Where does the difference of opinion come from? One obvious source is the poor knowledge of globalization and its various effects. There is surely a lack of empirical information about the effects of globalization on labour and labour standards. While the OECD publications offer much information about trade and investment, the topic of 'the relations between globalization and employment, particularly regarding restructuring of firms and shifts in their location and associated impacts on employment and human resources' is listed as an area of 'further work'. (OECD 1996, p. 63)

Another source of diverging views derives from the controversial nature of globalization. Since the 1980s globalization has become a neo-liberal project in a pack with free trade, deregulation, privatization, in short: less state and more market. Globalization is advocated because it is thought to bring advantages such as more efficient production, financial discipline in states, cheaper products and services in a greater variety, a global approach to problems of unemployment, and welfare. The neo-liberal view legitimizes globalization on the basis of the value of efficiency. On the other hand critics of this neo-liberal project hold globalization responsible for an uncontrolled concentration of power, an erosion of democracy, increasing social inequalities and ecological destruction. This view criticizes the normative bias towards efficiency and raises other values such as equity.

This brief sketch shows that globalization is a topic of major controversy, which will not be solved here as controversies by definition cannot be. Nevertheless, it is the aim of this volume and its contributors, first, to bring evidence to the debate about globalization and its effects on labour and labour relations. Theoretical and empirical papers will analyse and assess the effects of globalization and, secondly, evaluate the neo-liberal viewpoint of globalization on that basis. This second aim of a critical evaluation will be complemented by an exploration of the beginnings of regulation in a global context.

It is only the beginnings of transnational regulation that can be explored, because not only do states tend to have a narrow understanding of national interest and be reluctant to negotiate a transfer of power to supra-national bodies which are to guide and direct the globalization process (*cf.* Boyer and Drache 1996), but this is also true of trade unions, despite their longstanding ideals of international solidarity. In addition to the different meanings and normative evaluations which the various actors attach to globalization and national interest, another dimension is relevant for the prospect of supra-national regulation. In any social system modes of signifying or meaning constitution and normative sanctions are constitutive structures of that system, but so are power resources. Actors structure their interactions not only in terms of the meaning and the normative evaluation they attribute to their situation, but also by drawing on the resources they can dispose of. (*cf.* Giddens 1984) The relevance of this general observation in this context lies in the fact that the economic recession and neo-liberal political backlash of the 1980s and early 1990s drastically shifted the balance of power between employers and trade unions. Workers and unions were weakened by economic restructuring and high unemployment as indicated by falling union density rates and loss of influence in negotiations and tripartite consultation structures. The effect was that unions had fewer resources to enforce their criticisms of neo-liberal globalization policies *vis-à-vis* employers and the state. Thus, by focusing on globalization and labour relations, this volume intends to examine the effects of globalization on labour both in a descriptive sense, entailing outcomes which can be described in terms of jobs, wages and other aspects of employment conditions, and in an explanatory sense, meaning that labour relations are the indicator of the distribution of power resources which in combination with the signification and legitimation by collective actors explain why particular outcomes, such as the chances of global regulation, are more or less viable.

As an introduction to the topics and questions on which this book focuses, this chapter will first elaborate on our approach to globalization, putting it in perspective as *Triadization* and indicating the broader context of informational capitalism and the different spheres of economy, society and culture which interact in making the globalization process manifest. The sections that follow will deal with the normative claims of efficiency and equity in diverging views on globalization, and the impact of globalization on labour and trade unions, which can be indicated in such concrete terms as employment and wages, or more generally as increasing polarization and inequality. If competition becomes increasingly global what are the prospects of regulation in this global context? The section which tries to answer this question draws on the chapters in this book and focuses on trade-union strategies but will also include social movements, campaigns and opportunities which national states could make use of. The final section will outline the structure of this volume and introduce the chapters and the questions which they examine.

The Approach to Globalization

Various disciplines offer different definitions of globalization[1]. It is beyond the scope of this chapter to discuss them in detail, but it is useful to review a number of definitions with the aim of indicating the domain which this volume will explore.

An economic definition of 'globalization of industry refers to an evolving pattern of cross-border activities of firms involving international investment, trade and collaboration for purposes of product development, production and sourcing, and marketing'. (OECD 1996, p. 9) A political economic definition emphasizes that globalization indicates the changes in the organization and functioning of capitalism, including the emergence of really integrated markets and globalized enterprises and the lagging behind of supra-national institutions. (Went 1996, p. 11) Apart from these general definitions, more specific ones exist. Distinguishing internationalization, as in the case of the OECD definition above, from globalization, Hirst and Thompson (1996) describe a strong version of globalization which involves the development of a new economic structure, in which distinct national economies are subsumed and rearticulated into the global system by international processes and transactions in which transnational firms are the principal actors. Another more specific definition is offered by Ruigrok and Van Tulder (1995), who distinguish between different areas of globalization including finance, competition, technology and regulatory capabilities, and define globalization in the area of firm strategies as the strategy that entails a world-wide intra-firm division of labour (while glocalization refers to a strategy of a geographically concentrated, inter-firm division of labour).

Sociologists explicitly or implicitly distance themselves from an understanding of globalization as only or primarily an economic phenomenon. For instance, Giddens (1990, p. 64) initially defines globalization as 'the intensification of worldwide social relations which link distant localities in such a way that local happenings are shaped by events occurring many miles away and vice versa'. In a later publication he defines globalization more succinctly as 'action at distance' and clarifies: "Globalization does not only concern the creation of large-scale systems, but also the transformation of local, and even personal, contexts of social experience. Our day-to-day happenings are increasingly influenced by events happening on the other side of the world. Conversely, local lifestyle habits have become globally consequential." (Giddens 1994, pp. 4-5) Waters, another sociologist, defines globalization as 'a social process in which the constraints of geography on social and cultural arrangements recede and in which people become increasingly aware that they are receding' and differentiates between the economy, the polity and the sphere of culture. (Waters 1995, chapter 1)

These definitions and distinctions help to outline the domain which this volume explores, of course with relative differences of focus between the chapters. First, there is a substantial interest in the economic aspects of globalization. Several chapters, which adopt different levels of analysis ranging from national economies to sectors and to corporations, explore patterns of international trade, investment and the organization of production to assess the degree and/or type of internationalization *casu quo* globalization. In addition, most chapters that deal with the effects of globalization on labour analyse these effects in terms of segmentation and social stratification, and include (welfare) state policies in their analysis so as to evaluate the broader impact of globalization on society. Finally, the cultural sphere is also present in some chapters, notably in Vilrokx's analysis of the impact which the managerial emphasis on client orientation has on workers' class consciousness, in Du Gay's examination of the globalization-inspired discourse of the 'entrepreneurial self', and in Hyman's analysis of the ongoing project of solidarity, and his proposal to revitalize this through reclaiming topics such as flexibility, employability and opportunity.

From the many studies on globalization a number of general observations can be drawn which are relevant for the approach taken by this volume. First, economic studies have shown that the globalization hypothesis is untenable in terms of both its historical (time) and its geographic (place) dimension. Chapter 2 in this book, contributed by Hirst and Thompson, cogently argues this position. As regards the historical dimension of globalization, Hirst and Thompson (also Ruigrok and Van Tulder 1995, 1995a) point out that most developed countries now, by and large, do not trade more internationally than they did in 1913. This observation puts the globalization debate in its historical perspective. Having said that, one should not fail to appreciate the process of globalization: from the low level of international trade in 1950, the amount of international trade has risen in many countries since (with the exception of Japan) and economies have become more open as average tariffs on industrial products came down from more than 40 per cent in 1947 to 6 per cent in 1994. (World Bank 1995, p. 57)

As regards the geographic dimension of globalization, many publications (for instance Castells 1996; Hirst and Thompson 1996; Nierop 1995; Petrella 1996; Ruigrok and Van Tulder 1995, 1995a; Went 1996) demonstrate that, although there is a process of growing internationalization assessed by indicators such as trade and direct investment, the present state is one of *Triadization*. Economic exchanges and interrelationships involve the three most developed regions of the world: Western Europe, North America, and Japan and the South-East Asian newly industrialized countries. Almost all countries of Africa, most parts of Latin America and Asia, and substantial parts of Eastern Europe and the former Soviet Union are largely excluded from the global economy, as can be demonstrated by their low share in direct investment flows and world trade. The current pattern of economic inclusion and exclusion clearly demonstrates that 'global' is not an adequate characteristic of the actual scope of the capitalist economy. Since corporations are the dominant agents of the world capitalist economy, and since their production and trading activities are directed by profit, the spread of their influence has led to an extension of markets but also to a segmentation which excludes some territories and people, and to ecological destruction. (Korten 1995) In this respect Castells (1996, pp. 102-3) makes an important distinction between on the one hand the actual operation and structure of the global economy, which concerns only segments of economic structures, countries and regions in proportions that vary according to the particular position of a country or region in the international division of labour, and, on the other hand, the direct and indirect impact of the global economy on the livelihood of all mankind.

A second general observation which is relevant for this volume concerns the interrelatedness of the process of globalization and the informational economy. This is one of the fundamental insights from Castells's study of the network society, which can best be explained by a quotation.

A new economy has emerged in the last two decades on a worldwide scale. I call it informational and global to identify its fundamental distinctive features and to emphasize their intertwining. It is *informational* because the productivity and competitiveness of units or agents in this economy (be it firms, regions, or nations) fundamentally depend upon their capacity to generate, process, and apply efficiently knowledge-based information. It is *global* because the core activities of production, consumption, and circulation, as well as their components (capital, labor, raw materials, management, information, technology, markets) are organized on a global scale, either directly or through a network of linkages between economic agents. It is informational *and* global because under the new historical conditions, productivity is generated through and competition is played out in a global network of interaction. (Castells 1996, p. 66)

Some authors (*cf.* Went 1996) mistake the inclusion of information technology in the explanation of the spread of global capitalism as technological determinism, but Castells (1996, p. 81) is explicit in saying that firms are motivated by profitability, and that profitability and competitiveness are the actual determinants of technological innovation and productivity growth. Increasing profitability was what firms looked for in the economic crisis of the 1970s. In the short term, cutting production costs, including those of labour, was one way of increasing profitability, but broadening markets and expanding market share was more attractive. In both these strategies information technologies were essential tools, as well as in others, such as increasing productivity, and longer-term strategies such as organizational decentralization. According to Castells (1996, p. 82) this is at the root of the substantial expansion of trade relative to output and of foreign direct investment. To open up new markets, capital required extreme mobility and firms needed enhanced communication capabilities, and these conditions were provided by the deregulation of markets and new information technologies in close interaction. (Castells 1996, p. 85; for a similar analysis see ILO 1997, pp. 83-4)

The interactive development of an information infrastructure, of a deregulation of markets and a globalization of capital, is directly relevant for a hard core of high-technology firms (such as in microelectronics, microcomputers, telecommunications) and financial corporations. In fact, around this hard core, low-productivity service activities persist and the largest proportion of gross domestic product and employment of most countries continues to depend on activities aimed at the domestic economy rather than at the global market. According to Castells, however, what happens to competition in the global markets of finance, telecommunications and entertainment determines the share of wealth appropriated by firms and ultimately by nations, and that is why the interests of nation states have become directly linked with the competitive performance of 'their' firms, and why states have engaged in strengthening their economies' competitiveness, and in deregulation and privatization (Castells 1996, pp. 85-90). It is also because of the role of governments in fostering their own national interests, and of the firms in their territory, in the global competition, that the international economy is not global in the sense of a fully integrated open world market, but the overall dominant trend points toward the increasing interpenetration of markets. (Castells 1996, pp. 88-106)

Thirdly, studies of globalization have a strong preoccupation with economic indicators – trade, investment, production – and with quantitative effects such as employment numbers and income inequality. Such effects are rarely unmediated, except in explicit business decisions to relocate production. In general, globalization acts in conjunction with a transformation of the organization of production, as Vilrokx contends in chapter 3, including well-known reforms such as lean production, just-in-time management and quality circles. (see also Boyer and Drache 1996; Stokvis 1995) Indeed, in its study of the globalization of industry, the OECD explicitly recognizes as part of the policy implications of its study that businesses need to improve their competitive performance by adopting new organizational methods such as lean production methods, outsourcing of production and services, workforce reorganization and training. (OECD 1996, p. 55) For this book, which focuses on the impact of globalization on labour relations, it is of course important to include the processes that interact with globalization.

In addition, economic studies of globalization but also publications that pay attention to this associated organizational transformation (for instance, Boyer and Drache 1996), show little interest in the cultural dimension and impact of globalization: how people's awareness of globalization, to which Waters' definition refers, is brought about culturally and how the enterprising culture being promoted collides with traditional working class culture, or is assimilated, or results in some kind of *bricolage*. While we have a relatively large amount of information on effects, such as decreasing union density rates, and trade-union responses such as mergers and new financial services to members, less is known about the implications of globalization's cultural redefinition of workers as entrepreneurs for traditional worker values.(Du Gay 1998) As the next section will show, however, the cultural sphere of values and norms is clearly implicated in the globalization of competition and production.

Justifications, Promises and Evidence

When the cultural dimension of viewpoints of globalization is opened up, a difference in explicit reflection emerges between the neo-liberal proponents and their critics. Here we will study on the one hand, the OECD, which analyses globalization as if it were a process that is ultimately justified in itself, while on the other hand World Bank and ILO publications elaborate the grounds for their criticism more reflexively.

In conformity with the positivist philosophy of science, the neo-classical economic paradigm keeps clear of normative statements, including reflection on the normative perspective that is embodied in its theoretical assumptions. Thus the OECD publication on the globalization of industry does not explicitly go beyond normative statements which encourage countries to see to it 'that the potential welfare and efficiency gains from globalization are attained'. (OECD 1996, p. 9) In its analyses the OECD reasons from the intrinsic good of globalization, and from this normative assumption it argues that governments should make efforts to further liberalize international trade and investments, and to reduce trade and non-trade barriers to the international flow of goods and services[2]. Thus, these analyses demonstrate a means to ends thinking, which the sociologist Max Weber called functional rationality, according to which action is increasingly oriented to efficiency as such without reflection on the values of the ends at stake.

In view of its promise that globalization will bring greater welfare, the OECD is aware of the existence of public perceptions that globalization has a negative impact on employment. Referring to other studies, it claims that international trade and foreign direct investments have had a minor impact on employment only and suggests that technological changes have been more important than globalization in reducing demand for low-skilled labour. (OECD 1996, p. 10) This narrow understanding of globalization, as involving international trade and investment only, can also be found in other economic studies. For instance, Van der Zwet (1996) refers to a study by Krugman and Lawrence, which shows that the process of de-industrialization in the US would also have occurred without the effect of international trade, and in her research on Dutch industry along similar lines, she concludes that international trade

has had a positive sales effect and that, therefore, de-industrialization in
the Netherlands is not caused by international trade. However, Van der
Zwet recognizes that firms may have introduced labour-saving technology as a response to increased international competition and that
employment in some sectors such as the shipbuilding and the textile
industry have suffered strongly from competition by low-wage countries. She concludes, however, that businesses would also have invested
in labour-saving technology with a view to domestic competition, and
that, therefore, the loss of employment cannot only be attributed to
international trade caused by globalization. The normative evaluation
implicit in such publications boils down to a reinforcement of positive
associations with the concept of globalization.

The empirical examination and normative evaluation of globalization
which the World Bank offers in its *World Development Report 1995*
differs substantially from the OECD's. This is a remarkable fact in itself,
because in earlier publications the World Bank was highly critical of
labour legislation and regulations as inhibiting the capacity to adjust to
changing circumstances. (*cf.* Plant 1994) To be clear, the World Bank
does not abandon the goal of efficiency but the *World Development
Report 1995* explicitly brings equity into the analysis as well. Upholding
the value of equity requires that governments preserve open trading
relations, because market-based development is considered as the best
way to deliver growth and rising living standards for workers. (World
Bank 1995, p. 3) Starting from the foreword the World Bank emphasizes
that increased integration between countries can benefit workers in poor
and rich countries at the same time, but also that governments have an
important role in helping workers who are adversely affected by changes
in trade patterns and capital flows. This role of governments involves
measures like providing a social safety net, setting the legal and regulatory frameworks within which trade unions and firms can operate,
defining minimum standards and preventing exploitation and discrimination. (World Bank 1995, p. iii) The same balanced approach is
necessary, according to the World Bank to prevent the 'substantial risk
that inequality between rich and poor countries will grow over the
coming decades, while poverty deepens'. This need not take place if
countries preserve open trading relations and strive for high and stable
growth, but 'of even greater importance' are policies that promote
labour-demanding growth and sound labour policy, involving 'using
markets to create opportunities, taking care of those who are vulnerable
or left out, and providing workers with the conditions to make their job

choices freely, bargain over their conditions of work and take advantage of better educational opportunities for their children'. (World Bank 1995, p. 8)

Contrary to the OECD, the World Bank promises not just greater welfare as a result of globalization – this is just one possible outcome – but recognizes that there is also a substantial risk of rising inequality within and between countries. The various outcomes are illustrated by cases of a market-based strategy in conjunction with a particular type of government intervention[3]. In the group of developing countries Colombia, Indonesia, Malaysia and Morocco are mentioned as instances of long-term growth that has gone along with reduced intra-state inequality. However, Chile and Mexico are illustrations of the opposite, and in other countries intra-state inequality increased as well, in particular through job losses by unskilled workers and rising wage inequality. In general, so the World Bank (1995, pp. 43-7) argues on the basis of extensive empirical evidence, three types of inequality have proved particularly difficult to resolve through market forces alone: inequalities between men and women, inequalities between different ethnic and social groups, and inequalities across regions. In these respects governments have a role to play. The implications which the World Bank draws from this analysis are explicitly normative: 'Government policy should, wherever possible, fight discrimination and draw these excluded groups back into the mainstream. But above all, governments should ensure that the children of disadvantaged households do not remain trapped in poverty but instead have the chance to fulfil their potential.' (World Bank 1995, p. 47) Such public interventions the World Bank deems crucial, both to encouraging faster growth and to reducing inequality, thereby again underlining a balance of values.

The differences between rich and poor countries will certainly not disappear rapidly, the World Bank predicts. (World Bank 1995, pp. 53-4) In fact, although some poorer countries especially in East Asia are catching up with the rich countries, overall divergence has been the rule: the ratio of income per capita in the richest countries to that in the poorest increased fivefold between 1870 and 1985.

The values of efficiency and equity, which the World Development Report 1995 advocates, as well as the empirical analysis of the ongoing process of globalization and its effects within and between states, are basic to the World Bank's arguments for public intervention and labour standards. Direct government intervention is considered in order for achieving protection of workers against exploitation. Instances of such standards include a ban on child labour, protection for women, equality of treatment and the setting of minimum standards for wages, social security and health and safety at work. In addition, governments are thought to have an important role in establishing the legal framework for collective bargaining by trade unions and employers, and for the settling of disputes.

From the point of view of equity these interventions are justified because they provide a basis to tackle severe social abuses, for instance in 1991 80 million children were engaged in arduous work that interfered with their development, according to UNICEF (World Bank 1995, p. 72), and to redress the balance of power between employer and workers. From the point of efficiency, however, a neo-liberal type of argument could be raised that these regulations distort the operation of the market and prevent the adjustment to conditions of a more competitive international environment. This latter type of argument has been the topic of a number of publications by the International Institute for Labour Studies of the International Labour Office. (Plant 1994; Sengenberger and Campbell 1994)

The International Labour Organization was set up in 1919 as a tripartite organization in the cause of social justice. The realization of this objective through conventions was as much the subject of debates about the smooth functioning of markets then as it is today; the belief that any country introducing labour standards would raise the cost of labour, and thus impair its competitive position *vis-à-vis* other countries, was the reason for attempts to strive for internationally binding standards. The 1980s surge of neo-liberal policies and, in conjunction, the neo-classical economic paradigm, which are both antithetical to the ILO philosophy by essentially ignoring the value of labour standards as instruments of social justice, more or less forced the ILO to defend labour standards. An interesting feature is that this was done not only by defending labour standards as instruments of social justice, but also by demonstrating their instrumentality in enhancing productive efficiency.

The OECD study of globalization emphasizes the need for adjustment as a condition for attaining the welfare and efficiency gains from globalization. The neo-liberal or neo-classical view likewise stresses the necessity of adjustment as a condition of successful industrial restructuring and considers labour standards as impediments in this respect. Adjustment, among other objectives, entails the promotion of the openness of the economy through trade liberalization and deregulation. *Vis-à-vis* this view, Sengenberger and Campbell (1994) emphasize the conducive role of labour institutions on adjustment and restructuring, and support their view both by an analysis of the arguments concerning the economic rationality of labour standards, and empirical studies on the impact of standards on the restructuring of industries and regions.

The critics who regard labour standards as a distortion of the free operation of market forces, evaluate the effects of standards from the vantage point of individual firms, so Sengenberger (1994, p. 5) argues. However, labour standards are not set to optimize economies at the level of the individual enterprise but rather to prevent the shifting of negative effects on to other firms or on to society. Taking the vantage point of the individual firm implies that one fails to take into account this wider perspective of economic rationality. More importantly, the two approaches to adjustment and restructuring are connected with different views of labour standards. (Sengenberger 1994, pp. 18-32) Where labour standards are absent or of marginal importance, a situation preferred by those taking the view that labour standards are a distortion of the market seen from the point of view of the individual firm, adjustment takes place through concessions in wages and other conditions of employment. However, this type of short-term adjustment through downward-directed wage competition not only results in declining real wages for workers (to the point of creating working poor), but also engenders low productivity growth, a lack of international competitiveness, and a real risk of being locked up in low labour cost production while the exposure to international labour cost competition is intense. On the other hand, a view of labour standards as an enabling framework is a prerequisite to an approach to restructuring that is geared to efficiency enhancement and innovation through better management of resources and better organization of the value-added process. In this view, labour standards contribute to various forms of intra- and inter-firm co-operation, can contribute to developing and utilizing labour (for instance, by organizing training in generic skills based on sharing the costs and the risks collectively), can boost productivity and competitiveness, and facilitate functional and organizational flexibility and innovation. Evidently, the opportunities for this latter approach to labour standards depend on the collectively binding enforcement of the standards.

Thus Sengenberger (also Campbell 1998) shows that labour standards constrain the freedom of firms in some ways, notably by blocking downward-directed competition, but should not be equated with rigidity in general, because they open up and promote other options of adjustment, which are seen as both socially desirable and enhancing the overall performance of the economy. The evidence of empirical studies on the impact of standards on adjustment and restructuring supports this view.

Thus, there are valid arguments to support a regulated approach to globalization in which economic efficiency and social justice are combined. However, the force of argument does not operate in a social vacuum. Interests and power relationships determine which arguments and definitions of the general interest can be included in the dominant vision. (*cf.* Bourdieu 1987) A major disadvantage for arguments supporting the case of social justice is that one of the forces which can mobilize and organize social support for this case, namely the labour movement, has been seriously weakened. The next section will explore globalization's impact on the position of trade unions.

The Impact of Globalization on Labour and Trade Unions

Most OECD countries share the features of the socio-economic situation which Bechterman (1996) describes for Canada: a growing unemployment rate, an increasing proportion of structural unemployment, a growth of new jobs which for an important part are non-standard jobs (such as contract labour, agency work, involuntary self-employment) and an increasingly unequal and polarized distribution of wages since the late 1960s.

Variations in specific aspects exist between the countries. For instance, income inequality started to increase in the Netherlands only from the 1980s, indicating the influence of domestic policy; official unemployment figures decreased to about 5 per cent but unofficial data which include not only the unemployed but also the disabled, workers over 57 years and other categories continued to be about three to four times as high; and a significant proportion of 10 per cent of employment consists of non-stable jobs. The example of the Netherlands is pertinent in this respect, because it is now considered to be one of the more successful economies in the European Union (Leisink 1997; Visser and Hemerijck 1997); in fact, the International Institute for Management Development, a Swiss business school which assesses the competitiveness of economies annually, ranks the Netherlands as the world's fourth and Europe's first most competitive economy. (*de Volkskrant* 22 April 1998)

In the context of this general socio-economic situation specific implications of globalization can be indicated. Thus Bechterman suggests that the creation of the NAFTA regional block has implied for Canadian labour that while the aggregate employment impact in terms of numbers of jobs is likely to be insignificant the actual impact is significantly concentrated in sectors where low Mexican labour costs do matter, and that wage polarization is likely to be intensified with highly skilled Canadian workers best situated to benefit and unskilled labour facing further downward pressure on their wages. (Bechterman 1996, pp. 258-9) Case studies of Japanese car transplants in Canada broaden this picture by giving a more direct insight into the impact of major trans-national corporations on labour: lean production has intensified the work effort, employment security in the long term is doubtful, labour costs are cut by contracting-out or by the introduction of work teams making foremen and supervisors redundant, and two of the three transplants are non-unionized as a result of deliberate management policy. (Drache 1996)

The case of Canada exemplifies many features that fit in with a more general assessment of the impact of globalization on labour and labour relations in the advanced economies, on which the *World Labour Report 1997-98* (ILO 1997) offers much information.

Financial globalization puts constraints on government economic policies in several respects, to say the least, but can also fully destabilize economies as Asia felt in 1997 and Russia in 1998. The sheer capital volume of speculative hedge funds, which the International Monetary Fund estimates at some 400 billion dollars, is more than any central bank's reserves which can be used to maintain the value of the national currency against speculative pressure. International financial markets thus impose a discipline on states, which leads monetary authorities and governments to search for price stability as the principal objective of their monetary and fiscal policies. (ILO 1997, p.10) This also means, the ILO goes on to argue, that macro-economic policies to encourage full employment through counter-cyclical government spending are no lon-ger viable because of the constraints that financial globalization places on states, and thus trade unions, which advocate this type of policy, see their influence weakened. In fact, the objective of price stability leads to policies of austerity which reduce demand and slow down economic growth, which in turn cause a rise in unemployment and a concomitant decline of union membership as well as rising wage inequality. (ILO 1997, pp. 11-13)

Capital mobility not only of speculative but also of industrial capital or at least the possibility of locational choice and the threat of relocation influence state policies and trade unions in other respects. Multinational enterprises have seen their locational freedom increase and are thus in a position to elicit industry-friendly state policies and trade-union restraint. (*cf.* Lane 1995; Marginson and Sisson 1994; Marginson *et al.* 1996) Despite regional policies as in the European Union to guard against unfair inter-state competition, national states are intent on providing fiscal and other incentives in order to attract foreign direct investments, irrespective of whether such measures are effective. (ILO 1997, pp. 70-4) In addition, states attempt to make it attractive for enterprises to locate or to remain in their territory by reducing the burden of bureaucratic regulations, including labour regulations. Apart from direct state initiatives such as introducing a greater extent of labour-market flexibility and reducing direct and indirect labour costs, states have also involved trade unions in their attempts to increase their national comparative advantages. An illustration of this is provided by debates over the issue of strengthening the national economy's position in the global economy, *Standortdebatte* as the Germans call these. Neo-corporatist traditions have in some countries proved helpful in inducing trade unions not only to accept changes in labour regulation but also to initiate policies of wage restraint, themselves a feature which is regarded as one of the reasons for the success of the so-called Dutch *polder-model*. (Visser and Hemerijck 1997) In general, however, governments have favoured a neo-liberal redesign of labour relations without corporatist participation of collective actors involving deregulation, decentralization and curbing labour costs, because it appears less risky than an economic strategy aimed at quality and innovation. (Traxler, Kittel, Lengauer 1997, pp. 800-4)

Wage restraint policies by trade unions are not so much the effect of direct open threats by employers, at least in the European countries, but rather emerge as a result and as a part of broader changes in the cultural and political environment, as instanced by the shift in responses which topics such as uncertainty, solidarity, competition, profit and entrepreneurship evoke. In fact, when direct threats of relocation of production are manifest, which happens relatively rarely, trade unions do not hesitate to oppose firm closure or at least forced redundancies. For instance, when Philips announced its decisions to relocate the assembly of light bulbs and the production of vacuum cleaners and coffee makers from the Netherlands to Poland (1995, 1997, 1998), the union of metal workers organized strikes, which helped to prevent forced redundancies but not the relocation, which was only phased. Similarly, in 1996 union action blocked Akzo Nobel's plan to relocate 600 jobs in the production of textile fibers from the Netherlands to Poland, which the union considered morally unjust because it would destroy the low-paid segment of the Dutch labour market; the union regarded its actions as successful because forced redundancies were prevented, yet the success of the Dutch unions entailed an extra loss of jobs in German Akzo-plants. (*NRC Handelsblad*, 1 October 1996) This latter example illustrates that in the *Standortdebatte* it is not easy for the unions to avoid the approach to globalization that boils down to suggesting opportunities of strengthening the national economy's position at the cost of competitors. (*cf.* Mahnkopf and Altvater 1995) In general they only differ from the employers' approach by favouring investments in human capital, education, infrastructure and the like, rather than reduction of labour costs. (Simons and Westermann 1997)

Trade unions have also adapted to employers' claims that, in order to cope with the turbulence of the global market, firms need more flexibility in the organization of work and production and in the regulation of employment conditions[4]. Trade unions have tried to fight extreme forms of flexibility, including, for instance, temporary and casual work, and advocated negotiated forms of numerical and functional flexibility. Likewise, in Western European countries where centralized bargaining structures existed, unions have long sought to maintain those structures because of the worker solidarity which they can underpin against frequent employer pressure for decentralization (which is not to say that a general trend towards decentralization exists). (*cf.* Traxler, Kittel, Lengauer 1997) However, in many countries they have gradually consented to a partial decentralization of collective bargaining to the firm level, a limited transfer of the representative function to works councils and the introduction of some degree of flexibility in employment conditions themselves, for instance in the form of performance related pay and order-volume related bandwidths of working hours. (Ferner and Hyman 1992; Lane 1995; Leisink 1995) Such policies are accepted as unfortunate but inevitable by some categories of the union membership while others welcome them as a modernization showing recognition for the cultural diversity of the labour force. (Beukema 1995; Zoll 1996)

Despite, and partially because of, these policies some segments of the labour force have suffered from the direct and indirect effects of globalization more than others. Increased trade and increased competition have led to job losses in the advanced economies, probably not too many in aggregate terms but concentrated in low-skilled labour intensive industries with high labour costs, high in a comparative sense that is, for instance Mexico's low labour costs as compared with Canada's high labour costs, or Poland's as compared with Germany's. These job losses have been painful, both for the workers concerned whose lack of skills made it difficult for them to find another job, and for the unions whose membership consisted significantly of workers in these industries. In addition, organizational changes, such as contracting-out, downsizing permanent staff in combination with resorting to precarious forms of employment, which enterprises have introduced with a view to staying competitive, have affected low-skilled workers more than high-skilled and have contributed to widening wage disparities. (ILO 1997, pp. 15-17, 74-6) However, despite the exposure of all advanced economies to increased international competition and despite the overall rise of income inequality, there is a clear difference between them as regards the extent to which they are able and politically willing to redistribute economic wealth and prevent poverty. It is an illustration of the continued significance of the difference between the so-called Rhineland model and the Anglo-Saxon model of capitalism (*cf.* Albert 1991; also Lane 1995[5]) that countries like Sweden, the Netherlands and Germany have the smallest percentage of poverty (10 per cent or less) while the UK, Ireland and the USA have the highest percentage (15 per cent and more) according to the Human Development Report 1998. (UNDP 1998)

For the developing countries the impact of globalization is differentiated as well, but in a more extreme way than for the developed economies. On the one hand, Japan and a number of other South-East Asian countries, Hong Kong, Taiwan, South Korea, Malaysia, Singapore, India, experienced a period of rapid economic growth and decreasing income inequality which lasted at least until the recent financial crisis. On the other hand, Latin American countries had an uneven economic development and an increase in income inequality, for instance in Argentina, Bolivia, Brazil, Peru and Venezuela. Sub-Saharan Africa has suffered an overall decline in living conditions and has shifted, as Castells (1998, p. 162) has it, to a position of structural irrelevance from the perspective of dominant interests in global, informational capitalism. Economic reforms in this region including devaluation of currency, reduction of tariffs, deregulation, privatization have led to massive job losses, a consequent significant reduction of employment in the formal sector to less than a quarter of the active population in Sub-Saharan Africa, and a loss of trade-union membership. (ILO 1997, pp. 14-15) Despite their adjustment measures the integration of these economies in the global economy has been frustrated by protective actions by the Triad regions. A recent illustration is the opposition of EU member states to negotiating a trade agreement with Mercosur Argentina, Brazil, Paraguay, Uruguay and Chile which would include agricultural products. While the Brazilian President Cardoso stated that 'it is incredibly unjust to put up barriers to freer trade on agriculture products while it is precisely the area where developing countries have the opportunity to grow more rapidly', which is also the view of the World Bank (1995, p. 119), the EU's decision to start talks was made dependent by EU member states' farming ministries on safeguards and compensations for the agricultural sector. (*Financial Times*, 25-26 July 1998)

In the process of globalization the power of trade unions, as measured by trade-union density, has declined almost everywhere around the world, in developed as well as in developing countries. Evidently, some other factors have contributed to the evolution of trade-union membership such as the demise of state socialism in Central and Eastern Europe and the process of economic restructuring, the shift from manufacturing to service employment, in the advanced economies. Nevertheless, globalization as such has involved a number of effects on labour and labour relations as the above analysis has demonstrated and this has contributed considerably to the significant decline of trade-union density since the mid 1980s. In this respect ILO's *World Labour Report 1997-98* provides interesting empirical evidence on trade-union density for 65 countries in 1985 and 1995 (Table 1.2 of the Statistical Annex), which can be summarized as follows:
– 51 per cent (33) of the countries saw a decline of union membership by more than 20 per cent;
– 25 per cent (16) of the countries saw a decline by more than 5 and less than 20 per cent;
– 11 per cent (7) of the countries had a more or less stable union density (5 per cent);
– 3 per cent (2) of the countries experienced a growth of more than 5 and less than 20 per cent;
– 11 per cent (7) of the countries experienced a growth of more than 20 per cent membership.

These data clearly show the decline of the power of trade unions in general. In the South-East Asian dynamic economies the trade-union position worsened throughout the region with the exception of Hong

Kong and the Philippines, where union density increased, and the Republic of Korea and Thailand, where union density was more or less stable. In the majority of OECD countries union density declined substantially, with only Finland, Sweden and Spain showing an increase in union density from 1985 to 1995.

The globalization of the economy is believed by international organizations, not only the OECD but also the World Bank and the ILO, to 'offer promising prospects in the long term' (ILO 1997, p. 12) for the developing countries. Such global optimism may be part of the job of international organizations, but in the face of empirical evidence the impact of globalization on labour to date must be judged less positively. Only some developing countries have benefited from globalization. At the global level, the polarization in the distribution of wealth between states has increased, however. (Castells 1998; World Bank 1995) In many countries, including the advanced economies, income inequality has increased and poverty has grown everywhere. Among the industrialized countries the rise in the degree of income inequality differs, which is related to the extent of their welfare state provisions and the political and institutional support for the welfare state. In the countries of the Rhineland model of capitalism, the continued support for the values of equity and solidarity led to the maintenance of social citizenship rights, although less generally and less unconditionally than used to be the case, while in the Anglo-Saxon countries successive neo-liberal governments cut back on the welfare state on ideological and financial grounds, and the labour movement was unable to prevent this. (*cf.* Coenen and Leisink 1993; Roche and Van Berkel 1997) The overall decline in power of the trade unions and the decentralization of collective bargaining, which makes co-ordination of solidaristic union demands less viable (Traxler, Kittel, Lengauer 1997), are among the main reasons why the trend in the developed economies has reversed into increasing income inequality and growing poverty.

Given the erosion of trade-union power and the less than unequivocal support for an equitable transnational distribution of wealth, the question concerning the possibilities of regulation at the global level presents itself without much hope of a positive answer. Nevertheless, if the social abuses of the global economy are to be prevented, regulation at the global level is an essential precondition.

The Prospect of Regulation in a Global Context

This section will examine the prospects of regulation in a global context, thereby drawing on the opportunities and threats which the contributors to this book see. The starting point is that stronger regulation and more vigorous enforcement are called for, both from a normative and from a socio-economic point of view. The neo-liberal argument that regulation is undesirable because it interferes with the efficient working of the free market, and has a negative effect on economic growth and job creation, was refuted in previous sections on the basis of theoretical and empirical evidence. (Plant 1994; Sengenberger and Campbell 1994; also Crouch 1996) This position still leaves many aspects of regulation in a global context to be clarified, including the kind of regulation, the level(s), the main actors and their strategic opportunities.

It could well be that the neo-liberal viewpoint which has dominated this recent stage of the globalization process has paradoxically created the chances for (re-)regulation. The increased interdependence of economies has certainly contributed to the spread of the financial crisis and economic recession from Asia to Russia and Latin America and to its beginning impact on the Western economies, with the effect that now economists and politicians argue the need for stronger regulation and control. Thus the American economist Krugman argued in *Fortune* (August 1998) that re-regulation of exchange rates is required to cope with the financial and economic problems in Asia, and the political leaders of the G-7 suggest reorganizing the IMF and the World Bank, to impose more vigorous financial control on countries which apply for IMF support and to require more public control of speculative capital. Earlier in 1998 the talks about a Multilateral Agreement on Investments (MAI) had to be suspended both because of opposition by governments, which see their national interests threatened, like Canada and France did their film and culture industries, and because of opposition by non-governmental organizations (NGOs) which criticize the MAI for putting transnational capital over national states and for constraining the authority of governments in the field of environmental and labour standards. These events, and others, certainly mark the growing opposition to the neo-liberal approach to globalization.

From this growing opposition it cannot be concluded, of course, that there would be a wide acceptance of stronger global regulation and control of capital. The question remains pertinent what resources states and organizations can mobilize to impose stronger regulation and what kind of regulation would be adequate.

With respect to the former it is interesting to observe that on the one hand Shell, whose annual sales exceed the gross national product of many countries, is the world's most powerful corporation according to *Forbes*, while on the other hand European environmental organizations were able to force Shell to abandon plans to sink the Brent Spar oil platform. It shows that big corporations, especially those which serve brand products in a global market in which other competitors operate, are sensitive to consumer pressure and want to keep a favourable public image as a basis for continued sales. In a similar way NGOs, consumer organizations and trade unions have been able to put pressure on multi-nationals such as Nike, Reebok, IKEA, Levi Strauss and C&A to observe labour codes. In the case of Nike, boycott action forced the firm to introduce a code of conduct which requires subcontractors to respect local labour laws, to respect the right to organize, to ban child labour, to pay the local minimum wage and so on; public opinion campaigns forced IKEA to sign an agreement with an undertaking to observe a code of conduct for its subcontractors in Roumania and other East European countries. Of course the problem is to ensure the enforcement of such codes, but this point does not detract from the significant observation that NGOs and trade unions dispose of power resources which can effectively be used *vis-à-vis* multinationals.

While NGOs will primarily be in a position to mobilize public opinion and organize boycott actions, governments have their own possibilities. In chapter 2 of this volume, Hirst and Thompson argue that contrary to the assumption of footloose capital, most companies remain rooted in distinct national bases and thus states have real opportunities to initiate and enforce regulation. (also Boyer and Drache 1996; Hirst and Thompson 1996; Sassen 1996) States can create an attractive location for business, not only in a fiscal sense but also by promoting and investing in a transport and communication infrastructure, a highly skilled labour-force, a knowledge infrastructure of universities and R&D centres, a cultural environment which is attractive for highly skilled workers to live in, and so on. As part of such an arrangement other measures can be included such as those concerning worker participation, health and safety at work and social security. While this type of arrangement clearly relates to the national level, and is dependent on the nation state's power and resources relative to multinational corporations as well as to other states, states can also strengthen their own position and regulatory powers by transferring part of their power to supra-national bodies and enforcing the implementation of their codes. The central problem here is, as Hirst and Thompson point out, the divergent national interests of states and the belief that global competition makes co-operation hopeless. However, contrary to what states tend to regard as a loss of sovereignty and control, the transfer of power to create supra-national regulations can enhance the power and control by states *vis-à-vis* multinationals.

The nature of supra-national regulations continues to be a matter of debate despite the fact that the International Labour Conference has passed more than 350 conventions and recommendations since its inception in 1919. One issue is the lack of collective character of ILO recommendations. Only on ratification does the recommendation involve a dual obligation for a member state, which involves a formal commitment to apply the provisions of the convention and a willingness to accept a measure of international supervision. However, even in the case of such core conventions as No. 87, the freedom of association and protection of the right to organize (adopted in 1948), and No. 98, the right to organize and collective bargaining (adopted in 1949), one out of five countries (of a total of 147 listed in Table 5 of the Statistical Annex of ILO 1997) has not ratified No. 87 and one out of ten has not ratified No. 98. Another issue of debate, not only in the context of the ILO but also in meetings of the World Trade Organization (WTO), concerns the level of standards, and the competitive advantages and disadvantages which follow from them for states in a differential way. While Western states such as France, Norway and the USA criticized the developing countries for violating conventions on the right to organize and to collective bargaining as well as for instance the minimum age convention which aims at the abolition of child labour, developing countries have accused Western states of insisting on these conventions for reasons of protectionism. The chances which the globalization of the economy offers for the developing countries would be minimized if, for instance, the advanced economies imposed their standards of minimum wages, so the developed countries argued at the WTO meeting in Singapore in 1996.

The WTO meeting in Singapore compromised by recognizing the importance of the core labour standards and transferring them to the ILO instead of including them in a WTO agreement. This may partly satisfy critics who observe that the developed countries do tend to use these trade clauses to protect their own markets from the less developed countries, but it does not solve their criticism that ILO conventions are not very effective and cannot be enforced in countries where their application is most urgent. (Bechterman 1996, p. 264; Went 1996) It appears therefore logical to adopt a dual strategy. One part of this is the established practice of including labour standards in supra-national agreements such as the ILO conventions and turning these into collectively binding agreements. This should be restricted to core labour standards. Although every standard can be criticized for imposing a particular norm which derives from a Western culture which is inevitably true because norms without culture-bound suppositions cannot exist (*cf.* Van den Brink 1997) this would seem to hold least for the already existing ILO conventions concerning the right to organize and the right to collective bargaining, because these conventions enable or empower local actors to make their own arrangements without imposing substantive outcomes. In addition, core labour standards should also include basic human rights such as the abolition of child labour and discrimination. What issues should be included in this list of core labour standards is open to debate, since any issue can in principle be criticized as disguised protectionism posing as a basic human right. The other part of a dual strategy can consist of agreements between developed and less developed countries at bi- or multilateral level, which are not disguised protectionism. For this to be the case, Bechterman (1996, p. 265) suggests that developed countries make access to their markets the 'carrot' for less developed countries to upgrade their labour regimes. This is an attractive suggestion as a means of making a real deal and making protectionism an explicit matter of debate, but the conflict between Mercosur and the EU about agricultural products as part of a trade agreement illustrates that only economic interests are on the agenda and that (developed) countries do not take the initiative themselves to make labour standards part of an agreement. Obviously, here is a role which trade unions could play by pressing their governments to broaden the agenda in international negotiations. In combination these two strategic elements will result in a situation in which labour standards are elaborated at various levels of economic organization. (Campbell 1994)

So far the chances of regulation in a global context have been discussed as dependent on the effectiveness of public opinion campaigns and supra-national conventions and recommendations. In bringing about these forms of regulation trade unions have assisted in such diverse roles as partner in a social movement and in a neo-corporatist arrangement. What about the prospect of global regulation through normative contracts which are negotiated between trade unions and employers or employer associations?

Europe is looked upon by some (*cf.* ILO 1997, p. 44; Lambert in chapter 10) as the region where the evolution of economic and political integration offers the best chances of supra-national regulation, which could gradually expand into more encompassing labour standards. European industrial relations researchers, however, are not too optimistic about the prospect of European collective agreements for various reasons. (Mahnkopf and Altvater 1995; Marginson and Sisson 1996) On the employer side there is not much interest in collective bargaining at the European level. On the one hand small and medium-size businesses mostly operate in a local or national market, while multinational companies have often transferred responsibility for economic strategies to the level of transnational business units, and for production and employment policies to the level of the individual organization. Thus their diverse markets do not provide a basis for a joint interest in collective bargaining and, significantly, in many sectors of industry representative employer associations do not exist at the European level. On the trade-union side, collective bargaining policies have been oriented at the national level and their organizational structures are ill-adapted to both the supra-national and enterprise level. It is true that the Industry Committees have gained more weight in the European Trade Union Confederation (ETUC) but national trade unions have not been willing to transfer authority to European-level negotiating bodies[6]. The result of this is that collective bargaining is mostly still the prerogative of national unions which also decide to what extent they co-ordinate their bargaining policies across countries. Thus European collective agreements determining pay and other substantive conditions are unlikely in the immediate future, Marginson and Sisson (1996, p. 15) conclude.

However, Marginson and Sisson observe emerging forms of European-level collective bargaining which they describe as 'virtual collective bargaining'. This refers to the social dialogue at the EU level and at the level of the Euro-company, as well as to the voluntary anticipation and co-ordination of policies by collective bargaining actors across EU member states. While the outcome of such dialogues, like the agreement which specifies minimum provisions for parental leave, are valuable elements of social standards, they can hardly be regarded as the promising beginning of robust global regulation. First, employers engage in these agreements only reluctantly and under the threat of directives by the European Commission, which is rare[7]. As a consequence, EU wide social standards are fragmentary and do not prevent severe social abuses such as child labour, which is estimated for instance to involve 300 000 children in Italy. (*de Volkskrant*, 9 January 1998) Second, such agreements have a framework character which means that specific matters must be negotiated subsequently at the national level where the unions are thrown back on themselves. Therefore, the economic integration and competition in Europe causes continued fears of social dumping (Mahnkopf and Altvater 1995, p. 105) and it is hard to see how Europe could thus pave the way for a progressive transfer of social standards to the rest of the world.

While the general prospect for supra-national regulation through collective bargaining at the sectoral and regional level does not appear very positive, there are some interesting developments through other forums. A promising example of achieving global labour standards for multinational companies was given by the European Works Council of the French *Compagnie Générale des Eaux*, which succeeded in signing a 'charter of basic social rights' to be applied to all foreign activities including subcontractors. (Bach, 1997)

Given continued employer opposition to European-wide labour standards, unions will have to (re)build their power base at the company level and at the same time strengthen the authority of supra-national union bodies at the European level and at the global level. One element of such a strategy must undoubtedly be a substantive re-orientation on the definition of workers' interests and solidarity, as Hyman cogently argues in chapter 5. Another element is that unions not only co-ordinate their national bargaining policies but engage in a real transfer of negotiating authority. It appears difficult for unions in Europe to take the step from co-ordination to authorization of supra-national union bodies – yet chapter 8 by Leisink reports of such initiatives by some national unions in the media industries – and the idea of a loss of sovereignty interferes with the recognition that union strength in the national arena depends increasingly on supra-national power. Perhaps European unions should, therefore, study the recent experience of the Australian unions, described by Lambert in chapter 10. Faced with growing competition of low-wage Asian competitors, Australian unions did not choose a purely protective strategy but, as a longer term strategy, decided to sponsor building local union organizations in these Asian countries, so that these would be able to oppose exploitation and demand fair wages and employment conditions, and indeed also reduce the competitive discrepancies in the Asian region, from which Australian workers would also benefit in the long run. In 1998, when Australian unions fought to secure the basis of a regulated economy, they enjoyed support from these international union links.

The logical conclusion that, when competition is increasingly global, regulation must also be global is not enough to spur on the unions to adapt their organizational structures and strategies. However, the awareness of such necessities is growing, and several chapters in this book show that unions in particular sectors such as the media industries and in particular regions such as Australia-Asia are stepping up their activities of co-ordination to the point of creating supra-national bodies with a certain degree of authority and resources.

Outline of this Volume

The preceding sections have introduced the main aspects of globalization and labour relations on which this book will focus and which can be summarized by three straightforward questions. To what extent and how does globalization manifest itself? What are the effects of globalization on labour and on labour relations, including the position of trade unions and their possibilities to bring about economic regulation and labour standards? What is the response of organized labour to the growing polarization and inequalities between and within states and what beginning of strategies aiming at global regulation can be observed?

The chapters in this book will focus on these questions in a differential way. For instance, Hirst and Thompson open by questioning the very concept of economic globalization on the basis of extensive empirical data, thus paving the way for other chapters that concentrate more on analyses of globalization in a specific sector of industry. Similarly, Hyman will analyse the trade-union position in a more theoretical-analytical way while the chapters by Beukema and Coenen, Leisink and Lambert present empirical accounts of how trade unions attempt to cope with the impact of globalization. Together these different foci of analysis contribute to an elaborate analysis of the central aspects of globalization and labour relations. The following overview will present the main topics of the different chapters in the context of the book's central questions.

Hirst and Thompson closely examine the notion of globalization, involving a highly internationalized and uncontrollable global economy, and find, on the basis of extensive economic evidence, that this notion does not hold. Therefore, the claim that neo-liberal deregulation and global economic integration are irreversible and undermine the viability of social democratic policies of economic regulation and redistribution of wealth can be resisted, and should be resisted, Hirst and Thompson argue, because of the inequalities and unfairness inherent in the present world economy. National and multilateral governance and regulation are possible, but they require clear political choices.

Macro-economic change and structural transformations at the company level are interrelated, Vilrokx argues in chapter 3, producing both the transition from a production to a financially oriented capitalism and a global division of production. The management strategies that have developed in this context – competence optimalization and client orientation – alter class-legitimized control relations in the workplace. The consequent reformulation of the worker's identity as a manager of tasks which are executed for the benefit of clients, confronts the trade unions with the major problem of defining a collective identity as a basis of organization and challenges the class-based nature of industrial relations.

Du Gay, chapter 4, seeks to show how the discourse of globalization constructs a particular vision of the world, to which certain practices of national economic management, organizational governance and individual self-regulation are linked. More concretely, the discourse of globalization has powerful effects in demanding states to free the market and to enhance entrepreneurship. The concomitant adoption of a rational economic model influences the way in which the state defines public sector provisions and relationships as governed by contract and the way in which man is redefined as the 'entrepreneur of the self'. The power of this discourse is shown by the fact that counterfactual evidence concerning the globalization thesis and evidence as to the social consequences of the policies which it has inspired are unable to stop economic and political decisions being taken in its name.

In chapter 5 Hyman considers that the trade-union task of constructing solidarity has become more difficult. The restructuring of work and employment has increased the differentiation of the labour force; globalization has broken national labour markets and systems of industrial relations open, while intensified competition has led to organizational restructuring and to a fragmentation of hitherto standardized forms of collective employment regulation. Hyman concludes that if solidarity is to survive, it must be re-invented as organic solidarity which recognizes and respects differences of circumstances and interests. Themes that are of crucial relevance are those of flexibility, security and opportunity. If unions succeed in engaging in internal social dialogue and in elaborating worker-oriented meanings of these concepts, they can construct an agenda which links the interests of the precarious, the unemployed and the relatively secure.

A detailed analysis of changes in the labour market is undertaken by Rubery in chapter 6. She finds a destabilization of internal labour-market systems (caused by such developments as subcontracting and flexibilization) which coincides with the deregulation of external labour markets. The effect is a fragmentation of internal labour markets and increasing divisions between the core and the growing periphery. An explanation of these changes must take on board the power changes in society which leave organizations fewer restraints on the form of their internal labour markets and employment systems. It is not, Rubery argues, globalization in the sense of relocation of production that can be held to account for the widening inequalities, but the broader phenomenon of increased competition and the related move towards more flexible markets. She concludes that the changes require new forms of regulation and proposes a citizenship approach to employment.

The increasing momentum of the globalization process after World War II has been helped by the development of information and transport technology. The costs of transportation of persons, goods and information measured in time and money have decreased significantly during this century (Lash and Urry 1994; Nierop 1995; World Bank 1995, p. 51) and have been a major factor behind global integration. Given this significance of transport and information technology it is of great interest to take a closer look at the transport and media sectors themselves to examine what impact the globalization process has had on the organization of production and labour relations.

Beukema and Coenen, chapter 7, concentrate on the organization of distribution, which is highly relevant for understanding the globalization process, because distribution is directly involved in the strategies of those manufacturing firms which aim at a global division of production, which requires cheap and just-in-time transport technologies. The position which a distribution firm holds in the logistic networks which emerge, has implications for its business strategy and for labour. The dynamics of power relationships vary between types of networks but contacts with customers is certainly a resource for distribution firms which seek to control the network. The impact of this strategy on labour becomes obvious in terms of the conditions of work – for instance, higher job requirements in terms of customer orientation and communication skills and a segmentation of the workforce, which make a solidaristic union answer not easy to find.

The media industries are in a complex process of restructuring, Leisink shows in chapter 8. One feature is a differential segment sensitivity to globalization, and a polarization between global multi-media conglomerates and small firms which are mainly oriented at local markets. Another feature is the convergence of different segments of the information, communication and culture industries. The restructuring process creates winners and losers among workers. For the trade unions the challenge is both to adapt their strategy – protection of their traditional membership and recruitment of employees in the new industries – and to modernize their organizational structures. The unions appear divided in answering this challenge. In some countries unions are engaged in adding new items to their agenda and in promoting union co-operation close to merger at a national and international level, to cope with both convergence and globalization.

In chapter 9 Heycock reports on the impact of globalization on the potash mining industry. In a British mine a reorganization process involved a reduction of jobs, job flexibility and a programme for continuous improvement strategies. The question is to what extent this process is the result of global economic forces and of globally informed managerial choices. Global economic pressures can be observed in the drive to increase profits and production at lower costs. The methods chosen have also been influenced by local management studying other sites of the global company which owns the British mine. In addition, there is a general management awareness of Post-Fordist organization of work philosophies, which may explain why similar new forms of work organization were promoted in Britain and Canada. Further research is to make clear how much of this is a conscious global search for best practices.

The final chapter by Lambert brings together many of the topics that are implicated in the globalization process. He makes clear that globalization's urge for competitiveness not only erodes employment conditions but threatens democracy and citizens' rights. This development stands out clearly in Australia because of the geographic proximity of the Asian region, where labour-market institutions have an authoritarian character, as Lambert shows. Analysing the impact of the Asian regimes on Australian industrial relations and highlighting the 1998 waterfront conflict, he shows the contradictions of globalization and the broader significance of this conflict for the future development of (Australian) industrial relations, either in the direction of trade-union decline and further deregulation or in the direction of opportunities for a new style of global social movement unionism. His detailed account of the conflict between stevedoring companies and conservative government on the one hand, and unions on the other provides an insight into anti-union tactics spawned by globalization ideology, but it also reveals the resilience of international trade-union action and the wider popular support for trade unionism when democratic institutions themselves are at stake.

Notes

1. In the French-speaking parts of the world the term 'mondialization' is preferred, which usually refers to the same phenomenon of stretching and intensifying relationships over large geographic distances (*cf.* Heilbron and Wilterdink, 1995); but see the chapter by Vilrokx in this volume for a more specific use of the term 'mondialization'.

2. The theoretical assumptions of this economic paradigm are analysed, for instance, by Wilkinson (1994), who shows that the nature of the labour market is such that, when it is left to operate freely, endemic inefficiencies are generated which can only be offset by regulatory structures.

3. As the World Bank emphasizes, the policy issue is not one of *laissez-faire* versus government intervention. (World Bank 1995, p. 14) Rather the issue is whether government action only supports the efficient functioning of markets or also responds to the particular needs of workers who are discriminated against or otherwise disadvantaged.

4. Although this analysis generalizes about firms' aims of flexibility in the restructuring of work organization and industrial relations, and about (European) unions' adaptation to such demands, this is not to suggest some simple convergence towards a new production and labour relations paradigm. Societal differences, including industrial relations traditions, do matter in the way in which transnational pressures are accommodated. (*cf.* Lane 1995; Smith and Elger 1997)

5. A related typology is the one developed by Lane (1995). According to Lane Britain is the European exemplar of market-led capitalism, with firms oriented to short-term stock market performance, weak trade-union organization at the central level and fragmented industrial relations. The Rhineland model of capitalism is differentiated between Germany, representing the North European pattern of neo-corporatist centralized interest mediation, and France, representing a variant of the South European pattern of capitalist modernization in which the state is a principal actor. Germany and France share a closer coupling between financial and industrial capital and a commitment to long-termism in investment in both fixed and human capital. This makes it fundamentally different, according to Albert (1991), from the Anglo-Saxon model with its free-market individualism and short-term profit orientation.

6. A Dutch trade-union official operating in the banking sector reports in his union magazine about a debate in the European Federation of Commercial, Clerical, Professional and Technical Employees (FIET). His union's suggestion to strengthen the negotiating power of the FIET was jeered by other national unions because they did not want to lose their authority to an international union body. (*FNV Magazine*, 12 March 1998)
7. It is not too difficult to understand that this is only rarely the case. The European Economic Community, as the Union was previously called, has been brought about by the forces of economic integration, not political and social integration, and as Fortress Europe it represents the response to growing global competition. (Mahnkopf and Altvater 1995; Nierop 1995)

References

Albert, M. (1991), *Capitalisme contre capitalisme*, Paris: Editions du Seuil.

Bach, H. (1997), 'Social standards and global players', *Transfer*, 3 (2), 418-20.

Bechterman, G. (1996), 'Globalization, labour markets and public policy', in R. Boyer and D. Drache (eds), *States against Markets; The Limits of Globalization*, London and New York: Routledge, pp. 250-69.

Beukema, L. (1995), 'Differentiatie van belangen als uitgangspunt voor nieuw beleid', in H. Coenen (ed.), *De Vakbeweging na 2000*, Utrecht: Jan van Arkel, pp. 143-68.

Bourdieu, P. (1987), 'What makes a social class? On the theoretical and practical existence of groups', *Berkeley Journal of Sociology*, XXXII, 1-17.

Boyer, R. and D. Drache (eds) (1996), *States against Markets; the Limits of Globalization,* London and New York: Routledge.

Brink, B. Van den (1997), *The Tragedy of Liberalism*, Utrecht: Department of Philosophy (Ph.D. thesis).

Campbell, D. (1994), 'The rationale for multi-level labour standards', in W. Sengenberger and D. Campbell (eds), *Creating Economic Opportunities; The Role of Labour Standards in Industrial Restructuring*, Geneva: International Labour Office, pp.139-71.

Campbell, D. (1998), 'Labour Standards, Flexibility, Economic Performance', in T. Wilthagen (ed), *Advancing Theory in Labour Law and Industrial Relations in a Global Context*, Amsterdam/Oxford/New York/Tokyo: North Holland, pp. 229-43.

Castells, M. (1996), *The Rise of the Network Society*, Cambridge Mass./Oxford: Blackwell.

Castells, M. (1998), *End of Millennium*, Malden Mass./Oxford: Blackwell.

Coenen, H. and P. Leisink (eds) (1993), *Work and Citizenship in the New Europe*, Aldershot: Edward Elgar.

Crouch, C. (1996), 'Revised diversity: from the neo-liberal decade to beyond Maastricht', in J. Van Ruysseveldt and J.Visser (eds), *Industrial Relations in Europe; Traditions and Transitions*, London, Thousand Oaks, New Delhi: Sage, pp. 358-75.

Drache, D. (1996), 'New work and employment relations: lean production in Japanese auto transplants in Canada', in R. Boyer and D. Drache (eds), *States against Markets; The Limits of Globalization*, London and New York: Routledge, pp. 227-49.

Du Gay, P. (1998), 'Globalization, contemporary organizational discourse and the constitution of work identity', in T. Wilthagen (ed.), *Advancing Theory in Labour Law and Industrial Relations in a Global Context*, Amsterdam/Oxford/New York/Tokyo: North Holland, pp. 165-79.

Ferner, A. and R. Hyman (eds) (1992), *Industrial Relations in the New Europe*, Oxford: Blackwell.

Giddens, A. (1984), *The Constitution of Society*. Cambridge: Polity Press.

Giddens, A. (1990), *The Consequences of Modernity*, Cambridge: Polity Press.

Giddens, A. (1994), *Beyond Left and Right*, Cambridge: Polity Press.

Heilbron, J. and N. Wilterdink (1995), 'Inleiding', in J. Heilbron and N. Wilterdink (eds), *Mondialisering: de wording van de wereldsamenleving*, Amsterdam: Amsterdams Sociologisch Tijdschrift; Groningen: Wolters-Noordhoff.

Hirst, P. and G.Thompson (1996), *Globalization in Question*, Cambridge: Polity Press.

ILO (1997), *World Labour Report 1997-98: Industrial Relations, Democracy and Social Stability*, Geneva: International Labour Office.

Korten, D. (1995), *When Corporations Rule the World*, West Hartford: Kumarian Press; San Francisco: Berrett-Koehler Publishers.

Lane, C. (1995), *Industry and Society in Europe; Stability and Change in Britain, Germany and France*, Aldershot: Edward Elgar.

Lash, S. and J. Urry (1994), *Economies of Signs and Space*, London, Thousand Oaks, New Delhi: Sage.

Leisink, P. (1995), 'Vakbondswerk in de onderneming tussen ledenwerving en emancipatie', in H. Coenen (ed.), *De Vakbeweging na 2000*, Utrecht: Jan van Arkel, pp. 110-41.

Leisink, P. (1997), 'Work and Citizenship in Europe', in M. Roche and R. Van Berkel (eds), *European Citizenship and Social Exclusion*, Aldershot: Ashgate, pp. 51-65.

Mahnkopf, B. and E. Altvater (1995), 'Transmission Belts of Transnational Competition? Trade Unions and Collective Bargaining in the Context of European Integration', *European Journal of Industrial Relations*, 1 (1), 101-17.

Marginson, P. and K. Sisson (1994), 'The Structure of Transnational Capital in Europe: the Emerging Euro-company and its Implications for Industrial Relations', in R. Hyman and A. Ferner (eds), *New Frontiers in European Industrial Relations*, Oxford: Blackwell, pp. 15-51.

Marginson, P. and K. Sisson (1996), *European Collective Bargaining: A Virtual Prospect?*, Brussels: European Trade Union Institute.

Marginson, P., P. Armstrong, P. Edwards and J. Purcell (1996), 'Facing the Multinational Challenge', in P. Leisink, J. Van Leemput and J. Vilrokx (eds), *The Challenges to Trade Unions in Europe; Innovation or Adaptation*, Cheltenham: Edward Elgar, pp. 187-204.

Nierop, T. (1995), 'Globalisering, internationale netwerken en de regionale paradox', in J. Heilbron and N. Wilterdink (eds), *Mondialisering: de wording van de wereldsamenleving*, Amsterdam: Amsterdams Sociologisch Tijdschrift; Groningen: Wolters-Noordhoff, pp. 36-60.

OECD (1996), *Globalization of Industry*, Paris: OECD.

Petrella, R. (1996), 'Globalization and Internationalization: the Dynamics of the Emerging World Order', in R. Boyer and D. Drache (eds), *States against Markets; the Limits of Globalization*, London and New York: Routledge, pp. 62-83.

Plant, R. (1994), *Labour Standards and Structural Adjustment*, Geneva: International Labour Office.

Roche, M. and R. Van Berkel (eds), (1997), *European Citizenship and Social Exclusion*, Aldershot: Ashgate.

Ruigrok, W. and R. Van Tulder (1995), *The Logic of International Restructuring*, London and New York: Routledge.

Ruigrok, W. and R. Van Tulder (1995a), 'Misverstand: Globalisering', *ESB*, 80 (4038), 1140-3.

Sassen, S. (1996), *Losing Control? Sovereignty in an Age of Globalization*, New York: Columbia University Press.

Sengenberger, W. (1994), 'Labour standards: An institutional framework for restructuring and development', in W. Sengenberger and D. Campbell (eds), *Creating Economic Opportunities; The Role of Labour Standards in Industrial Restructuring*, Geneva: International Labour Office, pp. 3-41.

Sengenberger, W. and D. Campbell (eds) (1994), *Creating Economic Opportunities; The Role of Labour Standards in Industrial Restructuring*, Geneva: International Labour Office.

Simons, R. and K. Westermann (eds) (1997), *Standortdebatte und Globalisierung der Wirtschaft*, Marburg: Schüren.

Smith, C. and T. Elger (1997), 'International Competition, Inward Investment and the Restructuring of European Work and Industrial Relations', *European Journal of Industrial Relations*, 3 (3), 279-304.

Stokvis, R. (1995), 'Strategie en structuur van multinationale ondernemingen', in J. Heilbron and N. Wilterdink (eds), *Mondialisering: de wording van de wereldsamenleving*, Amsterdam: Amsterdams Sociologisch Tijdschrift; Groningen: Wolters Noordhoff, pp. 61-79.

Traxler, F., B. Kittel and S. Lengauer (1997), 'Globalization, collective bargaining and performance', *Transfer*, **3** (4), 787-806.

United Nations Development Programme (UNDP) (1998), *Human Development Report 1998*, New York: Oxford University Press.

Visser, J. and A. Hemerijck, (1997), *A Dutch Miracle, job growth, welfare reform and corporatism in the Netherlands*, Amsterdam: Amsterdam University Press.

Waters, M. (1995), *Globalization*, London and New York: Routledge.

Went, R. (1996), *Grenzen aan de Globalisering?* Amsterdam: Het Spinhuis.

Wilkinson, F. (1994), 'Equality, efficiency and economic progress: The case for universally applied equitable standards for wages and conditions of work', in W. Sengenberger and D. Campbell (eds), *Creating Economic Opportunities; The Role of Labour Standards in Industrial Restructuring*, Geneva: International Labour Office, pp. 61-86.

World Bank (1995), *World Development Report 1995. Workers in an Integrating World*, New York: Oxford University Press.

Zoll, R. (1996), 'Modernization, Trade Unions and Solidarity', in P. Leisink, J. Van Leemput and J. Vilrokx (eds), *The Challenges to Trade Unions in Europe; Innovation or Adaptation*, Cheltenham: Edward Elgar, pp. 77-87.

Zwet, A. Van der (1996), 'Globalisering en de Nederlandse economie', *ESB*, 81 (4045), 138-42.

2. Globalization – Frequently Asked Questions and Some Surprising Answers

Paul Hirst and Grahame Thompson

We challenge the fashionable view that a process of globalization has created a new kind of international economic system in recent decades, citing evidence relating to a number of key questions to disprove the more extreme globalizers' claims. In particular we argue that national economies continue to exist, that distinct social welfare policies can be followed, and that world market forces are not beyond governance.[1]

Globalization is the greatest threat to the existence of the pragmatic reforming left since 1945. What is at stake can be seen from a recent influential pamphlet by John Gray. (Gray 1996) He claims that economic globalization has developed to the point that social democratic policies of national economic regulation and egalitarian redistribution are no longer viable. National governments and organized labour are powerless when faced with international marketization, neo-liberal deregulation and global economic integration. These changes are irreversible and social democratic national strategies have become so ineffective that they will have to be scrapped in favour of other methods of meliorating the effects of capitalist markets.

This claim seems plausible, not least because social democratic parties have been politically unsuccessful and conventional strategies of reflationary macro-economic management have proved ineffective. It needs to be firmly resisted. Firstly, because many of the sources of failure of the reformist left have domestic rather than global causes, and because many of the left's problems have been created by the left itself. Secondly, because the notion of globalization is just plain wrong. The idea of a new, highly-internationalized, virtually uncontrollable global economy based on world market forces has taken root very strongly. It is being used to tell workers and the poor that they must accept whatever is left when their lives and hopes have been sacrificed on the altar of international competitiveness. Fortunately, the story is very different in fact and

36

our options much greater. In what follows we will concentrate on marshalling the evidence to answer ten frequently-asked questions about the world economy and thus show why the rhetoric of the globalizers is wide of the mark. The answers are surprising and we hope that in most cases the surprises are welcome too.

1. Is globalization new?

If we interpret globalization to mean an open international economy with large and growing flows of trade and capital investment between countries, then the answer to the question is clearly negative. The international economy has a complex history of relative openness and closure, since a truly integrated world trading system was created in the second half of the nineteenth century. Submarine telegraph cables from the 1860s onwards connected inter-continental markets. They made possible day-to-day trading and price-making across thousands of miles, a far greater innovation than the advent of electronic trading today. Chicago and London, Melbourne and Manchester were linked in close to real time. Bond markets also became closely inter-connected, and large-scale international lending – both portfolio and direct investment – grew rapidly during this period.

The economy of the *Belle Époque* from 1870 to 1914 was remarkably internationalized, and we have only begun to return to those levels of openness today. First we will consider merchandise trade. The key measure is exports and imports combined as a proportion of gross domestic product (GDP). In 1913 the UK's trade was 44.7 per cent of its GDP, after a dramatic fall in the inter-war years, it had risen to 39.3 per cent in 1973 and still had not equalled its pre-World War I level in 1993 at 40.5. France and Germany offer a similar picture: France has still not returned to 1913 levels of openness (35.4), in 1973 its ratio stood at 29.0 per cent, in 1993 at 32.4 per cent; for Germany the figures are 1913 35.1 per cent, 1973 35.2 per cent, 1993 38.3 per cent, a modest increase but hardly enough to sustain the notion of massive globalization in recent years. In Japan's case the figures show a marked decline from 31.4 per cent in 1913, to 18.3 per cent in 1973, to 14.4 per cent in 1993. (Hirst and Thompson 1996a, p. 60; Wolf 1995, p. 25) Clearly, Japan has been reducing its imports, but it still exports a relatively low percentage of its GDP – 8.8 per cent in 1991-3, down from a high of 11.8 per cent in 1979-1981. (Bairoch 1996, p. 176) For exports alone, we find that Western Europe exported 18.3 per cent of its GDP in 1913, 17.4 per cent in 1970 and 21.7 per cent in 1992; the USA exported 6.4 per cent in

1913, 4 per cent in 1970 and 7.5 per cent in 1992 and Japan 12.5 per cent in 1913, 9.7 per cent in 1970 and 8.8 per cent in 1992. (Bairoch and Kozul-Wright 1996, p. 6) Thus, apart from the increased openness of the USA in both exports and imports since the 1970s, the economies of the major developed countries are not markedly more open in trade-to-GDP ratio terms than they were before 1914 – although the volume of trade has increased massively.

Capital mobility was as marked a feature of the *Belle Époque* international economy as it is of the world economy today. Bairoch and Kozul-Wright comment, for example, that the stock of foreign direct investment (FDI) in 1913 reached over 9 per cent of world output and note that this figure was still not surpassed in the early 1990s. (Bairoch and Kozul-Wright 1996, p. 10) They also point out that between 1870 and 1913 foreign portfolio investment grew faster than trade, FDI and output. *Plus ça change*. The UK, France and Germany were the major capital exporters – the UK exporting an average of 4 per cent of national income per annum in 1870-1914 and an astounding 9 per cent at the end of the period.

The world economy is, of course, markedly different now from that before 1914. But it is still dominated by roughly the same main players. In 1914 there were eight military-economic Great Powers: Austria-Hungary, France, Germany, Great Britain, Italy, Japan, Russia and the USA. Today there is a G7 standing conference of the major economic nations; the difference is that Canada has replaced the defunct Austria-Hungary and that Russia attends the top table as an eighth impoverished Great Power with observer status.

World trade has a complex and chequered history. It was severely damaged by the Great Depression of the 1930s, when countries with high trade-to-GDP ratios like Britain and Germany suffered devastating losses of about 40 per cent in their foreign trade. The open international economy restructured by the *Pax Americana* after 1945 promoted rapid growth in world trade. Between 1950 and 1973 trade grew at an average annual rate of 9.4 per cent as against an average of 5.3 per cent for output. The figures for 1973-84 were 3.6 per cent for trade and 2.1 per cent for output. In the period 1872-1914 trade grew at an average of 3.5 per cent and output at 3.45 per cent (Hirst and Thompson 1996, p. 22). If there was a period of rapid internationalization it was the managed multilateralism of the Keynesian era. Growth in world merchandise trade only returned to the levels of the Great Boom in 1994 at 9.5 per cent (trade

grew between 1983 and 1990 at an average annual rate of 9 per cent).
(World Trade Organisation 1995, p. 7)

The more naive advocates of rapid and recent globalization have short
memories and they tend to see the international economy in post-1973
terms. A longer perspective is sobering, not merely for what it reveals
about the pre-1914 world economy, but because it shows how volatile,
how subject to conjunctural change, and how vulnerable to the effects
of political conflict the international economy is. No major regime has
lasted for longer than 30 to 40 years and periods of considerable
openness and growth have been replaced by closure and decline. It would
be naive, therefore, to project current trends towards openness and
integration forward as if they are inevitable or irreversible. People in
1914 from Norman Angell to Rudolf Hilferding thought that war between the Great Powers would be so disruptive of the highly integrated
trading and financial system that either it must be short or it would be
unsustainable. How wrong they were. War is unlikely between the major
powers today, but a return to protectionist policies by the advanced
countries could have a damaging effect.

An open international economy is worth preserving. To support free
trade against a return to generalized protectionism does not mean that
we are thereby tied to all the institutions and circumstances of the present
world economy with all its inequalities and unfairness. An unregulated
free-market international economy, organized solely for the benefit of
the richest nations and largest companies, is unlikely to be socially or
environmentally sustainable. Genuine economic openness requires multilateral regulation to prevent unfair competition, to redress the debt
burden on the poorest countries, to distribute investment more equitably,
and to compensate poorer countries for declining forms of trade. Such a
policy requires new priorities on the part of the advanced countries and
international institutions like the IMF, the World Bank, and the World
Trade Organization. Alarmist rhetoric about globalization is counter-
productive in this context because it makes people afraid of an open
trading economy and more inclined to support protectionism.

2. Is capital mobility a threat to jobs and living standards?
   ## Is capital now chasing low wages?

These questions can be more accurately, if ponderously, re-phrased thus:
Is the new international capital mobility made possible by the deregulation of financial markets and the removal of exchange controls in major
advanced economies in the early 1980s leading to a significant loss of

employment and output in the advanced nations as production shifts to exploit the benefits of low wages in the newly industrializing countries (NICs)?

This is a fear that unites sections of the left and the populist right. For example, prior to the conclusion of the North American Free Trade Agreement, both sections of the US trade union movement and Ross Perot argued that it would result in a massive loss of jobs in the USA as firms shifted south of the Mexican border to exploit low wages.

The evidence flatly contradicts the notion of a massive flight of capital from the advanced nations to low-wage countries in the Third World since the early 1980s. In 1993 capital flows from advanced nations to the NICs totalled over $100 billion. Surely this staggering figure must represent a massive loss of potential investment? One of the great bugbears of globalization talk is the quoting of apparently large numbers out of context. As Paul Krugman points out the combined GNP of North America, Western Europe and Japan in 1993 was $18 trillion, their investment $3.5 trillion and their capital stock about $60 trillion: $100 billion thus represents 3 per cent of investment in the rich Triad countries and 0.2 per cent of their capital stock. (Krugman 1996, p. 63) He calculates that between 1990 and 1993, the boom in investment in Third World markets reduced the stock of capital of the advanced world by 0.5 per cent.

Even if such foreign investment had no other effect than reducing Western employment and output, the figures are just not big enough to generate the kind of panic one currently sees in the West. Given the pitiful levels of foreign aid provided by most rich countries, these transfers of capital could be seen as a modest contribution to reducing the vast disparities in wealth and industrial output between the First and Third Worlds. Foreign direct investment in Third World countries is not necessarily negative for Western workers, it may also create demand for Western goods by promoting output and national income elsewhere – just as Britain's foreign investment generated expanded commerce with and exports to countries like Argentina and Uruguay before 1914.

Job losses and unemployment in the advanced world are just too big to be explained by trade with low-wage countries. It has been calculated that if the USA had enjoyed balanced trade in manufactured goods rather than a large deficit, the decline in manufacturing as a share of GDP between 1970 and 1990 would have been from 24.9 per cent to 19.2 per cent – the actual figure was from 25 per cent to 18.4 per cent. (Krugman 1996, p. 36) The USA became a far more open economy after 1970, suffering massive import penetration, mainly from advanced economies like Japan. If a relatively small part of US job losses is represented by import penetration, then a tiny fraction of those losses in turn are due to Third World imports of manufactured goods. Manufacturing exports from low-wage countries are only a small part of the market for manufactured goods in the advanced countries: 4.3 per cent in the USA in the second half of the 1980s, approximately 3 per cent in the major EU countries and 2.6 per cent in Japan. (Glynn 1995) The main causes of job losses are domestic to the advanced countries.

Foreign Direct Investment (FDI) has since the early 1980s been growing at over 3.5 times the rate of merchandise trade (1983-90 34 per cent per annum vs. 9 per cent per annum). FDI is an alternative to trade in manufactures, it creates branch plants and assembly operations, and it is also the main way in which countries can export marketed services, such as hotels or retailing. FDI and trade remain massively concentrated within the advanced countries. Closer integration is above all between the three major blocs of the Triad: North America, the EU and Japan. In 1992, including inter-EU trade, the Triad represented 70 per cent of world trade and, excluding inter-European trade, the figure was still 60 per cent. The ten most important recipients of FDI among the developing countries represented 18.2 per cent of total world trade (excluding inter-EU trade). In the case of FDI flows, between 1981 and 1991 North America, Western Europe and Japan represented 75 per cent of the total. The Triad's members invest mainly in each other and in other advanced countries. The ten major developing country recipients of FDI absorbed 16.5 per cent of the total flows during this period; representing with the Triad 91.5 per cent of total FDI. In population terms the Triad, the nine most important developing countries in respect of FDI, and the eight coastal provinces of China plus Beijing are 28 per cent of the world's population. This leaves the other 72 per cent, most of whom are very poor, with less than 10 per cent of total FDI. (Hirst and Thompson 1996, pp. 68-9) If FDI is changing the world it is to make the rich richer, and to propel a small number of developing countries, like Taiwan, close to advanced country status.

In the developing world FDI is highly concentrated. Of the total of $126.1 billion of FDI going to the ten largest recipients in 1988-92, $47.3 went to just two countries – China and Singapore – and $78 billion (or roughly two-thirds of the total) went to just four countries. (*The Economist* 1 October 1994, p. 29) Africa and the poorest countries in Asia like Bangladesh have been all but excluded from the 1990s boom in FDI.

Moreover, the figures for investment do not just represent Western firms investing in low-wage manufacturing sectors abroad. Foreign investment in China has surged from around $5 billion per annum in 1990 to over $25 billion in 1993. But the IMF notes that much of FDI comes not from the West but from near neighbours (Hong Kong, Macau and Taiwan), that it is highly concentrated in the coastal provinces, and that it is highly concentrated in certain sectors like real estate and natural resources. (International Monetary Fund 1994, p. 52)

If Western capitalists are moving capital abroad to take advantage of low wages in order to produce cheap manufactured goods in order to export them to the West, then they are making a bad job of it.

3. Is Third World competition destroying First World jobs?
Must wages in newly industrialized countries remain low?

Alarmists are not just concerned by capital mobility but by Third World industrialization in general. Countries like South Korea and Taiwan have industrialized primarily by domestic capital formation, rather than by high levels of FDI or international borrowing. The fear is that Third World newly industrializing countries will be able to exploit low wages to gain competitive edge and penetrate Western markets, and that a combination of relatively well-educated workers and technology transfer will enable them to match Western quality in manufacturers. The result will be a collapse of manufacturing employment and output in the West.

But how is this scenario possible? Falling output and employment would restrict demand in the West, and a loss of tradeable manufacturing goods would restrict the advanced countries' ability to trade. Trade is not like inter-company competition. If company A outsells company B and drives it to bankruptcy that is the end of the matter. But international trade requires some rough approximation of balance overall; other things being equal, a country must have goods it can trade with others if it is to continue to import. Manufactured goods are central to trade between the advanced countries and also a key component of their trade with the developing world. Low-wage exporters can only displace this trade if Western countries find other things to make and to sell abroad. Exporters who are highly competitive but have low domestic demand because of low home-country wages can only exist in particular niches. If they came to dominate trade in manufactures then world markets would begin to collapse. Some elementary trade theory and macro-economics will show why. Output and employment are falling in the advanced countries.

Output is rising in the low-wage exporters but not domestic demand. Trade will not balance and there will be a massive shortage of effective demand. This is madhouse economics on a world scale and need not be taken seriously.

The only sustainable option for international trade is the win-win outcome, in which rising output and employment in newly industrializing countries leads to rapid growth and rising real incomes. Thus markets for Western goods will grow in developing countries. Of course, certain sectors or products are displaced in the advanced countries and others face intensified competition and have to respond with improvements in productivity and technical innovation, Thus Western countries continue to have a range of goods they can trade internationally and emerging markets in which they can sell them. This may seem optimistic and hypothetical, it covers over a good deal of dislocation and job losses that are possible within the bigger picture, but in the end trade is driven by the crude logic that countries must have goods that others want.

Moreover, there is evidence that the most successful newly industrializing countries are experiencing rapid growth in domestic living standards. Labour costs per employee have grown faster in South Korea than in any advanced industrial country – in 1979-83 21.6 per cent, 1983-84 39.5 per cent, 1987-89 73.1 per cent and total growth over the period 1979-89 of 193.7 per cent. The comparable rates of growth in the UK and Japan over the same period were 88.2 per cent and 71.4 per cent respectively (Thompson 1995). This is of course growth from a very low base, but table 2.1 shows the likely outcome of Korea's successful industrialization and its rising incomes on its cost structure.

Table 2.1
Extrapolated Total Labour Costs per Employee 1989-99 in $

	France	Germany	Italy	UK	USA	Japan	S. Korea
Labour cost in 1989	29,423	31,857	28,630	21,301	30,829	30,963	12,464
Labour cost in 1999	37,600	47,785	56,006	40,088	44,918	53,071	36,607

Source: Thompson (1995), table 2, p. 103

This is a relatively crude extrapolation from rates of change that could easily alter, but it makes the point that South Korea could be nearly as expensive a producer as France and the UK early in the 21st century. It will thus have to follow a variant of the Japanese path, a route made harder by the fact that its home market is much smaller than Japan's (44 million against 124 million people in 1992). Japan has had a favourable balance of trade for a considerable time, but its exports are a small percentage of GDP. The greater part of Japan's output is consumed domestically.

Countries like Singapore and Hong Kong are seen as economic miracles in the West and silly politicians imagine that they are the new models for the 21st century, but there is little that is surprising in their economic success. Both are entrepôts with high ratios of re-exports to exports in merchandise trade. Singapore exported $58.3 billion of domestic goods in 1994 and re-exported $38.5 billion and Hong Kong exported $28.7 billion of domestic goods in 1994 and re-exported $122.7 billion. In both cases domestic imports at $64.2 billion and $43.2 billion respectively were greater than domestic exports. (World Trade Organisation 1995, p. 13) Neither conforms to the high-export, low-import, low-wage producer that some Western politicians and commentators fear. But Western Tiger watchers are afraid of an almost impossible entity: the economic equivalent of the frictionless machine.

4. Do multinationals now dominate world output and trade? Are such companies becoming transnational and ceasing to have national loyalties?

Many people are concerned that a globalized economy means the dominance of uncontrollable world-market forces and that multinational companies will become the dominant actors in such markets, having escaped from the scope of national regulation. Such firms will locate wherever economic advantage dictates. They will seek to dump costs on local governments and taxpayers, they will threaten to move if challenged, and they will seek to drive down both wages and social overhead costs.

Multinational companies can be defined as those with subsidiaries and affiliates in more than one national jurisdiction. The question is whether output and employment in the internationally-traded sectors of the world economy and in the major industrialized nations is becoming dominated by such companies. The answer seems to be not. The most exhaustive recent survey of the evidence concludes: ' .... the share of internationalized production (i.e. production by multinational firms outside their home countries) in world output was only about 7 per cent of world output in 1990 ...'. (Lipsey, Blomström and Ramstetter 1995) The authors of this survey generate various measures but calculate the share of output from multinational affiliates as a percentage of world GDP as follows (estimated from home country data): 1970 4.5 per cent; 1977 5.4 per cent; 1982 5.7 per cent; 1988 6.6 per cent; and 1990 6.8 per cent. (Lipsey, Blomström and Ramstetter 1995, p. 45) These figures show steady growth in production by multinationals, but hardly a share of world output that would dominate world markets in the way the more pessimistic proponents of the globalization thesis would claim.

Capital mobility and free trade are not creating footloose companies either. Most companies remain rooted in distinct national bases, even if they produce and trade in more than one country. Winfried Ruigrok and Rob van Tulder have produced a good deal of evidence to support their conclusion that 'none of the world's largest companies in 1993 could truly be called global'. Most companies continue to have the bulk of their productive assets in one national location – Daimler Benz and British Aerospace generated 57 per cent and 65 per cent of their sales abroad but only 19 per cent and 18 per cent of their respective assets were located abroad. Most major companies' top management boards are dominated by main location nationals. Most of the top 100 international companies in 1993 had gained at some time from public policies – as Ruigrok points out at least 20 of them would not have survived without some form of government assistance in the relatively recent past. (Ruigrok and Van Tulder 1995)

Our own evidence bears out this scarcity of truly transnational companies. Multinational companies typically have about two thirds of their assets in their home region/country, and sell about the same proportion of their goods and services in their home region/country. Germany and Japan both seem to have concentrated their sales of manufactured goods in their home region/country between 1987 and 1992-93, the respective percentages being 72 per cent to 75 per cent in the case of Germany and 64 per cent to 75 per cent in that of Japan; the figures for the UK and USA in 1992-93 were 65 per cent and 67 per cent. In 1992-93 Japanese multinationals held 97 per cent of their manufacturing assets in Asia; the figures for UK and US multinationals home assets were 62 per cent and 73 per cent respectively. (Hirst and Thompson 1996, p. 96) Multinational firms thus operate from distinct national bases, and, although export sales and levels of foreign competition in their home markets are significant for their strategies and operations, they are not rootless capital. In particular they cannot ignore their central home region/country markets. They are, therefore, not beyond the scope of national regulation, nor can they be indifferent to national public policy. Hence they can both be influenced by and will try to influence national governments. This does not make companies benign. National companies can just as easily try to bully their governments and labour forces, but the image of transnational companies beyond all governance is largely false.

5. Do international financial markets dictate national monetary and fiscal policies?

Some advocates of the globalization thesis might concede all that we have claimed so far, and yet argue that the central difference between the post-1945 era and now is the scale and power of integrated world financial markets. It is perfectly true that under the Bretton-Woods – GATT system trade was liberalizing but that capital movements were controlled. The aim of semi-fixed exchange rates was to ensure stability and, therefore, to give certainty to actor's expectations, thus promoting growth. Foreign exchange transactions were linked principally to trade and to long-term capital investments. This system was not without constraints. Throughout the Bretton Woods era the UK operated under a balance of payments constraint and this helped to contribute to the stop-go cycle of UK growth.

The scale of short-term transactions in the international foreign exchange markets – one trillion dollars a day – dwarfs the flows of foreign trade and direct investment. It also means that the major central banks just do not have the reserves (singly or collectively) to defend a given exchange rate if the markets have made up their mind that it will move up or down. Traders and commentators undoubtedly have prejudices; they favour low inflation, sound money public policies. There is little conflict with national governments of the major industrial powers here because most central bankers and national economic policy-makers think the same way. These policies undoubtedly inhibit growth and they establish the short-term interest of major financial institutions as the supreme economic wisdom.

This is not a satisfactory situation. The advanced world is trading jobs and growth for low inflation – the price is the growth of unemployment and poverty in the major industrial nations. But this is not quite the disaster of volatile casino-like financial markets wrecking real economies that the most alarmist counsels of the danger of unregulated international markets claim. Moreover, the markets are no longer that volatile or unregulated – they are probably governed just about enough to prevent meltdown. After the break-up of the Bretton Woods system in the early 1970s and the 1973 and 1979 oil price hikes there was a period of floating and highly volatile exchange rates. The turbulence was gradually brought under control; with the Plaza Accord of 1985 and the Louvre Accord of 1987 governments restored some minimal stability to the international monetary system. Throughout the 1980s, the dismantling of exchange controls has been accompanied by the re-regulation of financial institutions and markets through the Bank of International Settlements and other agencies. This sets the rules for such activities but does not attempt to steer or alter the price-making functions of markets. (Hirst and Thompson 1996, pp. 129-36)

This is not enough, but it shows that governance is possible. The vast majority of actors in the financial markets have an interest in a minimum degree of calculability in the international system too – not just exporters and long-term international investors. Incalculable risks undermine expectations, and thus extreme volatility is a growth and investment killer. Markets and institutions accept this for the turbulence caused by high inflation; they need to be made to realize that the turbulence created by exchange-rate crises and financial markets crashes can be equally problematic. Perhaps only a grave crisis will do this, but attitudes are slowly changing. Most international trading is done by major financial institutions that have definite expectations to meet – those of pensioners, bulk depositors, maturing policy-holders, and not least, those of their own shareholders for dividends. They have used the markets to make profits on short-term dealing and to hedge against risk. The Barings and Sumitomo scandals may well force the senior managements of the major institutions to seek greater regulation within their companies and also greater regulation of the major international markets. In the long run the markets will only be further re-regulated if the major actors in them see the benefits of doing so or if a combination of powerful governments decides to act in a co-ordinated way. At present neither of these things is likely. The world financial markets are not inherently ungovernable. The problem is the will to govern them, not the want of means. Given the will there is a variety of possible options, like James Tobin's turnover tax on short-term international financial movements.

6. Will globalization drive down both wages and welfare provision in the advanced countries?

Again this needs to be re-phrased somewhat more ponderously, as follows: do wages, levels of welfare provision and ratios of public spending to GDP in the advanced nations have to converge to the lowest possible level as a result of competition between them and with the developing nations to attract and retain capital?

Consider wages first. There is some evidence that for unskilled wages in manufacturing Third World competition does have a depressive effect. This is strongly argued by Adrian Wood. (1995, pp. 57-80; 1994) However, in most major economies in the developed world, such low-wage manufacturing sectors are not large enough to affect overall wages for the unskilled – most of whom work in low-productivity service jobs in sectors that are not internationally tradeable. In the case of the USA imports from low-wage countries (less than 50 per cent US wage levels) were a mere 2.8 per cent of GDP – far too little to affect overall wage rates significantly. (Krugman 1996, p. 47) Trying to compete with the Third World in wage costs in manufacturing is impossible – from China to Indonesia workers are available at a tiny fraction of the hourly rate for Western manufacturing employees whether skilled or unskilled.

Cutting wage costs may restore comparative advantage against other comparable advanced country producers, offsetting productivity differentials. The UK has recently followed a strategy of wage-cutting and competitive devaluation, mainly against its European Union partners. This is a short-term strategy that might make some sense if the UK were at the same time attempting to address by other means the problem of differential productivity. But, if it becomes a substitute for sustained productivity enhancement (and in the UK's case it seems to be) then it locks the country in question on a low-wage path and into having to export a larger proportion of its output to match imports. It appears that wages are not being greatly depressed by Third World competition and that the strategy of low-wage competition against other advanced countries is not sustainable in the long term except at the price of falling ever further behind in relative standards of living.

This does not stop illiterate politicians and ideologically-crazed economists claiming that the UK will become more competitive if the wages of British office cleaners are reduced to starvation levels. How they are competing with their equivalents in Jakarta or Shanghai is not clear, since most unskilled services will never be internationally tradeable. This low-wage strategy is best described as seeking competitive advantage by sweating – but it is mad. In the tradeable sector we cannot compete on wages with very low-wage countries – what are we going to pay? 50 pennies or 30 pennies an hour? In the non-tradeable sector trying to force down unskilled wages to poverty levels will mainly have the effect of shifting income from labour to profits. Moreover, a generalized strategy of wage-cutting will depress domestic effective demand, output and employment. Public officials who believe they are saving public money by such strategies ought to be sacked; ultimately they are undermining the national economy to line the pockets of bottom-of-the-bucket cheapskate employers. The sources of such policies are not global pressures, but a mixture of domestic interest groups using this rhetoric to feather their own nests and a failure of nerve by those who should be offering clear alternative policies, a timidity reinforced by the belief in global competitive threats. Radical reflationary policies face serious domestic constraints at the moment, but that is no reason to further inhibit domestic performance by self-defeating attitudes on wages and working conditions. (Hirst and Thomspon 1996a)

Many globalizers see current European levels of welfare spending and public expenditure to GDP ratios as unsustainable. Robert Skidelsky argues, for example, that public expenditure ratios need to be pushed back to the 30 per cent of GDP that they were in most cases in the 1960s. (Skidelsky 1995; 1996) Andrew Marr contends that high ratios of public spending to national income are a reflection of economic failure and unemployment. (Marr 1995; 1996) The state will have to tax and spend less in the long run; it will have to take the medicine imposed by global competitive pressures or face capital flight.

Such arguments are not supported by either economic theory or evidence. Why 30 per cent? Why not 10 per cent or 48 per cent? Who says current levels of public expenditure in Europe are unsustainable? *The Economist,* not noted for its opposition to the notion of globalization, recognizes that there are wide and persisting variations in the percentage of GDP devoted to public spending – in 1994 20 per cent in Singapore, 33 per cent in the USA, 49 per cent in Germany and 68 per cent in Sweden. (*Economist* 7 October 1995 'The Myth of the Powerless State') Table 2.2 gives comparative data on government expenditures as a percentage of GDP. All the countries listed show a growth in the ratio, despite in the case of the UK and USA attempts to cut government expenditure in the 1980s.

Globalization and Labour Relations

Table 2.2
General Government Total Expenditure 1960-1995 (per cent GDP at market prices)

	1960	1970	1980	1990	1995
Austria	35.6	39.2	48.8	49.3	52.7
France	34.6	38.9	46.6	50.5	54.1
W. Germany	32.5	38.5	48.0	45.3	49.1*
Italy	30.1	34.2	41.9	53.2	53.5
Japan	n/a	19.4	32.6	32.3	34.9
Sweden	n/a	43.7	61.2	60.7	69.4
UK	32.2	37.3	43.2	40.3	42.5
USA	27.0	31.6	33.7	36.7	36.1
NOTES	*United Germany n/a = not available				

Source: European Economy No. 60 (1996) Derived from table 61, pp. 212-13

The data also show persistent differences in ratios of government expenditures to GDP between states over the last 25 years. Austria has been at the high end and the USA at the bottom end throughout, for example. Moreover, there has been no consistent effect on growth rates. Thus Japan and the USA both have low GDP ratios for public expenditure but very different rates of growth. Slemrod (1995) in a thorough survey of the relationships between taxation and government expenditure on the one hand and GDP growth rates and prosperity on the other, found no systematic or robust empirical relationship between high government expenditure and poor economic performance. (Slemrod 1995) This is not to say there is no level of public expenditure to GDP that would not be growth-inhibiting, but that the opponents of the current levels have yet to make a coherent case for such a general effect.

Moreover, it is by no means clear that public expenditures are driven primarily by welfare spending or that such spending varies markedly over time or that current levels are unsustainable. Table 2.3 measures social protection – health, pensions, unemployment benefits and other income support. It shows considerable stability rather than relentless and insupportable growth.

Table 2.3
Total Public Expenditure on Social Protection (per cent of GDP)

	1980	1981	1982	1983	1984	1985	1986	1987	1988	1989	1990
EC countries											
Belgium	25.4	27.4	28.1	28.4	27.9	27.5	27.2	26.6	25.2	25.2	25.2
Denmark	26.0	27.6	28.1	28.0	26.8	26.0	24.8	25.7	27.8	27.8	27.8
France	23.9	25.4	26.5	27.3	27.8	27.9	27.4	27.0	26.4	26.4	26.5
Germany	25.4	26.3	26.6	25.8	25.4	25.2	24.7	25.0	24.1	24.1	23.5
Greece	13.4	14.9	17.9	18.4	19.1	20.1	20.6	20.8	20.9	20.9	*
Ireland	20.6	21.1	22.5	23.5	23.0	23.1	23.3	22.5	19.6	19.6	19.7
Italy	19.8	20.8	21.5	23.0	22.2	22.7	22.5	23.2	23.7	23.7	24.5
Luxembourg	26.0	27.2	26.4	26.0	25.0	25.0	24.4	25.9	26.6	26.6	27.3
Netherlands	27.2	28.4	30.2	30.8	29.7	28.8	28.4	29.0	27.9	27.9	28.8
Portugal	13.6	15.2	14.1	13.6	13.6	13.8	14.3	14.9	14.9	14.9	15.3
Spain	16.8	17.9	18.0	18.7	18.5	19.0	18.4	18.2	18.8	18.8	19.3
UK	21.3	23.3	23.6	24.0	24.0	24.1	23.9	22.9	21.9	21.3	22.3
EFTA countries											
Austria	23.4	24.2	24.1	24.4	24.4	24.8	25.1	25.4	25.3	25.1	24.5
Finland	21.4	22.1	23.3	24.2	24.6	25.9	26.3	26.7	25.6	25.4	27.1
Norway	21.4	22.0	22.5	23.0	23.0	22.1	24.2	26.2	27.0	28.1	28.7
Sweden	32.4	33.3	33.5	33.8	32.7	32.6	33.9	33.5	34.1	33.3	33.1
North America											
Canada	*	*	17.3	17.5	17.1	17.1	17.7	17.4	17.0	17.2	18.8
USA	14.1	14.3	15.0	15.3	14.3	14.3	14.4	14.4	14.4	14.5	14.6
NOTES											

* Data not aviable

Source: OECD Social Protection database table 4.7, p. 151; OECD Employment Outlook July 1994

If this is the case, why is there so much concern about social spending? In part because governments in the bulk of the advanced world have been running more or less substantial budgetary deficits and social expenditures seem easier to freeze and cut than some other programmes. The figure of 3 per cent of GDP as a desirable upper limit for government net borrowing in the Maastricht criteria for EMU is exerting a clear depressive pressure on government expenditures in the EU. It certainly helps to try and justify the cuts thus imposed by appealing to the needs of international competitiveness, even if the real reason is the consequence of seeking to make economies with divergent performances converge in order to pursue the goal of monetary union with low inflation. Government receipts have fallen relative to expenditure in many countries. In some cases this is as a result of tax-cutting strategies, or because of poor macro-economic management and miscalculations about the timing and strength of economic recoveries. But these are domestic choices and policy errors by national economic managers, not the relentless and direct pressure of global markets. Provided a country remains competitive in the goods and services it trades internationally, it can still choose high levels of social spending and collective consumption. There is no clear evidence that public expenditure *per se* undermines growth or economic performance.

7. Is the world economy now ungovernable and must global market forces inevitably overwhelm and subvert distinctive national projects of governance?

It should be clear by now that globalization has not swept away national economies. The political and business elites of advanced Western nations have found globalization a convenient cloak for the domestic policies they have chosen to follow – especially in the UK and USA. There are many reasons why full employment is difficult to attain, why social solidarity and social welfare are under severe pressure, why electorates are tax-averse, and why organized labour has much less power than it once did. But these changes are common to the social structures of many advanced societies and are not primarily the consequence of international competitive pressures. It is equally true that, while a great deal can be accomplished by national policies for economic management and social renewal, the national is merely one level in a complex division of economic and social governance.

Regional and local government has become more salient as industry has become more diversified and has moved away from the Fordist norm of large-scale standardized mass production. Those societies that have exploited the new trends best are those in which national and sub-national governments have achieved, whether deliberately or by happenstance, an appropriate division of labour. Equally, national governance is not in itself adequate for economic management; co-ordinated national action, and international agencies and regimes, are crucial for control of the world economy. This is not new. After 1945 effective national economic management in the advanced countries rested on a firm framework of international institutions underpinned by US hegemony. The true era of national policies, the 1930s, was one of trade crises, bitter rivalry, economic depression, and militarism.

The need for regulation of market economies at national level and the requirement for an appropriate system of management of the international economy are linked. Globalizers try to convince us that the international economy is inherently ungovernable and that it is absorbing and subsuming national economies; projects of regulation are thus futile. This is just not true, but national governance does require an effective international framework and the advanced nations must co-operate to provide it. The central problem here is not global markets but divergent national interests – those of the USA, Japan, and the major European states. These differences are exacerbated by the fear of global competition and the belief that co-operation is hopeless given the power of the markets. The rhetoric of competitiveness makes people scared, afraid of their own failure, and, therefore, indifferent to the fate of the poor in their own countries and in the Third World. Counterposing the declining role of national sovereignty and the growing salience of international markets and global problems is not useful – modern problems can only be coped with by a complex division of labour in governance. Clinging to national sovereignty is not effective either – national governments are effective only when they co-operate with effective sub-national and supra-national governing powers with a definite sphere of autonomy. If we can work towards such an extended division of labour in governance, if we can reduce fear that economies and societies are beyond control, then peoples and elites in the advanced countries may be willing to pursue more generous and egalitarian policies nationally and internationally.

What might those policies be? First, consider the level of international economic governance, where a great deal more could not be accomplished by the economic great powers of the G7 and major international institutions like the World Bank and IMF. A less cautious and more expansionary policy pursued across the advanced world might begin to reduce unemployment and increase the rate of growth. A co-ordinated policy would leave the financial markets less room to sanction policies they fear, given their instinctive preference for low inflation rather than growth. This would need to be reinforced by greater regulation of the markets to render short-term movements less profitable and to reduce volatility and rogue trading. A growth-oriented policy in the advanced countries needs to be coupled with a determined attempt to reduce debt for the poorest countries, to increase aid and to distribute foreign direct investment more widely – by tax incentives and levies that steer firms away from the top ten developing countries towards some of the poorer ones. Such policies could be achieved in the near future by more active and co-ordinated policies on the part of the advanced states – what stands in the way is not globalization but perceptions of national interest by key elites.

At the national level in the advanced countries radical go-it-alone expansionary policies are unlikely to succeed – not just because international markets may disapprove but primarily because, in a changed economic conjuncture, stimulus to demand does not lead to the major and rapid falls in unemployment that Keynes anticipated in the 1930s; most jobs require investment. However that does not mean that countries have to run actively deflationary policies. Equally, in a period of relatively low growth and strong demands on public welfare, it is difficult dramatically to increase levels of public spending. This does not mean that current levels of public expenditure are unsustainable or that existing welfare provision is unsupportable. In Europe the conditions for monetary union under the Maastricht Treaty are deflationary. Perhaps this means that we should slow down the process of monetary union because of the danger that the cuts required to implement it will damage the European Union politically with key constituencies in a number of major member states.

At the regional level new forms of economic governance have been emerging in recent decades, spurred on by the shift from standardized mass production to more customized and quality-oriented manufacturing and services – such diversity has favoured localization, it has also put a premium on intimate knowledge in the governance of economic sectors and, therefore, emphasized distinctive regional rather than uniform national industrial policies. The effect of this is to favour those countries where well-developed industrial districts are coupled with effective local and regional governments able to provide support and collective services for industry. Highly-centralized states like the UK are at a disadvantage in this respect. The future for governing the economy lies with a division of labour and co-ordination between the international, national and regional levels. This will be difficult to achieve and sustain; governance is more difficult than if the national state were a sovereign economic regulator. But that is an illusion, states have always been most effective when they have operated in an appropriate context of international institutions and policies – like the managed multilateralism after 1945. The myth of globalization works to undermine the very notion of such a division of labour, it tells us that the international economy is ungovernable and that national governments are ineffective. That is why it needs to be resisted and refuted.

Note

1.   This chapter originally appeared in *Soundings*, Issue 4, 1996.

References

Bairoch, P. (1996), 'Globalisation Myths and Realities', in Boyer, R. and D. Drache (eds), *States Against Markets – The Limits of Globalisation*, London: Routledge.

Bairoch, P. and R. Kozul-Wright (1996), 'Globalisation Myths: Some Historical Reflections on Integration, Industrialisation and Growth in the World Economy', UNCTAD Discussion Paper No. 113, March 1996.

Glynn, A. (1995), 'The Assessment: Unemployment and Inequality', *Oxford Review of Economic Policy*, **11** (1), 1-25.

Gray, J. (1996), *After Social Democracy*, London: Demos.

Hirst, P. and G. Thompson (1996), *Globalisation in Question*, Cambridge: Polity Press.

Hirst, P. and G. Thompson (1996a), 'Global Myths and National Policies, *Renewal*, **4** (2).

International Monetary Fund (1994), *World Economic Outlook*, Washington, DC: IMF.

Krugman, P. (1996), *Pop Internationalism,* Cambridge MA: MIT Press.

Lipsey, R.E., M. Blomström and E. Ramstetter (1995), 'Internationalized Production in World Output', NBER Working Paper 5385 Dec. 1995.

Marr, A. (1995), 'Stuck between the flab and a hard place', *Independent*, 19 October 1995.

Marr, A. (1996), *Ruling Britannia*, London: Penguin Books.

Ruigrok, W. and R. van Tulder (1995), *The Logic of International Restructuring*, London: Routledge.

Skidelsky, R. (1995), *The World After Communism*, London: Macmillan.

Skidelsky, R. (1996), 'Welfare without the State', *Prospect*, January, 38-43.

Slemrod, J. (1995), 'What do Cross-Country Studies Teach about Government Involvement, Prosperity and Economic Growth', *Brookings Papers on Economic Activity*, 2, pp. 373-431.

Thompson, G. (1995), 'A Comment on the Crisis of Cost Recovery and the Waste of the Industrialised Nations', *Competition and Change*, **1**, 101-10.

Wolf, M. (1995), 'Globalisation and the State', *Financial Times*, 18 September.

Wood, A. (1994), *North-South Trade, Employment and Inequality – Changing Fortunes in a Skill-Driven World*, Oxford: Clarendon Press.

Wood, A. (1995), 'How Trade Hurt Unskilled Workers', *Journal of Economic Perspectives*, **9** (3), 57-80.

World Trade Organisation (1995), *International Trade Trends and Statistics 1993*, Geneva: WTO.

3. Towards the Denaturing of Class Relations?

The Political Economy of the Firm in Global Capitalism

Jacques Vilrokx

> *Face à l'entrée du labyrinthe moderne, il convient d'abord de se remettre dans l'antique état d'esprit du nomade, pour comprendre physiquement ce que sont ces méandres. Faire de cette errance apparemment obscure une avancé constructive, vivre cette traversée comme une libération, lui donner un sens, la rendre créatrice.*

Jacques Attali (1996, p.160)

Introduction

Generally, macro-economists have paid little attention to the structural transformations that have occurred within organizations as a consequence of the world economy since the 1980s. Additionally, the broader economic environment in which organization change took place has been narrowed down by micro-economists and organization (and management) experts to the need to be increasingly competitive in the global market. The objective of competitiveness being self-evident and proclaimed as a fact of life, it is considered in no need of any further qualification. In this respect it is somewhat more than just illustrative that the chairman of the European Round Table of Industrialists consistently uses Competitiveness (with capital C) in his foreword to a recent report.

In the present contribution we will try to connect both macro-economic and company-level transformations by hypothesizing the fundamental interrelatedness of change processes at these two levels. We will argue that the globalization of the economy was possible because at the level of the company, completely new objectives have been defined not only in economic terms but also with regard to the organization of the firm as a social system. At the same time, changes that pushed the economic globalization tendency, influenced the restructuring of organizations.

We will start by highlighting the two defining characteristics of the global or new economy: on the one hand, the transition from a production-oriented capitalism to a financially-oriented capitalism and, on the other hand, the global economic division of production. In this context a clear distinction will be made between four strategies that companies have historically pursued in their striving for economic survival and growth: internationalization, multinationalization, mondialization and globalization. Each of these four strategies can be identified as dominant for a particular sequential stage in capitalist development. They point to very specific growth strategies that companies have (cumulatively!) developed, and between which it is analytically important to differentiate.

Taking into account the above strategies, we concentrate, in the second part, on their consequences for employment relations at the level of the company, more particularly within the context of globalization. How have legitimation processes underlying systems of regulation of labour been modified by factors outside the firm? We argue that two management strategies, the organization of the optimalization of individual competence, and the clientification of workers, are altering class-legitimized control relations at the workplace. As far as the trade-union side is concerned, the definition of a collective identity (or solidarity) and the apparently lost possibilities of alliances with political parties will be mentioned as the major problem areas.

We will conclude by hypothesizing that these management strategies and problem areas the trade unions are faced with, challenge the class- and stratum-based organization of workers and, as a consequence, the nature of industrial relations and the regulation of labour.

This contribution touches upon an aspect of what is one of the more intriguing problems society is faced with as a consequence of the economic restructuring that has taken place during the last 25 years: to what extent do organizations (trade unions, employers organizations, companies, political parties and so on) still represent the interests of their members? The idea of representativeness has been of central importance in the conceptualization and institutionalization of post-war welfare state regimes and now seems more and more problematic as a mechanism for building solidarity. (Touraine 1994; Vilrokx 1996; Haarscher and Libois 1997)

The Two Dimensions of Global Capitalism

In 1997 the denomination new economy became widely used in the United States alongside the more common term global economy favoured throughout the 1990s. As such this is not unfortunate. New economy stresses the fact that current economic functioning is different from the old economy. Although it would be difficult to defend that new economy represents the ultimate in conceptual precision, it acknowledges, at least, the fact that as a result of the fundamental restructuring since the mid-1970s, a systemic change in the functioning of the economy has been brought about.

Such a consciousness has barely arisen in Europe where most economists, commentators and politicians alike, generally still use a kind of economic recession discourse when discussing the present situation. This is misleading and dangerous because it does not recognize (or conceals more or less consciously?) the discontinuity in the functioning of the economy that occurred in the 1970s. It leads policy-makers to propose the sort of old-economy measures as if we were not faced, since the 1970s, with an economic restructuring, a transition to a fundamentally different economic environment than the one that existed before that period.

Being unable to understand and, consequently, to assess the nature of the economic changes in terms of a historical discontinuity, policy-makers have also failed to recognize the need for the (re-)construction of social and political solidarity mechanisms. More and more indications with regard to individual and collective behaviour, point to possibly very disruptive situations in European countries. If this materializes, it can be feared that the effects will be quite disastrous for example at the level of a constructive European unification process, the coherence and stability of social and political systems and, of course, the social regulation of labour.

For reasons that will be made explicit we prefer the term global capitalism to the ones generally used. In the next section we briefly go into what are the two constituting elements of global capitalism: the shift from a production capitalism to a financial capitalism and the implementation of a global economic division of production.

Financial capitalism

There are many indications (increasing merger movements, stock exchange and monetary technology, speculation against national currencies, and so on) that suggest that financial aspects and the interests of stockholders determine strategic decisions of the key economic players more and more. Creation of wealth is increasingly generated by the manipulation of capital flows and by financial product innovations, involving huge risk-capital flows, rather than by the production of goods and services to people. A large part of the economy thus becomes virtual (Bourguinat 1995) or immaterial (Goldfinger 1994). As a result, purely financial transfers far outweigh capital movements related to selling and buying of goods and services. Goldfinger (1994, p. 29) reports that world wide the daily volume of stock exchange transactions is some $1,000 billion as against only $15-20 billion for the trade in goods. And while the international exchange of goods and services increased 3 per cent more than production in the 1960s, this figure was 2 per cent in the 1970s and 1 per cent in the 1980s as against a yearly increase of 10 per cent of certain financial flows in the first years of the 1990s. (Bourguinat 1995, p. 107)

The enormous amount of literature on this subject (e.g. Boyer *et al.*, 1997; Went 1996) suggests a quite strong consensus as far as the importance of the financial dimension in economic functioning is concerned. If, however, many contributions have documented this ever growing dominance of financial markets over product markets, a parallel evolution has attracted much less scientific attention. We refer here to the way the general public and the workers have been implicated in the new financial capitalist environment. This can be illustrated through the privatization wave that has accompanied the establishment of financial capitalism. 'Germans dive into the equity culture' was a characteristically concise and precise headline of the *Financial Times* (19 November 1996) reporting public reaction on the occasion of the privatization of *Deutsche Telekom*. Such mass support legitimizes the ongoing economic restructuring process even if the transformation of the worker into a worker-stockholder is relatively new in Europe compared to the United States. Anyway, it can be considered as one of the dimensions of the denaturing of class relations.

It is clear that from a sociological point of view, both the dimensions of the implication of the general public and the workers mentioned above have served as legitimation mechanisms for the financial capitalist development to be smooth and drastic. We will come back to the consequences this has for the regulation of labour.

The global economic division of production

As an introduction to this second characteristic, it is useful to make an analytical distinction between internationalization, multinationalization, mondialization and globalization. Often these concepts are used indiscriminately, thus leading to considerable conceptual confusion. Although all four have to do with economy-of-scale policies, they differ fundamentally at the level of their underlying strategic logic (see Table 3.1).

What we will argue in the first place is that each of these concepts indeed points to specific stages in the development of capitalism and is, therefore, connected with equally specific stages in the development of other sub-systems of societal organization. In the second place it will be stressed that with the gradual development of a new growth strategy from a certain period on (for example mondialization) the former strategies (internationalization and multinationalization) do not vanish and are not diluted but, on the contrary, strengthen because, respectively, industrial production and world markets continue to develop quantitatively and qualitatively. As a result, a new growth strategy does not replace the other ones but makes a supplementary growth technique available for companies. In practice it is most probable that companies will combine (elements of) two or more growth strategies in their striving for economies-of-scale. In summary, it can be said that these sequential strategies correspond to answers to new challenges at particular stages of the development of the capitalist-economic environment, but that each of these strategies continues to be valid in the ever more differentiated capitalist-economic environment and, once recognized, they essentially form cumulative options for companies to adopt at need.

By internationalization we mean the cross-border expansion of activities on a non-permanent basis by a particular company. It is, typically, a growth strategy based on the international enlargement of the firm's product market. Internationalization is historically the first stage of economic expansion. Even in pre-capitalist societies the international dimension of the commercialization of goods and services has been, of course, extremely important: precious products and services were traded internationally and highly specialized craftsmen and experts went to work abroad on prestigious projects. These two main forms of internationalization, by exporting both products and the expertise to make products, can still be distinguished.

Table 3.1
Trends in Socio-Economic Development

Stages in economic Development	Growth strategies of firms	Main macro-economic catalyst	Production organization	Type of worker representation	Time scale
Internationalization	Product market enlargement	Industrial production	Craft-based Small batch	Guild	End 18th C
Multinationalization	Financial-economic expansion	Development of the world market	Standardization	Sectoral	Mid 19th C
Mondialization	World-wide brand marketing	Core-periphery relations	Assembly line	Collective	Beginning 20th C
Globalization	Lean production	Information technology Transportation logistics	Nomadic integration	Specific interests	Third quarter 20th C

First, the selling of goods and services on foreign markets (for example Belgian trams for Istanbul's public transport) and, second, off-shore projects (for example the construction of the first East-European under-grounds by West-European companies and the building of nuclear plants or other turn-key plants in developing countries by consortiums of firms from the highly industrialized countries) are examples here.

The increased internationalization tendency from the end of the 18th century onwards can be considered a direct consequence of industrial capitalism and has accompanied inherently economic development since.

The next stage, multinationalization, is linked with the invention of standardization (and combinability and interchangeability). As a capital intensive concept, standardization can only be sustainable when production is organized in large batches. Its generalization, therefore, increased the need to create a world market.

Multinationalization is the growth strategy based on financial-economic consolidation. The development of world markets with sufficient purchasing power called for financial techniques in order to meet capital intensive expansion strategies. This process started around the mid-19th century and for reasons that are not difficult to understand America was the first of such a world market.

Two main action patterns have been deployed in pursuing a multinational environment. In the first place, firms can look for participations in existing companies (for example Westinghouse buying Belgian ACEC[1]), or acquire other companies. In the second place, companies can establish production units in other countries (for example Philips producing in several places in Belgium and other countries). Different options are open here: delocalization with decreasing activities on the home market, with expansion as well on the home market as on third markets, and diversification. The multinationalization of the economy could take off exponentially when from the mid-19th century a world-wide demand-and-supply situation for fairly standardized products developed.

Mondialization is a strategy pertaining to the expansion of markets for highly uniform mass-consumption products (Coca-Cola and Nike) and for more high-end brand products (Chanel and BMW) with world-wide appeal and strong life-style identification potential. Such a strategy can be pursued in close connection with the multinationalization strategy. The merger between LVHM and Guinness is an example of such a combination of strategies.

Globalization, finally, is the strategy towards the borderless organization of production of goods and services in order to obtain optimal integration of the different components and processes within that production system. It is based on just-in-time routines and the highest possible level of incorporation of subcontractors in the production process, not only in the definition of specifications of components but also in the research and development phase of the final product combined with responsibilities for the end assembly of that final product. In such an ideal world brand makers are not producers of brands anymore but conceptualizers and sellers of brands. The automobile sector (Lopez' Brazilian Resende project for Volkswagen is a good example), and the sportshoes industry (Nike) present some of the more advanced steps in this direction, at the level of the production of goods. As far as the service sector is concerned, recent mergers (perhaps most importantly in banking and assurances, and consultancy) are typical examples of the global production integration strategy. By definition, a globalization strategy can only be put in practice when products can be marketed world-wide and when extremely strong financial resources are available.

It is important to note that each of the four strategies of the above typology point to very distinct objectives and are characterized by specific action patterns. Moreover, internally these strategies can differ in degree of sophistication, managerial and material resources to be allocated, and so on. They are strictly cumulative (a globalization strategy implies incorporating and superseding the former strategies) but must, again, analytically be separated. The argument we will put forward is that the proposed classification also represents an ordinal scale of what we have called the tendency towards an increasing relative autonomy of lower level organizational units or relative autonomization. (Vilrokx 1987; 1996) The implementation of relative autonomy implies, and aims at, a certain independence of companies, or parts of them. It is a necessary condition for production organizations to be (potentially) nomadic on an international, multinational, mondial or global scale.

Many other conceptualizations (transnationality, multinational networks, and so on) have been used in this context. As the exemplary case of IBM shows (Hamill 1993, p. 90), responsibility or, using the more analytical terminology, accountability of lower level organizational units underlies most, if not all, organizational changes that have been carried out by (global) firms. We will briefly develop this theme.

Attali (1990) has suggested that our culture (or the way we interact with other people and create things) is increasingly determined by electronic data carrying nomadic objects. Portable PC's, walkmans, cellular telephones, and so on, are nomadic because their use is not limited to a specific location and they enable information manipulation in real-time. Nomadic objects, Attali argues, are becoming more and more important in the organization of social life. Many examples can be given of other forms of nomadic objects. To develop Attali's analysis somewhat further, we could say, for instance, that expert systems (in the medical, educational or legal sphere) are nomadic phenomena too. This is particularly relevant because it illustrates that not only information carriers become increasingly nomadic but also information itself can be disconnected from its traditional carriers (medical doctors, university professors, lawyers) and can be made (more) nomadic (than, for example, books previously).

We can take the argument one step further. Not only objects as information carriers are subject to such a trend, workers, who are also information carriers, are too. Atypical labour contracts (temporary workers are the most striking examples of the modern nomads) and many ideas about the new organization of work (multi-availability, employability) point to completely different conceptions and practices with regard to the labour process. Evidently these changes profoundly affect the relations workers have among each other, and with their organization.

But not only objects and workers as information carriers are becoming more and more nomadic, organizations also carry an information content and have become increasingly nomadic. Thus, delocalization of companies (or parts of them), subcontracting and outsourcing, to name just a few, can, of course, also be seen as forms of nomadic behaviour of the firm. Even the (re)organization of companies into business units is to be considered as creating a nomadic environment, because potentially a specific business unit can be replaced by another, internal or external, supplier when it does not meet preset productivity, financial or other standards. It follows from this that making workers and/or organizations nomadic implies giving them a certain level of autonomy. In fact, the construction of (relative) autonomy is the broader and more fundamental goal companies pursue, rather than the objective of nomadism. We could say, to use a well-known distinction, that the aim of the implementation of relative autonomy is strategic, while the objective of nomadism is operational.

Without going into any detail here, we would like to argue that the gradual construction of a relative autonomous environment constituted the (often unconscious) underlying principle of virtually all advances in (production) organization change and that it constitutes the (much more conscious) underlying principle of more recent organization theories and practices. Variants of Human Resources Management (as intervention strategies at the level of the optimalization of the use of labour) and variants of Business Process Reengineering (as intervention strategies at the level of the optimalization of the organizational structure) are, finally, all based on the implementation of relatively autonomous relations between workers and the organization, between workers themselves, and between components of the organization.

The organizational principle of relative autonomy applies to the micro-, meso- as well as the macro-level functioning of organizations. Individual intrapreneurship at 3M, business units now implemented in almost all companies of any size and the think globally, act locally strategy of the ABB group are, respectively, examples of the (relative) free-movers environment that is increasingly created on the three mentioned levels. The strict dependence relations between organizational components (branches, departments, teams, individuals, and so on) prevailing in traditional organizations are, thus, transformed into looser but, at the same time, more accountable relations.

Two elements must be highlighted in this respect. First, this tendency is called relative autonomization because autonomy and dependency simultaneously become the poles of attraction of the definition of relations within the organization. Second, on the one hand, binding forces (world-wide concentration of economic and financial power, strengthened authority structures in companies, and so on) are brought into existence and, on the other hand, possibilities are created for a differentiated development of smaller scale patterns of activities. The most important consequence to emphasize here is that such relative autonomy settings require new power and control mechanisms not only on the meso level of the organization of the group, but also on the micro level of the relations within the individual companies of the group. This conclusion brings us to the problem of the regulation of labour to be discussed in the second part of this chapter.

Globalization and the Regulation of Labour

Table 3.1 suggests a relation between the stages in economic development and the type of worker representation. From the guild and sectoral kind of organization in the 19th century, interprofessional organizations started to develop at the end of that century and in the beginning of the 20th century. Improved living and consumption conditions related to production organization innovations resulted, in the core countries, in more collective emancipatory expressions of the workers' power. This period came to an end with the restructuring of the economy which started in the 1970s. The challenges to trade unions are precisely how to cope with the transition of a mondialization into a globalization phase, or, in other words, how to develop counterstrategies when faced with new growth strategies and production organization innovations of companies. These strategies undermine the collectively based representation potential inherent in the mondialization type of economic development.

Campbell (1993, p. 267) has correctly observed that

> Globalization can affect labour and labour institutions in two ways. The first is through the creation of what might be called a 'regulatory deficit', where the national institutions which govern the labour market are rendered less effective by the internationalization of markets. ... The second is the multinational enterprise (MNE), the 'engine' of the tendency toward globalization. The process of globalization creates pressure on MNEs to become global actors, resulting in far-reaching organizational changes *within* and *between* these firms.

In this chapter we will concentrate on the second aspect. It is, however, necessary to specify that, although MNEs are (or have been) the engines of the globalization trend, the consequences of globalization are no longer limited to MNEs. Being caught in the rhetoric or reality (or both) of the globalization of production, virtually all companies are affected.

In this transition the balance of power between capital and labour has shifted toward capital, forcing labour into questioning traditional ways of acting and exploring answers to the new challenges that lie ahead (see for example Rosanvallon 1988; Regini 1992; Durand 1996; Leisink *et al.* 1996). In management visions on how a company should be organized in order to face global competition, two innovations, competence optimalization and client orientation, have shaped managements' approaches toward manpower utilization. The first one concerns the control of the available and needed qualification pool in the enterprise. The second one is the redefinition of the very concept of what a worker is and should be within the organization. To a very large extent one can say that these two objectives are at the core of all human resources policies. More important is that both directly challenge the class- and stratum-based nature of the regulation of employment relations that was dominant in the pre-globalization period.

It is, most probably, not allowed to make reference here to a conscious strategy of management against organized labour. Certain indications exist that an annihilation of organized labour is not the explicit aim (for example French employers' organizations regularly warning that trade unions are becoming too weak). The results of these strategies must be seen, then, as unanticipated consequences for organized labour. Exactly this fact makes it difficult for the trade unions to formulate adequate counterstrategies.

'To remain significant agents of employment regulation, unions must redefine utopias at transnational level while at the same time winning membership comprehension and enthusiasm for such ambitions. The ideal of a social Europe rescued from current evasive obfuscations and given concrete, intelligible meaning could be a starting point' concludes Hyman (1996b, p. 87) after his discussion of union identities and ideologies in Britain, Italy and Germany. It seems that management has had less trouble in redefining its own utopias. Moreover, aided by the ideology of globalization, it was quite successful in implementing significant parts of its utopian views.

Management strategies and actions: toward the objectification of management

Competence Optimalization: Versatility and Accountability

A straightforward definition of the act of organizing is that it tries to mobilize optimal competences in order to achieve an expected outcome, taking into account the internal and external constraints an organization may be confronted with. If we accept this formulation, competence deployment is a pivotal element in any organization. Recent personnel policies have, however, gone far beyond just trying to obtain, in Weick's formulation, 'the establishment of a workable level of certainty' (cited by Scott 1998, p. 98) and have, on the contrary, in quite extreme ways centred around the most efficient way to control the utilisation of competence resources. Behind the discourse on flexibility, employability and other legitimations for the redefinition of the labour process, two management strategies are central in this context: increasing the versatility and the accountability of workers. Both organization strategies are strongly linked, and they allow for the redefinition of the labour process through the optimalization of competence deployment.

Regulatory institutional settings and workers' resistance have often prevented organizational change from being as radical as management intended. Greenfield operations, union-free plants and no-strike deals have, to some extent, eliminated some of these external constraints. The two management innovations mentioned above, versatility and account-ability, are, however, much more far-reaching in scope and depth. They concern the qualitative (internal) aspects of the organization of work (or the terms of employment as opposed to the working conditions), a domain that has been largely neglected by the trade unions more keen on turning the changes in the organization of work asked for by manage-ment to good account.

An optimal competence deployment is primarily achieved through the creation of versatile workers. It is one of the results of the organization of a relatively autonomous environment. Several targets are pursued in this context. The most important one is a separation between worker and job. This involves, logically, two processes: tasks to be performed are redesigned in order to make them independent from their usual or traditional executors but, at the same time, workers are multi-skilled in order to be able to perform different tasks. An availability with respect to task content and a spatial availability are the two qualities of the versatile worker. The worker, made doubly nomadic, identifies less and less with his/her specific job and with his/her particular work spot. As a result, some of the constituting elements in the formation of working-class solidarities vanish in this process.

The trend to emphasize occupational identities and reinforce trade-union solidarities along those lines, is a clear indication that competence optimalization through the implementation of versatility and account-ability does not produce universal effects everywhere at the same time. It also shows that trade unions are reacting against strategies that atomize workers. But there are limits to the realization of such occupational identity building as well as to certain corporatist dangers. Sectors like printing, for example, have a strong, historically developed occupational identity and can resist the unravelling of collective solidarities. Qualifi-cation levels are relatively high and the relation between worker, pro-duction process and product is a very tangible one. In (subsectors of) metal working such favourable conditions also exist. Moreover, it is a well organized sector on the European level. Under these circumstances countervailing trade-union strategies can be imagined. This is much more difficult in sectors characterized by low qualifications and a substantial female workforce such as textiles or various sectors in the service industry. Even in situations with high levels of qualifications and with a high occupational identification, in the new sectors such as marketing and publicity, and information technology, occupation-based organization proves difficult if not impossible. In the latter sectors the level of atypicalization of the contractual labour relation is very high. In general, this aspect seems to be an increasingly crucial factor in the organization of occupational solidarities. In the Netherlands, for example, about half of all labour contracts are fixed term, part-time and interim contracts. Such a nomadic environment hampers occupational identification processes, of course.

The relative autonomization of the worker is also intended to loosen the dependence of the worker on the supervising organization structure and to enlarge the potential for creative co-operation with fellow workers. De-layering, teamwork and virtualization are perhaps the better known instruments in this respect. Referring to the discussion in the first part of this chapter, it can be put forward that the implementation of relative individual (or small group) autonomy, in order to achieve the highest level of accountability possible, becomes the crucial management target. On the basis of that implementation, responsibilities can be rather clearly defined with regard to qualitative and quantitative outputs and thus with payments and all other aspects of the relation between the worker and the company.

If one of the effects of the versatilization of the worker is the loss of identification with his/her job and his/her work spot, the most crucial result of autonomization is the increasing accountability of the worker for the tasks to be performed. The former is an expropriation process, the latter is an allocation process. In this dialectical situation the worker becomes a responsible executor of tasks: a manager.

Client Orientation

Connected with the versatility and accountability hypotheses is the introduction of a client-based orientation in production organizations. We are dealing here with a double tendency: workers are increasingly being defined as service providers to the clients of the company and, also, as service providers to their fellow workers as clients within the company. Two aspects have to be stressed in this context: the idea of a direct relationship between workers and external and internal clients which short-circuits the (intermediate) managerial authority level and, consequently, the concept of personal responsibility of the worker with regard to external and internal clients.

Several developments can be mentioned in this respect. The concept of total quality control has, for example, introduced the notion of individual responsibility of the worker for conformity and reliability of produced goods and services, even if such responsibility has not (yet?) gained legal status. In organization-sociological terms we are confronted here with a form of externalization of a specific function that was, normally, performed by the firm.

The idea that companies, even those which produce durable goods, are in fact delivering services to clients, is rapidly expanding. Customization in order to meet specific needs of individual clients is certainly a case in point here, but does not tell the whole story. More important is the trend that, with products such as aircraft engines, computers, and other high tech devices becoming increasingly sophisticated, no one but the manufacturer can better service these devices during their lifetime. This, moreover, binds the clients to the producer even after the product has been sold: in the ever more competitive environment in which companies operate, such durable relations can have substantial advantages.

Another example of the clientification of producers of goods (and services) is the steel industry as suppliers to the automobile industry. New metal body parts and coating methods are now being developed in close collaboration between the two sectors, which, in a mutual expertise exchange process, become each other's clients. And in the already mentioned Resende project, the traditional European concept of subcontractor, as a rather passive supplier to the automobile industry, has been completely abandoned. In this latter case we can indeed speak of an extremely complex chain of mutual clients.

Client-centredness is a relatively new dimension in company policies. From a passive supply orientation toward (end-)users that was common until the 1970s, companies have now explicitly shifted to an active demand-oriented relation with their clients. These clients can be internal to the company (other departments) or external (other companies, individual or collective consumers). One example, among many others, is a change project aiming at 'improving radically our customer focus' according to a February 1998 note of an important and large Belgian company. Direct supervisors, in this particular case the category comparable to foremen, 'will learn to use a flexible situational leadership style and [the category of employees supervised] will learn the essence of upward leadership and self-leadership. Our key tasks will be: Customer focussed behaviour – Quality – (Self)Leadership'.

Versatility and accountability are related to the actual labour process, that means to the way the production of goods and services is organized in a (following the very useful Weberian category) 'imperatively co-ordinated association'. (Dahrendorf 1959) Such an association implies an exclusive (class) relation between those co-ordinating and those co-ordinated. A client-based orientation, initiated by management, connects the actual producers of goods and services not only to management but also to the users of these goods and services. It pertains to what could be called the objectivation of management: management acts rather as an intermediate or regulator between the interests of workers and clients than as an actor defending class-related interests. We have already concluded that 'the versaccountable worker' is more and more transformed into a manager of tasks. Now we observe, moreover, that, according to management, these tasks are not executed anymore for the benefit of the company (and its shareholders), but for clients.

This latter aspect is extremely important. It means that the imperative co-ordination traditionally performed by management in the interests of shareholders is now defined as being mediated by the interests of clients. Since clients do not have a class-based relationship with workers, as shareholders have, the exclusively bilateral conception of class relations on the firm level, and its materialization into an industrial relations system in the previous mondialization phase, potentially comes under pressure.

Challenges to organized labour
Faced with the profound changes in the structural functioning of the organization and even the finality of the organization, the power basis of organized labour is severely undermined. The reason for this is, as argued, the blurring of the distinction between manager and worker and, consequently, the elimination of the opposition between capital and labour. The basic concept on which the regulation of industrial relations was grounded, was, in its various forms, worker participation or, more precisely, collective worker participation.

It is quite obvious that the very nature of participation within industrial relations settings is undergoing important changes and will continue to change if the tendencies analysed above become more concrete. Without going into any detail we will only mention what, in our view, are two of the main problems here.

The Definition of a (Collective) Identity

Forms of worker consciousness are four-fold and have traditionally been linked to an objective and/or subjective attachment to a class or a stratum (see Table 3.2).

Table 3.2
Definition of Social Inequality and Forms of Consciousness

Definition of the situation by workers	Behaviour corresponding to such a definition	Social consciousness
Structural oppression (definition of inequality in terms of exploitation by management)	Explicit rejection (theoretically and practically) of capitalist production relations	Vanguard consciousness
Structural dependency (definition of inequality in terms of control by management)	Defence of workers' interests on the basis of opposition between capital and labour	Class consciousness
Not accepted uncertainty (definition of inequality in terms of social stratification)	Corporatist defence of workers' interests	Trade union consciousness
Accepted uncertainty (definition of inequality as an unescapable or desirable condition of social organization)	Defence of own interests	Individual consciousness

Two forms of class consciousness can be distinguished: a vanguard class consciousness (a rare quality) and a class consciousness. From a class conscious point of view, analysis of the labour process is made in terms of fundamentally different interests between capital and labour, and actions are undertaken accordingly. Active trade-union members are among those who have such a consciousness. A third form is a trade-union consciousness. Those who think they have collective interests as workers (as opposed to class interests) and estimate that these interests are best represented by trade unions, belong to this group. This consciousness can be of a broader solidarity type or can be more occupational or even corporatist. The fourth consciousness is of an individualistic type. Except for possible *ad hoc* and small scale expressions of overlapping interests, individual action for individual advancement is pursued.[2] What has been said above on competence optimalization and client orientation, and their consequences, could give some plausibility to the possibility that the pursuit of specific interests can become a dominant feature in the workers' definition of their own position within society and thus lead to forms of consciousness of a more individualistic type.

As vehicles for, and as results of, the collective representation of material and immaterial consciousness expressions, trade unions face identity problems (see the Hyman trilogy 1994, 1996a and 1996b). Trade unions have always had these problems but, as can be said quite safely, the nature of these problems has changed under the conditions of globalization and they have now become existential. How do workers, then, select between alternative trade-union identities when catering for the interests of (potential) members has become more and more difficult for the trade unions since the socio-economic positive sum period is over and done?

This already extremely complicated question may be even more complicated than it looks. It may also be that the question only partly addresses the real issue, or conceals part of reality. What we have argued in this chapter is that the constituency for the establishment of trade-union identities, as we know them, has been (is being/could be) altered. Until now we have always defined trade-union identities in terms of subjective or objective class- or stratum-related interests definitions, forms of consciousness being subjective or objective intermediate processes.

If the two developments at the level of the functioning of organizations analysed above have any validity, then we must review quite a few of our already shaken assumptions. '... Les syndicats ne doivent-ils pas se professionnaliser?' in order to '... reconquérir les âmes des salariés qu'ils ont laissées filer', asks Durand (1996, p. 9). It would be difficult to find a more revealing formulation on the state of confusion of the labour movement and the, seemingly contradictory, dimensions of the challenges trade unions are confronted with at the level of both discourse and action.

Socio-Political Exchange

In the European welfare states, the objectives of the labour movement were for a very large part internalized by their (formerly) ideological counterparts in the political field and, subsequently, realized through political regulation. It is difficult to imagine such a political exchange dynamic now or in the near future. The *de facto* acceptance of (in some cases very high levels of) unemployment by all mainstream political parties in the European Community as a corollary of the deflationary, budgetary and *pensée unique* policy currently pursued, may serve as an illustration that the cleavage between political and trade-union objectives is, indeed, a fundamental dimension of the crisis of trade unionism. There is a striking, some might say frightening, parallel between the objectification of management and the making of the worker-manager at the level of the organization, and the objectification of politics, in other words, the making of European labour parties into administrators of things, using Saint-Simon's expression. The objectification of politics, exemplified by the Maastricht norms, reduces policy making (what politics should be about) to the achievement of purely budgetary criteria. Critical questioning of the objectives and the consequences of such politics equals (for the powers that be) uncivil behaviour and is, as Fitoussi (1995) has aptly observed, forbidden. The transformation of the labour parties in Europe into administrators of things, things meaning the same (for example in the case of Europe) budgetary targets as adopted by all other mainstream political parties, signifies the submitting to the idea that there is only one possible way of acting. This negation of the existence of alternatives, sadly enough, also means the abandonment of the Enlightment spirit without which politics (in its modernist content at least) is stripped of all meaningfulness.

Conclusion

Structural changes in the position of workers have almost exclusively been studied, theoretically and empirically, within embourgeoisement and convergence perspectives. The nature of current transformations in the political economy of the firm, leads us to suggest that such approaches may not be sufficient anymore to account for the socio-political impact of the global division of production taking shape now.

The objectification of management and the making of the worker-manager are two aspects of organizational innovation, possibly leading to an implicit or explicit denial that class- and stratum-related issues are a basis for the structuration of industrial relations. This may be a confusing situation for trade unions, it is also confusing for social scientists.

Notes

1. Of course, these strategies do not guarantee success in the long run: ACEC has virtually stopped its activities and Westinghouse ceased to exist in 1997.
2. The typology presented here is further developed and empirically used in J. Vilrokx (1981), *Werknemers in onzekerheid: Sociaal bewustzijn in een bedreigde onderneming*, Gent: Masereelfond.

References

Attali, J. (1990), *Lignes d'horizon*, Paris: Fayard.

Attali, J. (1996), *Chemins de sagesse: traité du babyrinthe*, Paris: Fayard.

Bourguinat, H. (1995), *La tyrannie des marchés: essai sur économie virtuelle*, Paris: Economica.

Boyer, R., *et al.* (1997), *Mondialization: Au-dela des mythes*, Paris: La Découverte.

Campbell, D. (1993), 'The Globalizing Firm and Labour Institutions', in P. Bailey, A. Parisotto and G. Renshaw (eds), *Multinationals and Employment: The Global Economy of the 1990s*, Geneva: ILO.

Dahrendorf, R. (1959), *Class and Class Conflict in Industrial Society*, Stanford: Stanford University Press.

Durand, J.P. (ed.) (1996), *Le syndicalisme au futur*, Paris: Syros.

Fitoussi, J.P. (1995), *Le débat interdit: monnaie, Europe, pauvreté*, n.p.: Arléa.

Goldfinger, C. (1994), *L'utile et le futile: l'économie de l'immatériel*, Paris: Odile Jacob.

Haarscher, G. and B. Libois (1997), *Mutations de la démocratie représentative*, Bruxelles: Editions de l'Université de Bruxelles.

Hamill, J. (1993), 'Employment Effects of the Changing Strategies of Multinational Enterprises', in P. Bailey, A. Parisotto and G. Renshaw (eds), *Multinationals and Employment: The Global Economy of the 1990s*, Geneva: ILO.

Hyman, R. (1994), 'Changing Trade Union Identities and Strategies', in R. Hyman and A. Ferner (eds), *New Frontiers in European Industrial Relations*, Oxford: Blackwell, pp. 108-39.

Hyman, R. (1996a), 'Changing Union Identities in Europe', in P. Leisink, J. Van Leemput and J. Vilrokx (eds), *The Challenges to Trade Unions in Europe: Innovation or Adaptation*, Cheltenham: Edward Elgar, pp. 53-73.

Hyman, R. (1996b), 'Union identities and ideologies in Europe', in P. Pasture, J. Verberckmoes and H. De Witte (eds), *The Lost Perspective?: Trade Unions Between Ideology and Social Action in the New Europe*, Aldershot: Avebury.

Leisink, P., J. Van Leemput and J. Vilrokx (eds) (1996), *The Challenges to Trade Unions in Europe: Innovation or Adaptation*, Cheltenham: Edward Elgar.

Regini, M. (ed.) (1992), *The Future of Labour Movements*, London: Sage.

Rosanvallon, P. (1988), *La question syndicale*, Paris: Calmann-Levy.

Scott, W.R. (1998), *Organizations. Rational, Natural, and Open Systems*, Upper Saddle River, New Jersey: Prentice Hall.

Touraine, A. (1994), *Qu'est-ce que la démocratie?*, Paris: Fayard.

Vilrokx, J. (1987), *Self-Employment in Europe as a Form of Relative Autonomy: Significance and Prospects*, Brussels: EC/FAST.

Vilrokx, J. (1996), 'Trade Unions in a Post-representative Society', in P. Leisink, J. Van Leemput and J. Vilrokx (eds), *The Challenges to Trade Unions: Innovation or Adaptation*, Cheltenham: Edward Elgar, pp. 31-51.

Went, R. (1996), *Grenzen aan de globalisering*, Amsterdam: Het Spinhuis.

4. In the Name of 'Globalization': Enterprising Up Nations, Organizations and Individuals

Paul Du Gay

Introduction

'Globalization' has become possibly the most fashionable concept in the social sciences, a core axiom in the prescriptions of management consultants, and a central element of contemporary political debate. As Hirst and Thompson (1996, p.1) have indicated, it is widely asserted that we live in an era in which the greater part of social life is determined by global processes, in which national cultures, national economies and national borders are dissolving. Central to this assertion is the notion of a truly globalized economy. The emergence of such an entity, it is claimed, makes distinct national economies and, therefore, domestic strategies of national economic management, irrelevant. The world economy is increasingly globalized in its basic dynamics, it is dominated by uncontrollable market forces, and it has as its principal economic actors and strategic agents of change truly transnational corporations, that owe allegiance to no nation state and locate wherever in the globe market advantage dictates. (Ohmae 1990; 1993; Reich 1990; 1992; Angell 1995)

This representation of 'globalization' connects with the most diverse outlooks and social interests. It covers the political spectrum from left to right, and it is endorsed in several, diverse academic disciplines – from economics to sociology, and from cultural studies to international relations.

Indeed, it has achieved such widespread exposure and has become such a powerful explanatory device and guide to action that it sometimes appears almost unquestionable. Certainly its effects have been quite pronounced. As Hirst and Thompson (1996) have also suggested, one such effect of the dominance of this representation of contemporary economic life has been the effective paralysis of radical reforming national strategies, rendering them seemingly unviable in the face of the judgement and sanction of global markets.

Although there remains considerable room for debate as to precisely how far and in what respects economic and other activities are in fact 'globalizing' (as opposed to 'internationalizing', for example) (Boyer and Drache 1996; Hirst and Thompson 1996; Lane 1995), there can be no doubt that this dominant conception of the problem of globalization has played a crucial role in transforming the character of Western government's perceptions of the ways in which their own national economies should be managed, with consequential changes on their governmental understanding of the relations between economic activity and other aspects of the life of a national community. In other words, regardless of whether this dominant 'globalization' hypothesis is over-stated or indeed just plain wrong, an awful lot of things are being done in its name.

In this chapter, I want briefly to delineate some of the ways in which this particular discourse of 'globalization' comes to problematize con-duct in a diverse range of sites and to indicate some of the diverse mechanisms through which authorities of various sorts seek to shape, normalize and instrumentalize the conduct of institutions and persons in the name of making 'globalization' manageable.

Globalization and National Economic Security

If the widespread consensus of the 1950s and 1960s was that the future belonged to a capitalism without losers, securely managed by national governments acting in concert, then the late 1980s and 1990s have been dominated by a consensus based on quite the opposite set of assumptions, that global markets are basically uncontrollable and that 'the only way to avoid becoming a loser – whether as a nation, an organization, or an individual – is to be as competitive as possible'. (Hirst and Thompson 1996, p. 6; see also Krugman 1996)

This zero-sum conception has serious implications for the ways in which states are encouraged to view their own security. Of course, security, and security of economic activity in particular, is a primary concern for any state. What the discourse of 'globalization' problem-atizes is the ways in which security is to be obtained under conditions of extreme uncertainty. Indeed, the discourse of globalization both defines the circumstances in which states find themselves and advocates particular mechanisms through which security might conceivably be obtained under those circumstances.

Simply stated, nation states embedded in (what is represented as) an increasingly competitive global market and hence exposed to (what are represented as) supra-nationally ungovernable economic forces are encouraged to guarantee their survival through devolving responsibility for the 'economy' to 'the market' – using what remains of their public powers of intervention to limit, as it were constitutionally, the claims that politics can make on the economy, and citizens on the polity. Streeck (1996a, p. 307), for example, testifies to the power of the discourse of globalization when he writes that 'in many countries today, disengagement of politics from the economy is defended with reference to constraints of economic internationalization that would frustrate any other economic strategy'.

In place of a representation of the national economy as a resource, and therefore as contributing to the well-being of the national community in other respects – and, of course, in place of technologies designed to make this practicable – we now find an inversion of that perception, with other aspects of the life of the national community increasingly perceived in terms of their contributions to economic efficiency. In this new light, security can only be obtained, it would appear, through allowing economic problems to rebound back on society, so that society is implicated in resolving them, where previously the economy was expected to provide for society's needs.

So what are the implications of this new image of the national economy for governmental perceptions of relations between national economic activity and other aspects of the life of the national community? Under the old regime, the national economy could be seen both as a largely self-regulating 'system' and as a resource for other component parts or domains of a larger national unity. Since prudential government would secure the conditions of economic growth its output, net of depreciation and replacement costs, could be deployed for investment on the one hand and for other crucial national purposes, such as defence and social welfare, on the other. These latter expenditures might or might not be seen as 'economic costs' but their net effect would only be to reduce the rate of growth to rather less than it might otherwise have been. (Hindess forthcoming)

Within the discourse of globalization the pursuit of national economic efficiency is the *sine qua non* of national security and well-being. This incessant hunt for economic efficiency appears as a foundation not only of economic growth but of all those other activities that must be financed from growth. As I indicated above, this strategy of economic governance undermines existing divisions between the economy and other spheres of existence within the nation state. The image of the well-ordered national economy providing resources for the national state and society is now replaced by the image of the extravagant 'big government' state and society undermining efficient national economic performance. This shift helps account for the seemingly paradoxical situation in which governmental discourse in the wealthiest nations on earth contains an assumption that social welfare regimes are not any longer affordable in the forms we have come to know them. Anything which might seem to have a bearing on economic life (and this includes education, defence, and health as well as social welfare) is assessed not only in terms of the availability of resources and the alternative uses to which those resources might be put, but primarily in terms of their consequences for promoting or inhibiting the pursuit of national economic efficiency. The aim here is not simply to save money in the short term but also to induce efficiency enhancing 'cultural change' in organizational and personal conduct through the introduction of market-type relationships into evermore spheres of existence.

Globalization, Enterprise and the Problematization of Conduct

The idea that organizations, for example, need to change and to change dramatically and immediately certainly appears to be one of the axioms of the present age. Rarely a day goes by without a new pundit appearing in the press or on TV exhorting organizations to 'delayer', 'downsize', 're-engineer' or 'enterprise up' in order simply to ensure their continued survival. While these pundits speak from different institutional locales and from ostensibly differing political positions, they nonetheless all assume that something called 'globalization' is driving the need for 'change', that 'change' is thus absolutely necessary and that the imperatives of 'change' require quite similar responses from organizations and from persons within organizations.

Indeed, it is quite interesting to note how ostensibly different texts, from the popular books of management 'gurus' such as Tom Peters and Rosabeth Kanter, through official reports published by bodies such as the Confederation of British Industry, to policy statements produced by both major political parties in the United Kingdom, draw upon a similar vocabulary of 'globalization' in seeking to delineate the problems facing organizations and the solutions they should adopt. While different texts highlight different combinations of phenomena – the dislocatory effects consequent upon the increasing deployment of new information and communication technologies; those associated with the competitive pressures resulting from increasingly 'global' systems of trade, finance and production – they all agree that an intensification of patterns of global interconnectedness is having serious repercussions for the con-duct of organizational life in every organizational domain – public, private and voluntary[1].

If a composite monster called 'globalization' constitutes the 'key' predicament, then more often than not another composite monster named 'bureaucracy' is positioned as the crucial impediment to the successful management of its effects (synonymous as this term has become with 'foolish' strategies of intervention, 'unnecessary regulation' and other uncompetitive, inefficient dysfunctions). Organizations, it is argued, now operate in an environment characterized first and foremost by 'massive uncertainty'. In such an environment, only those organizations that can rapidly and systematically 'change their conduct' and learn to 'become evermore enterprising' will survive and prosper. Because 'bureaucracy' is held to be a 'mechanistic' form of organization best suited to conditions of relative stability and predictability, it of necessity becomes the first casualty of such an uncertain environment.[2]

> In this environment, bureaucratic organizations – public and private – increasingly fail us. Today's environment demands institutions that are extremely flexible and adaptable. It demands institutions that deliver high-quality goods and services, squeezing ever more bang out of every buck. It demands institutions that are responsive to customers, offering choices of non-standardized services; that lead by persuasion and incentives rather than commands; that give their employees a sense of meaning and control, even ownership. (Osborne and Gaebler 1992, p. 15)

The dislocatory effects generated by the intensification of patterns of global inter-connectedness is thus held to require constant 'creativity' and 'innovation' and hence the continuous construction of collective operational spaces that rest less upon mechanistic forms and their related practices – 'bureaucracy' – and increasingly upon the development of more entrepreneurial organizational forms and modes of conduct. Invar-iably, then, organizations are offered stark alternatives: to survive in the dislocated, increasingly competitive and chaotic global economy, they 'must either move away from bureaucratic guarantees' to flexible entre-preneurialism 'or stagnate'. (Kanter 1990, p. 356)

The notion of 'enterprise' occupies an absolutely crucial position in contemporary discourses of organizational reform. It both provides a critique of 'bureaucratic culture' and offers itself as a solution to the problems posed by 'globalization' through delineating a new set of ideals and principles for conceiving of and acting upon organizational and personal conduct.

Enterprising up Organizations and Individuals

This emphasis on enterprise should come as no surprise given the foundational place accorded to market forces by advocates of the globalization hypothesis. (Ohmae 1990) If the winners and losers in the global economy are to be determined largely, if not exclusively, by their competitiveness, then obviously enterprise is a quality no player in the global market game can afford to be without, whether nation, firm or individual.

Accordingly, the foremost consideration for national governmental players is the necessity of constructing the legal, institutional and cultural conditions which will enable the game of entrepreneurial and competitive conduct to be played to best effect. For these anti-political liberals or neo-liberals, it is a question of extending a model of rational-economic conduct beyond the economy itself, of generalizing it as a principle both limiting and rationalizing government activity. National government must work for the game of market competition and as a kind of enterprise itself, and new quasi-entrepreneurial market models of action or practical systems must be invented for the conduct of individuals, groups and institutions within those areas of life hitherto seen as being either outside or even antagonistic to the economic.

Looking briefly at developments in the UK, for example, we can see that while the concrete ways in which this model of rational economic conduct has been operationalized in the public sector have varied quite considerably, the forms of action that have been made possible for different institutions and different types of person – schools, general practitioners, housing estates, prisons and so forth – do seem to share a general consistency and style.

One characteristic feature has been the crucial role allocated to 'contract' in re-defining organizational relationships. The changes affecting schools, hospitals, government departments and so on, in the United Kingdom, has often involved the re-constituting of institutional roles in terms of 'contracts strictly defined', and even more frequently has involved a 'contract-like way' of representing relationships between institutions, and between individuals and institutions. (Freedland 1994)

An example of the former, for instance, occurred when fund-holding medical practices contracted with hospital trusts for the provision of health care to particular patients where previously that provision was made directly by the National Health Service. Examples of the latter include the relationships between central government departments and the new executive or 'Next Steps' agencies – where no technical contract as such exists but where the relationship between the two is governed by a contract-like 'Framework Document' which defines the functions and goals of the agency, and the procedures whereby the department will set and monitor performance targets for the agency.

This process, which Donzelot (1991) has termed one of 'contractual implication', typically consists in assigning the performance of a function or an activity to a distinct unit of management – individual or collective – which is regarded as being accountable for the efficient (that is 'economic') performance of that function or conduct of that activity.

By assuming active responsibility for these activities and functions – both for carrying them out and their outcomes – these units of management are in effect affirming a certain type of identity. This identity is basically entrepreneurial in character because 'contractualization' requires these units of management to adopt a certain entrepreneurial form of relationship to themselves 'as a condition of their effectiveness and of the effectiveness of this type of government'. (Burchell 1993, p. 276) To put it another way, contractualization makes these units of management function like little businesses or 'enterprise forms'.

According to the social theorist Gordon (1991), entrepreneurial forms of governance such as contractualization involve the re-imagination of the social as a form of the economic. 'This operation works', he argues, 'by the progressive enlargement of the territory of economic theory by a series of re-definitions of its object'. He continues, 'economics thus becomes an "approach" capable in principle of addressing the totality of human behaviour, and, consequently, of envisaging a coherent, purely economic method of programming the totality of governmental action'. (Gordon 1991, p. 43)

According to Gordon (1991, p. 43), it would be a mistake to view these developments as simply expressing the latest and purest manifestation of the rise of *homo economicus*. For as he goes on to indicate, the subject of entrepreneurial discourse is both 'a reactivation and a radical inversion' of traditional representations of 'economic man'. The reactivation consists 'in positing a fundamental human faculty of choice, a principle which empowers economic calculation effectively to sweep aside the anthropological categories and frameworks of the human and social sciences'. The great innovation occurs, in his opinion, in the conception of the economic agent as an inherently manipulable or 'flexible' creation.

Gordon argues that whereas *homo economicus* was originally conceived of as a subject the well-springs of whose activity were ultimately 'untouchable by government', the subject of enterprise is imagined as an agent 'who is perpetually responsive to modifications in its environment'. As he suggests, 'economic government here joins hands with behaviourism'. (1991, p. 43) The resultant subject is in a novel sense not simply an 'enterprise' but rather 'the entrepreneur of himself or herself'. In other words, the discourse of enterprise makes up the individual as a particular sort of person – as 'an entrepreneur of the self'. (Gordon 1987, p. 300)

So what does it mean to conceptualize a human being as an 'entrepreneur of the self'? This idea of an individual human life as an 'enterprise' suggests that no matter what hand circumstance may have dealt a person, he or she remains always continuously engaged (even if 'technically 'unemployed') in that one enterprise, and that it is 'part of the continuous business of living to make adequate provision for the preservation, reproduction and reconstruction of one's own human capital'. (Gordon 1991, p. 44)

Once a human life is conceived of primarily in entrepreneurial terms, the 'owner' of that life becomes individually responsible for his or her own self-advancement and care; within the ideals of enterprise, individuals are charged with managing the conduct of the business of their own lives. The vocabulary of enterprise re-imagines activities and agents and their relationship to one another according to its own ideals. Thus, the entrepreneurial language of responsible self-advancement and care, for example, is linked to a new perception of those who are 'outside civility' – those who are excluded or marginalized because they cannot or will not conduct themselves in an appropriately 'entrepreneurial' and hence 'responsible' manner. In the UK, for example, pathologies that were until recently represented and acted upon 'socially' – homelessness, unemployment and so forth – have become re-individualized through their positioning within entrepreneurial discourse and hence subject to new, often more intense, forms of surveillance and control. Because they are now represented as responsible individuals with a moral duty to take care of themselves, pathological subjects can blame no one but themselves for the problems they face. This individualization of social problems is evidenced in the UK by the introduction of a new terminology to describe the unemployed person – 'job seeker' – and the homeless person – 'rough sleeper'.

Because a human being is considered to be continuously engaged in a project to shape his or her life as an autonomous, choosing individual driven by the desire to optimize the worth of his or her own existence, life for that person is represented as a single, basically undifferentiated, arena for the pursuit of that endeavour. As previously distinct forms of life are now classified as 'enterprise forms' the conceptions and practices of personhood – or forms of identity – they give rise to are remarkably consistent. Thus, as schools, prisons, charities, and government departments, in the UK for example, are represented as 'enterprises' they all accord an increased priority to the development of the 'enterprising subject' for their own success.

As I suggested earlier, this conception of the individual as an 'entrepreneur of the self' is firmly established at the heart of contemporary discourses of organizational reform. In keeping with the entrepreneurial mix of economic and behaviourist vocabularies contemporary discourses of organizational reform characterize employment not as a painful obligation imposed upon individuals, nor as an activity undertaken to meet purely instrumental needs, but rather as a means to self-development, 'self-responsibility' and individual 'empowerment'.

Organizational success is thus premised upon an engagement by the organization of the self-managing and 'self-optimizing' capacities of individuals as subjects, no matter what their formal organizational role or status. This ambition is to be made practicable within the workplace through techniques for reducing dependency by reducing management strata ('delayering' or 'downsizing'), for encouraging the breaking-down of occupational boundaries through the development of 'special project teams', for stimulating individual entrepreneurship through the introduction of new forms of staff evaluation and reward ('performance related pay') and so on and so forth.

Performance management and related techniques, for example, can be seen to involve a characteristically 'contractual' and 'entrepreneurial' relationship between individual employees and the organization for which they work. This can involve 'offering' individuals involvement in activities – such as managing budgets, assessing staff, delivering services – previously held to be the responsibility of other agents – such as supervisors, personnel departments and so forth. However, the price of this involvement is that individuals themselves must assume responsibility for carrying out these activities and for their outcomes. In keeping with the principles of enterprise as a rationality of government, performance management and related techniques function as 'responsibilizing' mechanisms, which are held to be both economically desirable and personally 'empowering'.

This requirement that individuals become more personally exposed to the risks of engaging in a particular activity is represented as a means to their 'empowerment' because within entrepreneurial discourse, individuals can only be 'free' if they are 'enabled' to build resources in themselves rather than relying on others to take risks and bear responsibilities on their behalf. According to Kanter (1990, pp. 357-8), for example, 'entrepreneurial strategies are more motivating for people' because they allow everyone the opportunity to be in business for themselves 'inside the large corporation'. They are also better for business because the corporation itself 'should reap benefits too, in increased productivity' .

Within entrepreneurial discourse, then, paid work (no matter how objectively 'alienated', 'deskilled' or 'degraded' it may appear to social scientists) is represented as a crucial element in the path to individual responsibility, freedom and self-fulfilment. However, the forms of conduct which individuals are encouraged to adopt at work are not exclusive to that domain. There is a real sense in the world of enterprise that 'one is always at it' because entrepreneurial discourse represents life as one big enterprise. As Gordon (1991, p. 42) has suggested, the discourse of enterprise advocates a diffusion of the enterprise form throughout the social fabric 'as its generalized principle of functioning'. This means that there is no domain of activity where entrepreneurial conduct is not appropriate because every individual life is, in effect, structured as an enterprise of the self which each person must take responsibility for managing to their own best advantage.

As a number of sociologists have pointed out, entrepreneurial discourse effectively blurs traditional distinctions between different spheres of existence by making certain (entrepreneurial) forms of conduct appropriate to the functioning of all of them. According to Sabel (1992, pp. 42-3), for example, whereas it once seemed easy for at least a proportion of the population (mainly men, of course) to know where work stopped and leisure began, contemporary entrepreneurialism makes it 'harder to say when one is working. Activities at work become preparation for turning the family into a family enterprise that absorbs all leisure, family and leisure activities become preconditions of employ-ability. Anticipation of these possibilities undermines the distinctions between work, leisure and family.'

What I take Sabel to be getting at here is that the forms of conduct expected of employees at work are now remarkably similar to those required of them outside of work. They and their families live life as 'an enterprise' in every sphere of existence, whether at work or at play, in order to guarantee their survival and reproduction. As a result, traditional boundaries between work and non-work, public and private spheres, are increasingly thrown into question.

As I indicated earlier, the price of being offered more 'autonomy' at work, and so forth, is accepting responsibility for one's use of that autonomy and for the outcomes its exercise produces. This means that 'managerial units' such as individuals or families are more exposed to the costs of engaging in any activity and more dependent on their own resources for successfully carrying it out. Once inside the discursive world of Enterprise, therefore, one cannot hand one's autonomy back. Instead, one is forced, in effect, to exercise one's freedom continuously in order to guarantee one's own reproduction. (Du Gay 1996)

As Sabel's comments suggest, the symbolic hierarchies through which we allocate distinct meanings and identities to particular sets of activities – in this case the symbolic divisions between work and non-work, public and private space – are put into question when those activities are given a different symbolic or discursive inflection.

As we have seen, at the core of these new classificatory ideals is the privileged place accorded to the model of the commercial enterprise and the free market, for the conduct of government, for any institutional organization of goods and services, and for the conduct of one's own individual existence.

Conclusion

A wealth of counter-factual evidence has been generated by academics and others indicating that the globalization hypothesis is remarkably overstated in many of its assertions. As Hirst and Thompson (1996, p. 199), for example, have argued, while classical national economic management now has only limited scope, this does not mean that economic relations at both international and national levels are beyond governance, that is, means of regulation and control. Much, they argue depends on political will and co-operation between the major economic powers.

In the absence of such regulation economic analysis shows that persisting unemployment, recurring financial crises, rising inequalities, under-investment in productive activities such as education and research, and cumulative asymmetries of information and power, are evermore likely outcomes of continuing reliance on 'pure' market functioning. (Boyer 1996, p. 108)

The events of the 1980s and 1990s provide ample evidence that these evils do not belong to the world of theory. Britain, for example, has become markedly more unequal, at a faster rate than any other country in Europe. In 1979, the poorest 10 per cent of the population claimed 4.3 per cent of the nation's income. By 1991 that was down to 2.9 per cent. Over the same period the share taken by the richest 10 per cent rose from 20.6 per cent to 26.1 per cent. The 'winner takes all' logic of market led reform in Britain is most evident in the controversial example of the pay increases awarded to so called 'fat cat' directors. The highest-paid directors of Britain's largest companies enjoyed an average pay increase of 12.6 per cent in 1996, while average earnings rose by just 3.75 per cent. In 1995 top director's pay rose by 9.9 per cent and the year before by 22 per cent. The most striking rises have been among directors of privatized utilities. (quoted in Leadbetter 1996, p. 9)

Similarly, in the United States, the average weekly earnings (adjusted for inflation) of 'production and non supervisory workers' fell by 18 per cent between the late 1970s and the early 1990s. By contrast, between 1979 and 1989 the real annual pay of corporate chief executives increased by 19 per cent, and by 66 per cent after taxes. Even Alan Greenspan was moved to warn Congress in 1995 that the growing inequality of income in the United States could become 'a major threat to our society'. (quoted in Head 1996, p. 47)

It might be objected that concentrating on evidence from two of the world's foremost exponents of market-led reform paints a rather one-sided picture as there is obviously more than one way of responding to concerns about national competitiveness in an international economy.

Scholars from a range of fields have convincingly argued, for example, that national institutional heritage still plays a crucial role in structuring the means chosen to pursue given economic goals, the capacity for adaptation in various domains, and the manner in which change is accomplished. (Lane 1995; Boyer 1996; Hirst and Thompson 1996) Streeck (1996a, p. 310) identifies two divergent political responses at the national level, both rather different from the social-democratic, welfare-state policies of the post-war period.

On the one hand, he points to those nation states, such as the UK and the USA, who may see their principal contribution to competitiveness in handing responsibility for it to 'market forces'. Such a policy has involved large-scale privatization, retrenchment of social protection, market-driven industrial re-structuring, restoration of managerial authority, downwardly flexible wages and working conditions, the disablement of organized interests, particularly trade unions, and the promotion of a low-wage, low-skill sector to absorb some of the unemployed (see also Rubery 1994).

The alternative response, what might remain in an era of 'over-diminished expectations', of social democracy, neo-corporatism and social partnership, is the construction at the national level of what Streeck (1996a, p. 311) terms 'coalitions to "modernize" the national economy, with all other political objectives subordinate to that of increasing national competitiveness'.

> Post-social-democratic coalition-building can draw on the institutional and economic nationalism of labour movements prevented from acting at the supra-national level by lack of state capacity and employer interlocutors. It may also count on the employers, whose main interest is to forestall supra-national state formation and economic intervention; who therefore benefit from labour being contained in national political circuits; and who can be certain that, in the face of external competitive pressures and because of their capacity to exit, they will be the alliance's senior partners. Finally, national governments can hope to increase their support from both business and labour for defending joint national interests in the international arena, thereby defending their own legitimacy as well and further reinforcing the national organization of politics and the intergovernmental character of international economic governance. (Streeck 1996a, p. 311)

Despite their obvious differences, these two governmental responses are by no means mutually exclusive. For one thing, it is still the case that the globalization hypothesis provides a discursive framework in relation to which both sets of policies are pursued. As Streeck (1996b) has argued in another context, the globalization hypothesis 'discriminates against modes of economic governance that require public intervention...it favours national systems like those in the United States and Britain that historically relied less on public-political and more on private-contractual economic governance'. (quoted in Milner 1996, p. 23) To this extent, it comes as no surprise to learn that the competitive coalition-building model is in many respects as dependent on the voluntarism of the marketplace as the neo-liberal deregulation model.

Under both, national governments refrain from imposing obligations on market participants, especially business, as much as possible, either because they believe that market intervention is by its very nature disfunctional, or because they are legally obliged by international treaty to restrict such public intervention to the creation of incentives and the removal of deterrents for mobile investors. At the same time, nationally based democracy in both models is constrained by a presumed need not only to respond to competitive pressures before responding to citizens' democratic demands – or to interpret the latter in terms of a technically correct response to the former – but also to make sure that it stays within the boundaries of the rules and regulations imposed on national economic decision-making by intergovernmental agreement. As constraints on national economic intervention become more severe, 'national governments... become dependent on *the voluntarism of the market-place*, having lost recourse to the "hard law" that used to be the main tool of state interventionism in the past'. (Streeck 1996a, p. 311; italics in original) While the main tenets of the globalization hypothesis have been subject to extensive and largely convincing academic critique, important economic and political decisions continue to be taken in their name. The effect of this is to make the system of international economic governance that is developing – one dominated, in Streeck's terms, by 'the voluntarism of the marketplace' – increasingly difficult to buck. Far from increasing the likelihood of an alternative system of governance emerging, one capable of civilizing and domesticating rampant market forces, current developments seem to be effectively negating this possibility. The danger is that what we have got is what we are stuck with for the foreseeable future and that this is far less than is needed to ensure that an increasingly internationalized economy is a viable social as well as economic entity.

Notes

1. The texts which I draw upon and refer to here are largely Anglo-American in origin. However, the discourses they articulate can be observed to have structured policy initiatives in national contexts from Canada to Australia and to have been advocated by political regimes of left and right of the political spectrum. However, that said, I do not want to over-exaggerate the convergence in the forms of organizational and personal conduct they engender in different societal contexts.

2. It is interesting to note that bureaucracy is always represented as an entirely passive organizational form. There never appears to be any acknowledgement of the productive capacities of bureaucratic organization; that 'bureaucracy' actively constructs a predictable environment rather than being 'suited to' some already pre-existing stable space.

References

Angell, I. (1995), 'Winners and losers in the information age', *LSE Magazine*, 7(1).

Boyer, R. (1996), 'State and market: a new engagement for the twenty-first century?, in R. Boyer and D. Drache (eds), *State against Markets: the Limits of Globalization*, London: Routledge, pp. 84-114.

Boyer, R. and D. Drache (1996), *States against Markets: the Limits of Globalization*, London: Routledge.

Burchell, G. (1993), 'Liberal government and techniques of the self', *Economy and Society*, **22** (3), 266-282.

Donzelot, J. (1991), 'The mobilization of society', in G. Burchell et al. (eds), *The Foucault Effect*, Brighton: Harvester Wheatsheaf, pp. 169-79.

Du Gay, P. (1996), *Consumption and Identity at Work*, London: Sage.

Freedland, M. (1994), 'Government by contract and public law', *Public Law*, Spring, 86-104.

Gordon, C. (1987), 'The soul of the citizen: Max Weber and Michel Foucault on rationality and government', in S. Whimster and S. Lash (eds), *Max Weber: Rationality and Modernity*, London: Allen and Unwin, pp. 293-316.

Gordon, C. (1991), 'Governmental rationality: an introduction', in G. Burchell *et al.* (eds), *The Foucault Effect*, Brighton: Harvester Wheatsheaf, pp. 1-51.

Head, S. (1996), 'The new ruthless economy', *The New York Review of Books*, February 29, 47-52.

Hindess, B. (forthcoming), 'Neo-Liberalism and the national economy', in M. Dean and B. Hindess (eds), *Governing Australia*, Sydney: Cambridge University Press.

Hirst, P. and G. Thompson (1996), *Globalization in Question*, Cambridge: Polity Press.

Kanter, R. (1990), *When Giants Learn to Dance*, London: Unwin Hyman.

Krugman, P. (1996), *Pop Internationalism*, Cambridge (Ma.): MIT Press.

Lane, C. (1995), *Industry and Society in Europe*, Aldershot: Edward Elgar.

Leadbetter, C. (1996), 'How fat cats rock the boat', *Independent on Sunday*, November 3, 9-11.

Milner, M. (1996), 'A timely global warning', *The Guardian*, 7 September 1996.

Ohmae, K. (1990), *The Borderless World*, London: Collins.

Ohmae, K. (1993), 'The rise of the region state', *Foreign Affairs*, **72** (2), 78-87.

Osborne, D. and T. Gaebler (1992), *Re-Inventing Government*, Reading (Ma.): Addison-Wesley.

Reich, R. (1990), 'Who is Us?' , *Harvard Business Review*, January-February, 53-64.

Reich, R. (1992), *The Work of Nations*, New York: Vintage.

Rubery, J. (1994) 'The British production regime: a societal specific system', *Economy and Society*, **23** (3), 335-354.

Sabel, C. (1992) 'Moebius strip organizations and open labour markets: some consequences of the re-integration of conception and execution in a volatile economy', in P. Bourdieu and J.S. Coleman (eds), *Social Theory for a Changing Society*, Boulder (Co.): Westview Press, pp. 23-54.

Streeck, W. (1996a), 'Public power beyond the nation state: the case of the European Community', in R. Boyer and D. Drache (eds), *States against Markets: the Limits of Globalization*, London: Routledge, pp. 299-315.

Streeck, W. (1996b), *German Capitalism: Does it Exist? Can it Survive?*, Köln: Max Planck Institute.

5. Imagined Solidarities: Can Trade Unions Resist Globalization?

Richard Hyman

My title 'Imagined Solidarities' is open to at least three interpretations.
1. The idea of worker or trade-union solidarity is today (and always was?) imaginary, illusory, fictitious, unattainable.
2. Solidarity is a utopia, a Sorelian myth, unrealizable yet perhaps capable of inspiring action which results in its partial accomplishment. This is the sense in which Anderson (1983) writes of nations as 'imagined communities': people conceive a commonality with others whom they do not know and of whose specific identities they are unaware, with such powerful sentiments that nationalism is probably the most significant mobilizing principle of our time.
3. The integration of diverse and competing (or indeed conflicting) employee interests cannot be achieved mechanically but requires creative imagination.

My argument is that any simple conception of solidarity ('mechanical solidarity' of the working class) is and was imaginary in the first sense; that mythic solidarity ('solidarity forever') may historically have provided inspiration and perhaps helped generate a reality approximating to the ideal, but probably can no longer do so; and that collectivism, particularly of an encompassing character, is therefore a project demanding new forms of strategic imagination.

In the discussion which follows I develop each of these themes, and consider how far the socio-economic transformations commonly identified as globalization have altered the problem of constructing solidarity.

The Unity of Labour: an Imagined Universal Class

From the revolutionary theories of Marx – a powerful influence on both trade-union activists and analysts of trade unionism – derive a conception of the unity of working-class interests and a conception of unions' historical mission to articulate this unity.

The 'classic' Marxian conception rested on at least three foundations. First, in his early 'philosophical' writings, Marx recast the Hegelian interpretation of history. Human emancipation required material force: and specifically, a class whose own particular interests could be achieved not within the existing society but only through transforming society as a whole. As he insisted in the *Introduction to the Critique of Hegel's Philosophy of Law*, the proletariat constituted 'a class with radical chains, a class within civil society that is not of civil society...'. Because of the totality of its oppression within bourgeois society, the working class suffered 'the complete loss of humanity and can only redeem itself through the total redemption of humanity'. Hence famously, 'the proletarians have nothing to lose but their chains. They have a world to win.'

Second, those who did enjoy distinctive interests and advantages in the labour market did so as relics of pre-capitalist relations of production; the advance of capitalism involved the degradation of traditional skills and the homogenization of the proletariat. Both the rationale and the result of mechanization involved the reduction of capitalists' dependence on the discretion of expert workers and on the availability of scarce and hence expensive labour power.

Third, the objective commonality of class interests (the proletariat as a class 'in itself') would lead inevitably to workers' subjective consciousness of their common identity and historical mission as a class 'for itself'.[1] The increasing inefficacy of defensive and particularistic struggles would persuade workers of the need to organize comprehensively as a class and to pursue the total transformation of society. Trade unions, as agencies of working-class collective struggle, would inevitably be shaped by this dynamic.

It is unnecessary to rehearse the problems underlying this conception; the critiques are all too familiar. The thesis of homogenization – as much sociological discussion of 'deskilling' in the last two decades witnesses – rests on a unilinear reading of the dynamics of the capitalist labour process and labour market. In practice, new differentiations arise as old ones are weakened (a process which Marx himself, in *Capital*, saw as characteristic of the era of 'manufacture', but as unable to persist with the advance of increasingly mechanized 'modern industry'). The idea of objective class unity seems to conflate the abstract (the structural relationship between wage-labour and capital) and the concrete (the circumstances of actually existing workers and their relations among themselves and with actually existing employers, among others); as Sayer and Walker (1992, p. 29) put it, 'division of labour is not merely a modifier in the grammar of class'. The conceptual and practical linkage between 'objective' class and 'subjective' consciousness is moreover inadequately theorized (primarily in *The Poverty of Philosophy* and the *Communist Manifesto*) by simple analogy with the rise of the bourgeoisie as a hegemonic class.

Reality is different. We are shaped by our direct experiences, immediate *milieux*, specific patterns of social relations. Broader identities and affiliations are founded on the direct, immediate and specific, through intersubjectivities which link these to the external and encompassing. Solidarity implies the perception of commonalities of interest and purpose which extend, but do not abolish, consciousness of distinct and particularistic circumstances.

Actually existing trade unions reflect these processes. The earliest unions typically emerged as organizations of distinct occupational communities of interest within local labour markets. The development of multi-occupational unionism with a broader geographical compass normally required either the external intervention of a politically driven class project, or the gradual experience of the limited efficacy of too narrow a representational base. The 'one big union' of syndicalist aspirations remained a dream.

The boundaries of union inclusion are also frontiers of exclusion. The perceived common interests of the members of a particular union (or confederation) are defined in part in contradistinction to those of workers outside. In compartmentalizing workers, unions traditionally have compartmentalized solidarity.

Constructing Labour Movements: Solidarity as a Mobilizing Myth

'Interests can only be met to the extent that they are partly redefined'. (Offe and Wiesenthal 1985, p. 184) It is a sociological truism that the elusive notion of interests has both objective and subjective dimensions, and that the relationship between the two is never fixed. Through their own internal processes of communication, discussion and debate – the 'mobilization of bias' – unions can help shape workers' own definitions of their individual and collective interests. Cumulatively, the outcomes compose the patterns of commonality and conflict among the interests of different groups and hence contribute to the dynamics of sectionalism and solidarity within labour movements.

Borrowing from Durkheim – though applying his concepts flexibly – one may define the classic form of interest definition and representation as 'mechanical solidarity'. Durkheim attributed order and stability in traditional society to the repressive imposition of standardized rules and values on members whose circumstances were relatively homogeneous. Traditional trade unionism displayed some similarities. The aggregation of interests, which is essential for any coherent collective action, involves establishing priorities among a variety of competing grievances and aspirations. One reason why many employers came to perceive the value (to themselves) of the existence of a recognized vehicle of employee 'voice' was that unions filtered out (or perhaps suppressed) certain demands and discontents while highlighting others. Another was that unions could be induced to share responsibility with management for disruptive initiatives and uncomfortable changes.

Trade unions, in other words, are agencies whose role in the aggregation of interests may also involve the (re-)distribution of gains and losses: not only between workers and employers but also among workers themselves. Typically the definition of union-relevant interests has reflected systematically the existing distribution of power within the working class.

What are often presented as expressions of the general interests of the class have traditionally been in large measure representations of the particular interests of relatively protected sections. In Britain in the nineteenth century, for example, craft unions representing a fraction of the labour force with distinctive (relative) advantages were nevertheless widely perceived (and often perceived themselves) as representatives of a general world of labour. In many European countries in the first half of the present century, coal-miners assumed the status of archetypal proletarians and helped inspire a particular iconography and discourse of the nature of collective solidarity and collective struggle. The 'mass worker' in engineering production (and above all, on car assembly lines) subsequently constituted the 'model trade unionist' in much of Europe.

In effect, the type of solidarity typically constitutive of twentieth century trade unionism tended to reflect and replicate on the one hand the discipline and standardization imposed by 'Fordist' mass production, on the other the patterns of differentiation within the working class between those who were central to this production process and those who were more marginal. Thus within companies and sectors, collective bargaining priorities were normally set by core groups of full-time production workers (typically male, white, with a stable place in the internal labour market); within national labour movements, priorities were imposed by the big battalions (typically the unions of manual manufacturing workers, notably metal workers).

Associated with this form of mechanical solidarity was clearly an implicit bias in terms of whose interests counted for most. But also affected was the conception of which interests were relevant for union representation and bargaining policy. A specific conception of the relationship between 'work' and 'life' has been seen in retrospect to have informed working-class organization; one which in particular counter-posed a full-time (male) wage-worker in mine, mill or factory and a full-time (female) domestic worker in the home. That reality was always more complex than this did not prevent the model from shaping firmly the conceptions of which issues were union-relevant and which were not.

The Crisis of Mechanical Solidarity

For over a decade, it has been common for academic writers to speak of a crisis of trade unionism. (Edwards *et al.* 1986; Regini 1992) Müller-Jentsch (1988) has identified three types of underlying challenge: increasing heterogeneity within the labour force, creating a 'crisis of interest aggregation'; decentralization of employment regulation to company and workplace levels, resulting in a 'crisis of workers' loyalty towards their unions'; and failure to organize effectively the key occupations in the dynamic sectors of the economy, giving rise to a 'crisis of union representation'. These factors may be viewed as elements in a series of interlocking transformations: a more unstable and segmented labour market; more strategic (or aggressive) employer approaches to the management of labour; intensified competitive pressures in product markets; the support (though to different degrees) of most European governments for deregulation of industrial relations.

Initially, many trade unionists resisted the very idea of a crisis. (Mouriaux 1995, p. 3) Increasingly, however, there has been an acceptance that traditional policies and forms of organization have lost their effectiveness; that if unions are to remain significant social actors in the new millennium they must be transformed and renewed. There is wide-spread discussion within European labour movements of the need for 'modernization' of trade unions (Mückenberger *et al.* 1996), even if as yet the evidence of its achievement is limited.

It is my thesis that what is normally conceived as a crisis of trade unionism as such may be better understood as a crisis of a particular model of trade unionism, one based on what I have termed mechanical solidarity. The debate on 'modernization' may thus be reconceptualized as a search for a new model, which again following Durkheim we may term 'organic solidarity'. Before elaborating on this thesis I will first outline three factors which are commonly identified as underlying causes of the crisis of traditional solidaristic projects:

1. increased internal differentiation within the working population (linked to diagnoses of 'individualism') (Zoll 1993);
2. intensified competition, restructuring and 'deregulation' (often conceptualized within a 'globalization' perspective) turning intra-class bargaining increasingly into a zero- (or negative-) sum game (Golden and Pontusson 1992) and encouraging micro-level 'solutions' to macro problems;
3. the erosion of egalitarian commitments within labour movements (Swenson 1989), reflected both in increased internal differentiation among trade unions and in the eclipse of the communist political model and the exhaustion of the social-democratic.

Internal differentiation

Without differentiation, there would be no need for solidarity. Solidarity is a project to reconcile differences of situation and of interest, to offer support and assistance to the claims of groups and individuals irrespective of immediate advantage in respect of one's own circumstances. Solidarity became a slogan of labour movements precisely because the working class was not a homogeneous unity, because divisive sectionalism was an ever-present possibility, and because painful experience showed that isolated and often competitive struggles by fragmented groups were more often than not mutually defeating.

Yet if vertical and horizontal differentiation is anything but new, has it assumed new forms which imply new obstacles to the attainment of solidarity? One argument is that the deviation from the mean, so to speak, has increased, and that this poses serious problems for union organization. Traditional patterns of unionization, in the private sector at least, appear to display the familiar inverted U curve. The most advantaged sections – those with high educational qualifications and favourable career expectations, for example – commonly saw no need for collective organization, or may have considered it a threat to promotion prospects to take what might be seen as anti-employer initiatives. Conversely, the poorest, most vulnerable and most insecure sections of the labour force – who may perhaps have had the greatest need for unionization – commonly lacked the resources to build stable collective organization, and were easily victimized if they did make the attempt. Unions built their strongholds among the relatively secure, relatively well paid 'core' working class (what some writers termed the 'mass worker'). (Paci 1973) It was in the era when such workers constituted the dominant section of the active labour force that union density in many countries reached its peak, and labour movements as a whole seemed best able to identify shared interests.

One distinct feature of the restructuring of work and employment in recent times has been a two-fold differentiation. At one extreme, the creation of new skills and the blurring of the manual/white-collar divide have had two important consequences. These trends have generated a significant category of 'winners' from the process of technological and organizational change: a new elite probably unresponsive to the appeals of traditional trade unionism; conversely there has been a rapid growth of a 'white-collar proletariat' (often female) whose security and prospects depend on the employer's goodwill. At the other extreme, there has been a substantial growth of precarious and 'atypical' forms of employment, particularly with the decline of manufacturing, the cutbacks in the public sector, and the expansion of an array of private-sector services. This peripheral workforce has in most countries proved painfully difficult to unionize, if indeed unions have even made the attempt. Unions face difficult choices in terms of the constituencies they seek to represent: they can either stick with a declining core, attempt to address the special interests (and advantages) of the new 'elite', or struggle to represent the periphery; but it is an enormous challenge to develop strategies which point effectively in all directions. Certainly this cannot be achieved by rhetorical assertions of a unity of interests.

Increased differentiation links to the issue of individualism. In many European countries it has become common to argue that one of the key problems confronting trade unions has been a socio-cultural transformation whereby traditional working-class values of collectivism have given way to more individualistic orientations. In one sense this argument is trite and simplistic. Collectivism has never represented an alternative to individual interests and individual identities: trade unionism has traditionally provided a pooling of resources allowing workers more effectively to defend and advance their personal interests. While union members may indeed have been conscious of common occupational or employmental interests, this did not negate their individual circumstances and projects. Trade unions have rarely been able to rely on a spontaneous urge to collectivism: to integrate diversity into an organization with a common set of objectives has been a task to accomplish, and with no guarantee of success.

This said, it is plausible to argue that the task has become more difficult in recent times. There is a stereotype of the traditional proletarian status which emphasizes a common work situation, an integrated and homogeneous local community, and a limited repertoire of shared cultural and social pursuits. Though exaggerated, this stereotype does identify a core of historical reality, particularly in the single-industry manual working-class milieux in which the 'modern' mass trade unionism had its strongest roots. By contrast, in contemporary society the spatial location and social organization of work, residence, consumption and sociability have become highly differentiated. Today the typical employee may live a considerable distance from fellow-workers, possess a largely 'privatized' domestic life or a circle of friends unconnected with work, and pursue cultural or recreational interests quite different from those of other employees in the same workplace.[2] This disjuncture between work and community (or indeed the destruction of community in much of its traditional meaning) entails the loss of many of the localized networks which strengthened the supports of union membership (and in some cases made the local union almost a 'total institution').

In consequence, trade unionism seems confronted with two main options. One is to develop a much more calculative attachment based on a narrowly specified set of occupational interests. The other is to appeal to a more diffuse set of interests which transcend local and particularistic identities: the classic project of 'social movement unionism'. (Johnson 1994; Waterman 1998)

Market coercion
In most Western European countries, 'modern' systems of industrial relations became consolidated around the middle of this century as a key element in post-war settlements which though nation-specific contained many common features. Their foundation was the existence of relative job security (at least for a substantial core of primarily male manufacturing workers in larger firms) under macroeconomic conditions of 'full' employment, often buttressed by legal supports. This was in turn facilitated by stable or expanding demand in key product markets and by institutional and other constraints on destructive market competition.

The organized capitalism which achieved its high point in the 1950s and 1960s helped establish trade unions as central actors in a variety of national systems of employment regulation. (Standing 1997)

The 'social market economy' which in different forms characterized post-war Western Europe (even if the term itself was exclusively German) is challenged by the intensified competitive restructuring of national economies. (Mahnkopf and Altvater 1995) Many writers refer to a process of globalization, and although this term has been questioned (Boyer and Drache 1996; Hirst and Thompson 1996) transnational concentration and centralization of capital certainly have occurred, though primarily within separate world areas (North America, Europe, the Asian Pacific).[3] In Europe this has been reflected (as was indeed one of the aims of the Single Market project) in an acceleration of foreign direct investment between EU countries and a rapid process of corporate consolidation through mergers, take-overs and joint ventures.

The past dozen years have witnessed the rise of the 'Euro-company' (Marginson and Sisson 1996) as a specific type of multinational corporation (MNC). In previous decades, the 'problem of MNCs' for European trade unions was relatively narrow and specific: how to contain foreign-owned (primarily American) enterprises within the regulatory frameworks of national industrial relations systems. In the 1990s the problem has become broader and more serious: the internationalization of significant segments of 'national capital' and the potential abdication of key companies from the role of interlocutor within a national system of 'social partnership'. The most dramatic instance, perhaps, is the case of Sweden: the major employers in effect 'joined' the EU long before the country's formal accession, and demolished the classic centralized 'Swedish model' of industrial relations the better to pursue more company-specific and internationalized employment policies. In most other European countries, analogous pressures are apparent. The growing importance of the Euro-company threatens established forms of cross-company standardization and solidarity while at the same time necessitating new forms of cross-national co-ordination on the part of labour.

The visible hand of the MNCs interacts with the increasingly coercive invisible hand of finance capital. The last two decades have seen a radical transformation involving: the liberalization and deregulation of international capital and currency markets; the acceleration of transactions (to the point of virtual instantaneity) as a result of advances in information and telecommunications technologies; and the breakdown of the American-dominated post-war system of international monetary stabilization.

The result is a highly volatile pattern of capital flows. Unpredictable (speculative) fluctuations in the paper values of company shares or national currencies are translated into disruptive oscillations in the physical economy.

The matrix for the formative period of capitalist industrialization, and for the various Keynesian-influenced systems of post-war macroeconomic management, was the regulatory capacity of the nation state. As Rogers has argued (1995, p. 370), the scope for pressure on the state to deliver material benefits of general application itself encouraged 'the political project of uniting across differences'. It is indeed true that in most European economies the pivotal importance of the export sector ensured that industrial relations policies were consistent with international competitiveness. Nevertheless the national state, and the parties to collective bargaining, could address the labour market as a more or less closed system. The consequence of globalization is that market dynamics are increasingly subject to exogenous determination: the 'confidence' of the institutions and agents of international financial transactions sets new, onerous and often unpredictable constraints on the agenda of national industrial relations. (Streeck 1992) It also means that the attraction to (some) employers of nationally co-ordinated collective bargaining as a means of 'taking wages out of competition' has been eroded. (Jacoby 1995, p. 8)

Another significant feature of intensified market coercion is the internal restructuring of the firm. The traditional large company was hierarchically organized with a high degree of internal standardization. This structure (which the development, within the largest firms, of divisionalization by product only partially modified) was conducive to similarly standardized and bureaucratic forms of collective employment regulation. Corporate structure encouraged a particular type of employee solidarity. By contrast, current principles of business organization have fragmented the terrain of collective action. Increasingly – though faster in some countries than in others – the centralized firm has given way to the 'hollow company'. (Sabel 1995) This process has three key elements: the externalization through sub-contracting and franchising of many of the non-core functions of the firm; the formal separation of conglomerate companies into legally differentiated subsidiaries; and the devolution of decision-making responsibility to a network of business units. The common characteristic of these changes is the spread of market relationships within the boundaries of the firm, imposing accountancy criteria as the key performance indicators and setting the various sub-units in competition one with another.(Coller 1996; Mueller 1996)

Intensified competitive pressures have reconstituted the patterns of employment security and insecurity. In the past, in most countries, there has been a rather close mapping between regulation by collective bargaining and a relatively secure labour-market position. Union organization and bargaining strength were facilitated by, and in turn reinforced, internal labour markets which protected the core workforce from the employer's ability to hire and fire at will. Conversely, in many countries there existed a substantial secondary labour market with far weaker (or non-existent) collective regulation, where employment was far more casualized. (A third category, those who constituted an occupational elite, were often also weakly covered by collective bargaining but possessed scarce professional qualifications which provided relative autonomy from adverse market forces.) The significance of intensified product market competition is that the link between collective regulation and employment security is more fundamentally ruptured: the protection of the internal labour market is undermined if the whole workplace becomes vulnerable to radical job loss or total closure. A substantial proportion of collectivized employees now constitutes an endangered labour force. To the extent that market forces or their proxies have been imposed in public employment, moreover, this vulnerability encompasses sectors previously completely protected from the vagaries of product competition and production rationalization.

The industrial relations consequences involve at least three major challenges to the trade-union role in interest representation. First, there are strong pressures to engage in concession bargaining in the interests of enhanced competitiveness: trading off employment guarantees for restraint in pay bargaining (or even real wage reductions), agreement to changes in the organization of production which conflict with established protective regulations, and/or more general acceptance of managerial authority. Unions which in previous decades based their appeal to workers on their ability to win tangible improvements in pay and working conditions have a far harder task to justify their existence if obliged to accept the reversal of their former achievements.

Second, the endangered status of unionized companies and workplaces encourages enterprise egoism: survival of the establishment assuming overriding importance for local negotiators. The outcome can become a cumulative undercutting of national/sectoral regulatory standards: a process often deliberately encouraged by MNCs with their ability to 'benchmark' the performance of their various subsidiaries and to base investment (and disinvestment) decisions on relative compliance with management requirements. If the workforce of each production unit becomes driven by the demands of mutual competition, the logical result is both intra- and international social dumping.

Third, within as well as between workforces the process of interest representation more sharply differentiates (relative) winners and (absolute) losers. For employees, the response to increasingly coercive market pressures seems to involve a negative-sum game. The logic of market relations is that competition reinforces disparities of power within as well as between classes. In the distribution of the costs of competitive restructuring, trade unions' own internal balance of power is likely to favour the relatively advantaged at the expense of the most insecure.

The eclipse of egalitarianism
In most countries the rise and consolidation of national labour movements involved clear egalitarian commitments: to a narrowing of income differentials, progressive taxation policy, and universal entitlement to social benefits and services. In many ways, one of the most impressive testimonies to the strength of solidaristic principles was the degree to which working-class organizations drawing their cadres of activists and leaders from the better-educated, higher-paid and more secure categories of the labour force nevertheless espoused policies of particular benefit to the less advantaged. Sectional interests, in other words, were perceived as best pursued through a more general commitment to social justice. The post-war consolidation of the Keynesian welfare state – whether through the political victory of labour or the acceptance by conservative regimes of the need to reform and humanise capitalism – represented the apparent victory of these principles.

Paradoxically, the form of this victory contained the seeds of its own defeat. The egalitarian project in most European countries was a type of 'socialism within one class' (and often, within one gender). The central achievement of most welfare states was to redistribute income within the working population across the life-cycle (a process which has come to generate increasing tensions with a change in demographic structure). Egalitarian wage policy primarily involved the narrowing of differentials within bargaining groups, to the particular advantage of manual workers classified as lower-skilled. In itself this helped reduce gender differentials; but to the extent that employment has tended to be demarcated between (higher-paid) primarily male industries and (lower-paid) primarily female industries, in those countries where the most important level of collective bargaining was the industry or sector then inequalities tended to remain large. There is also evidence that recent decentralization of collective bargaining has been associated with the blockage, or even reversal, of gender equalization. And indeed, the combination of economic stringency with an increased female rate of labour-market participation almost inevitably makes the issue of male-female pay relativities potentially conflictual.

In most countries the post-war decades saw some narrowing of income differentials between manual workers and white-collar employees. Yet to the extent that these categories were separately represented for purposes of pay determination, levelling was often greater within each group; and indeed, with the shift in the numerical balance between the two types of employee, white-collar unions often articulated the demand for the defence or even expansion of differentials. In the Swedish case, the result was that the lower range of white-collar salaries might be higher than the top manual wages. (Kjellberg 1992) As technological change blurred the (always to some extent artificial) boundary between the two categories, consciousness of inequity was inevitable: with higher-skilled manual workers either escaping through reclassification to staff status or demanding a widening of pay differentials. Sweden is also a clear example of the erosion of the previously hegemonic role of manual worker unionism, with the share of *Landsorganisationen* (LO) in total union membership falling from 80 per cent in 1950 to 56 per cent today. Both trends shift the balance of power towards the better off.

In part, then, the retreat from egalitarianism has involved a revolt of the (relatively) advantaged against the particular manifestations (rising taxes, narrowing differentials) of the specific form of the egalitarian project. But the retreat also reflects the erosion of the classic ideological foundations of this project. The exhaustion of Western communism, and the post-1989 collapse of the Soviet bloc, eliminated one point of reference for traditional notions of class solidarity. Ironically, indeed, in the 1990s the traditional class struggle rhetoric of the revolutionary left has commonly (most notably perhaps in Italy) lent endorsement to the sectional militancy of relatively privileged groups.

In the very period when most mainstream communist parties came to embrace social democracy, social-democratic egalitarianism itself was in decline, for reasons both domestic and external. Domestically, most European social-democratic parties identified a causal link between declining electoral success and the dwindling of their traditional manual working-class base; the typical conclusion was the need to appeal to the expanding 'new middle class' by diluting or abandoning former policy commitments to generous and universal social welfare funded by high and progressive taxation and to forms of labour-market intervention which offset the inegalitarian dynamics of market competition. Externally, intensified transnational competition seemed to spell the end of 'Keynesianism in one country'. As the French discovered at the beginning of the 1980s, and the Swedes at the end of the decade, the location decisions of MNCs and the speculative fluctuations of currency markets punished national governments whose defence of the Keynesian welfare state stood out against the general adoption of neo-liberal principles of fiscal rectitude. The pressures of regime competition – which underlie the German *Standort* debate of the 1990s – will be intensified by monetary union within the framework defined by the Maastricht convergence criteria. Having endorsed the Maastricht project, European social-democratic parties are weakly placed to propagate a programmatic alternative to the neo-liberalism which is at its core.[4]

Imagining Alternatives: Towards Organic Solidarity?

If solidarity is to survive, it must be reinvented. Here too, we may recall Durkheim and his conception of a better integrated social order based on flexible co-ordination of individuals who were both more differentiated and (as a necessary consequence) more interdependent. His vision (indeed excessively idealized) of 'organic solidarity' was expressed in the insistence that 'society becomes more capable of collective movement, at the same time that each of its elements has more freedom of movement'. (Durkheim 1933, p. 131) The task of moving from an old model of mechanical solidarity to a new model of organic solidarity – or as Heckscher (1988, p. 177) puts it, 'a kind of unionism that replaces organizational conformity with co-ordinated diversity' – demands new efforts of imagination.

Any project aiming to create such a model must recognize and respect differentiations of circumstances and interests: within the constituencies of individual trade unions, between unions within national labour movements, between workers in different countries. The alignment and integration of diverse interests is a complex and difficult task which requires continuous processes of negotiation; real solidarity cannot be imposed by administrative fiat, or even by majority vote.

To construct trade-union programmes with which vertically and hori-
zontally differentiated groups of workers can identify requires a sensitive redefinition of what interests are represented. If on the one hand
unions must be alert and receptive to (possibly altered) expectations and
aspirations on the part of actual and potential members, on the other a
priority must be to construct an agenda which can unite rather than
divide. The representation of workers' interests – and their definition,
which is necessarily a prior process – has never been straightforward.
Building collective solidarity is in part a question of organizational
capacity, but more fundamentally it is part of a battle of ideas. The crisis
of traditional trade unionism is reflected not only in the more obvious
indicators of loss of strength and efficacy, but also in the exhaustion of
a traditional discourse and a failure to respond to new ideological
challenges. It is those whose projects are hostile to what unions stand
for who have set the agenda of the past decades. Unions have to recapture
the ideological initiative.

As a starting point, the labour-market perspectives of the 'mass
worker' with a standard model of full-time employment, firm-specific
job security and limited scope for occupational advancement can no
longer dictate the central content of bargaining policy. Themes of crucial
relevance for contemporary trade unionism are those of flexibility,
security and opportunity. These concepts have inspired the offensive of
employers and the political right (many of the latter wearing the clothes
of social democracy); they must be reclaimed for different purposes.

Flexibility is of course primarily a slogan of those who wish to weaken
and restrict labour-market protections, making workers more disposable
and more adaptable to the changing requirements of the employer. Yet
flexibility can have alternative meanings. The 1970s objective of 'hu-
manization of work' was in essence a claim for flexibility in the interests
of workers through the human-centred application of technologies, the
adaptation of task cycles and work speeds to fit workers' own rhythms,
the introduction of new types of individual and collective autonomy in
the control of the labour process. This agenda has in large measure been
hijacked as part of the new managerialism of the 1980s and 1990s (with
its mendacious rhetoric of 'empowerment', 'teamwork' and 'human
resource development'). Can unions recapture the initiative? A key issue
in the contemporary world of work, in addition to those raised by
industrial workers and their unions a quarter-century ago, is that of
time-sovereignty: the temporal linkages between employment, leisure
and domestic life; the ability to influence the patterns of the working

day, week, year and lifetime. There is a worker-oriented meaning of flexible working time which can directly confront that of the employers – and which offers new potential for integrating very different types of employee interest. So too with other dimensions of flexibility; rigidity and standardization were impositions of a particular model of capitalist work organization; to the extent that some of the features of Taylorist-Fordist systems have lost their attractions to employers, space exists for unions to mobilize support for radical alternatives which transcend some of the divisions within the working class.

For example, changes in the organization of production and the employment relationship (such as teamworking, quality circles, performance related pay, personalized contracts) are often accompanied by a managerial propaganda offensive in which 'empowerment' is a central rhetorical device. Dr Goebbels would have been proud of such discourse, which provides a 'democratic' gloss to employer efforts to intensify production pressures, cut staffing numbers and undermine traditional forms of collective regulation. The 'new workplace' is one in which employees often have increased responsibilities but always with reduced power. By focusing their own demands and activities on this contradiction, trade unions have the potential to address current worker discontents in ways which generalize fragmented experiences and permit new forms of solidarity in the pursuit of genuine empowerment.[5]

The resurgence of market coercion is causally related to a massive growth of insecurity. Part of the function of trade unionism is to resist such trends. To the extent that such resistance is company- or sector-specific, however, its consequences may well prove divisive. The fight for company-level security, if successful, by stabilizing the position of 'insiders' may make the labour-market situation of 'outsiders' even more precarious. Where public employees struggle to retain protections which in the private sector were lost a decade ago, their unions may be seen as defenders of sectional privilege. (It may have been only because of very distinctive political circumstances that the public-sector strikes in France in 1995 and 1996 evoked considerable popular support.)

In constructing an agenda which links the interests of the precarious, the unemployed and the relatively secure, it is again possible to seek a distinctive trade-union application of current rhetoric which is often used mendaciously. One concept which has become increasingly popular among policy-makers is 'employability': the argument is that individuals can no longer anticipate unbroken employment within a single organization but can avoid labour-market vulnerability by acquiring valued competences (including adaptability). Commonly this rhetoric is no more than a means of individualizing the problem of unemployment and deficient job opportunities and scapegoating the unemployed for their own marginalization. Evidently, a purely supply-side labour-market policy will result primarily in a more qualified cohort of unemployed (and perhaps in a demographic shift in the structure of employment and unemployment). However, the concept of employability is in principle one which can be made central to trade-union policy, in ways which address what Leisink (1993; 1996) calls 'occupational interests'. This would imply the co-ordination and integration of demands which unions have indeed often embraced: first, for enhanced individual entitlements to education and training, and for flexible opportunities to benefit from these throughout the working life; second, for more effective (and worker-oriented) provision both by employers and by education and training institutions; third, for demand-side policies to encourage employment growth and, no less importantly, to provide appropriate employment opportunities for 'upskilled' workers.

Part of the difficulty is that these demands address different interlocutors and involve different levels of initiative, and hence may fail through lack of co-ordination. (To take a concrete example: the imaginative and innovative proposals of IG Metall's *Tarifreform 2000* were overwhelmed by the macroeconomic problems affecting the German labour market after unification.) The issue of policy formulation thus links to that of organizational capacity. Yet it is surely essential that to address workers' current consciousness of extreme job insecurity, trade unions develop programmes which offer hope of real employment opportunity yet do so in a non-divisive manner. The idea of employability is one which could unite rather than divide. But to achieve this, trade unions must develop new means of articulation with workers' current preoccupations as well as new persuasive capacities.

This connects to the third theme identified: opportunity. Again, this is a concept which has been appropriated by the right but should be reclaimed for the labour movement. For most of the twentieth century, the core workforce which formed the main basis of trade unionism achieved their employment status through the dull compulsion of circumstance. Career advancement and self-directed occupational mobility are aspirations increasingly salient for unions' actual and potential constituencies. The weakening of the ties to the existing occupation and employer is however emancipating only to the extent that real and preferable alternatives are open. The choice among alternative options is an individual project, but one which is illusory unless a genuine and favourable structure of opportunities exists. To enhance the opportunity structure is necessarily a collective project, one which challenges both employers' discretion and the anarchy of market forces. In many ways a redefinition of the traditional function of trade unionism, this is another key dimension of a union agenda which can appeal to diverse constituencies in solidaristic fashion.[6]

The logic of all these themes is the reassertion of rights of labour as against the imperatives of capital. Many of the most effective interventions by European unions in the last decade represent partial efforts to articulate a new discourse of workers' rights. To regain the initiative, and to provide the foundation for new forms of solidarity, European labour movements need to develop these aspects of their programmes in more ambitious and more systematic ways. What is at issue is nothing less than that much abused notion, a new hegemonic project.

To be more than mere paper interventions, such initiatives must connect to a reformulation of the how of trade-union representation. (Accornero 1992) Organizational forms are inherited from the past and institutionally embedded; while some adaptations have been occurring and others may be pursued, radical transformation cannot be anticipated. More may however be feasible in terms of organizational capacity, democracy and activism. In an epoch when the traditional arena of trade-union intervention – the national/sectoral level – has diminished in relevance in the face of challenges from above (global market forces and transnational capital) and below (decentralization to the individual company and workplace), traditional recipes are often ineffective. Current challenges evidently pose new demands in respect of union intelligence. Knowledge by officials and activists of union organizations, policies and activities in other countries is uneven; some unions and confederations possess significant international departments, in others there are minimal resources. European-level organizations possess extremely restricted capacity either to influence transnational capital or the EU decision-makers, or to communicate with the members whom they in theory represent. Even if it were financially possible to satisfy these requirements by a vast expansion of the bureaucratic apparatus of international trade unionism, this would scarcely be a desirable solution. What is necessary is the development of new channels for the production and communication of trade-union intelligence.

This links to the issues of strategic leadership and democratic activism. It is easy to recognize that an urgent current need is for new models of transnational solidarity and for enhanced capacity for transnational intervention. But neither can be manufactured from above. The dual challenge is to formulate more effective processes of strategic direction while sustaining and enhancing the scope for initiative and mobilization at the base, to develop both stronger centralized structures and the mechanisms for more vigorous grassroots participation: which entails new kinds of articulation between the various levels of union organization, representation and action.

Within the European Union, one of the more fatuous of recent rhetorical devices is the idea of 'social dialogue'. Much time and energy are spent by representatives of European labour in discussion with their counterparts on the employer side. Very exceptionally indeed this results in an agreement, couched in such general terms and with such limited content as to contain little of practical significance. Rather more frequently, discussions result in a 'joint opinion'. It may indeed be comforting (or perhaps not!) to know that union representatives may at times be able to align their opinions with those of employers; but the effect in the real world is imperceptible. But within and between trade unions themselves, the pursuit of dialogue and the search for common opinion are vital requirements. Hence the task of European trade unions today may be encapsulated in the slogan: develop the internal social dialogue! Enhanced organizational capacity and organic solidarity demand a high level of multi-directional discussion, communication and understanding. To be effective at international level, above all else, trade unionism must draw on the experience at national level of efforts to reconstitute unions as discursive organizations which foster interactive internal relationships and serve more as networks than as hierarchies.

Finally, modern information technologies offer the potential for labour movements to break out of the iron cage which for so long has trapped them in organizational structures which mimic those of capital. The Liverpool dockers, in their long but ultimately unsuccessful struggle against a ruthless employer, used e-mail and the world-wide web to great effect in campaigning for international solidarity. In more routine ways, intelligent use of new modes of information and communication can assist in the work of consciousness building and representation. (Müller 1996) With imagination, unions may transform themselves and build an emancipatory potential for labour in the new millennium. Forward to the 'virtual trade union' of the future!

Notes

1. Gorz (1982, p. 16) indeed argues that class consciousness was irrelevant for Marx, quoting the famous comment in The Holy Family: 'it is not a question of what this or that proletarian, or even the whole proletariat, at the moment *regards* as its aim. It is a question of *what the proletariat is*, and what, in accordance with its *being*, it will historically be compelled to do.' But this is to assume that Marx never developed his analysis beyond the position of his earliest writings. One may counterpose the Gorzian argument to that of Fantasia (1988, pp. 8-10), who insists (correctly in my view) that for Marx the apparent dualism of 'objective' and 'subjective' is bridged by collective human action.
2. In addition, as Vilrokx (1996) has argued, technological and organizational changes have increasingly fragmented the labour process itself in many work contexts; the consequence, he suggests a little dramatically, is the creation of a 'post-representative society'.
3. Hence Ruigrok and Van Tulder (1995) speak of 'triadization' rather than globalization.
4. The Jospin government which took office in France in June 1997 attempted to escape the constraints built into the iron cage of EMU, but (at the time of writing) with few signs of success.
5. Jefferys (1996, p. 183) develops a similar argument in suggesting that 'a union focus on sustaining or introducing a new "bilateral" content to the unilaterally-imposed management-led employment relationship may offer the required strategic direction'.
6. As Waddington and Whitston (1996, p. 163) note in their study of white-collar workers' attitudes, 'new union members... look to unions to negotiate a fair and equitable framework within which individualized aspects of the employment relationship – which are often career related – may be worked out.'

References

Accornero, A. (1992), *La Parabola del Sindacato: Ascesa e Declino di una Cultura*, Bologna: il Mulino.

Anderson, B. (1983), *Imagined Communities*, London: Verso.

Boyer, R. and D. Drache (eds) (1996), *States Against Markets*, London: Routledge.

Coller, X. (1996), 'Managing Flexibility in the Food Industry', *European Journal of Industrial Relations*, **3** (2), 153-72.

Durkheim, E. (1933), *The Division of Labour in Society*, London: Macmillan. [Originally published 1893 as *De la Division du Travail Social*.]

Edwards, R., P. Garonna and F. Tödtling (eds) (1986), *Unions in Crisis and Beyond*. Dover: Auburn House.

Fantasia, R. (1988), *Cultures of Solidarity*, Berkeley: University of California Press.

Golden, M. and J. Pontusson (eds) (1992), *Bargaining for Change: Union Politics in North America and Europe*, Ithaca: Cornell University Press.

Gorz, A. (1982), *Farewell to the Working Class*, London: Pluto.

Heckscher, C. C. (1988), *The New Unionism*, New York: Basic Books.

Hirst, P. and G. Thompson (1996), *Globalization in Question*, Cambridge: Polity.

IG Metall (1991), *Tarifreform 2000: ein Gestaltungsrahmen für die Industriearbeit der Zukunft,* Frankfurt: IGM.

Jacoby, S. M. (1995), 'Social Dimensions of Global Economic Integration', in S. M. Jacoby (ed), *The Workers of Nations*, New York: Oxford UP, pp. 3-29.

Jefferys, S. (1996), 'Strategic Choice for Unions in France and Britain' in P. Leisink, J. Van Leemput and J. Vilrokx (eds), *The Challenges to Trade Unions in Europe*, Cheltenham: Edward Elgar, pp. 171-85.

Johnson, P. (1994), *Success While Others Fail*. Ithaca, ILR Press.

Kjellberg, A. (1992), 'Sweden: Can the Model Survive?', in A. Ferner and R. Hyman (eds), *Industrial Relations in the New Europe,* Oxford: Blackwell, pp. 88-142.

Leisink, P. (1993), *Is Innovation a Management Prerogative?*, Coventry: IRRU.

Leisink, P. (1996), 'The Wavering Innovation of Trade Union Policy', in P. Leisink, J. Van Leemput and J. Vilrokx (eds), *The Challenges to Trade Unions in Europe*, Cheltenham: Edward Elgar, pp. 123-37.

Mahnkopf, B. and E. Altvater (1995), 'Trade Unions as Mediators of Transnational Economic Pressures?', *European Journal of Industrial Relations*, **1** (1), 101-17.

Marginson, P. and K. Sisson (1996), 'Multinational Companies and the Future of Collective Bargaining', *European Journal of Industrial Relations*, **2** (2), 173-97.

Mouriaux, R. (1995), 'The Disarray of Trade Unions in a State of Crisis', in P. Pasture, J. Verberckmoes and H. De Witte (eds), *The Lost Perspective*, 2, Aldershot: Avebury, pp. 3-18.

Mückenberger, U., E. Schmidt and R. Zoll. (eds) (1996), *Die Modernisierung der Gewerkschaften in Europa*, Münster: Westfälisches Dampfboot.

Mueller, F. (1996), 'National Stakeholders in the Global Contest for Corporate Investment', *European Journal of Industrial Relations*, **3** (3), 345-68.

Müller, W. (1996), 'Per E-Mail', *Mitbestimmung*, **7+8**/96, 6-7.

Müller-Jentsch, W. (1988), 'Trade Unions as Intermediary Organizations', *Economic and Industrial Democracy*, **6**, 3-33.

Offe, C. and H. Wiesenthal (1985), 'Two Logics of Collective Action', in C. Offe, *Disorganized Capitalism*, Cambridge: Polity, pp. 170-220.

Paci, M. (1973), *Mercato del Lavoro e Classi Sociale in Italia,* Bologna: il Mulino.

Regini, M. (ed.) (1992), *The Future of Labour Movements*, London: Sage.

Rogers, J. (1995), 'A Strategy for Labour', *Industrial Relations*, **34** (3), 367-81.

Ruigrok, W. and R. Van Tulder (1995), *The Logic of International Restructuring*, London: Routledge.

Sabel, C. (1995), 'Meta-Corporations and Open Labour Markets', in W. Littek and T. Charles (eds), *The New Division of Labour*, Berlin: Walter de Gruyter, pp. 57-94.

Sayer, A. and R. Walker (1992), *The New Social Economy*, Oxford: Blackwell.

Standing, G. (1997), 'Globalization, Labour Flexibility and Insecurity', *European Journal of Industrial Relations*, **3** (1), 7-37.

Streeck, W. (1992), 'National Diversity, Regime Competition and Institutional Deadlock', *Journal of Public Policy*, **12**, 301-30.

Swenson, P. (1989), *Fair Shares: Unions, Pay and Politics in Sweden and West Germany*, Ithaca: Cornell University Press.

Vilrokx, J. (1996), 'Trade Unions in a Post-representative Society', in P. Leisink, J. Van Leemput and J. Vilrokx (eds), *The Challenges to Trade Unions in Europe*, Cheltenham: Edward Elgar, pp. 31-51.

Waddington, J. and C. Whitston (1996), 'Collectivism in a Changing Context', in P. Leisink, J. Van Leemput and J. Vilrokx (eds), *The Challenges to Trade Unions in Europe*, Cheltenham: Edward Elgar, pp. 153-67.

Waterman, P. (1998), Globalization, *Social Movements and the New Internationalisms*, London: Mansell.

Zoll, R. (1993), *Alltagssolidarität und Individualismus*, Frankfurt: Suhrkamp.

6. Fragmenting the Internal Labour Market

Jill Rubery

A key characteristic of recent labour-market trends has been the de-stabilization of internal labour markets. These developments are often interpreted as a consequence of the changing world order. Globalization is argued to have increased uncertainty, restricting companies' ability to offer long tenure jobs and favouring the development of a fragmented industrial and employment system, flatter organizations and more individualized reward and career structures. These trends stand in contrast to the large-scale bureaucracies based on job ladders and promotion by seniority associated with standard internal labour-market theory. These changes are taken to reflect a move towards more market-determined pay and employment systems, and a reduced role for institutions and regulations in the organization of employment. Yet diversity within the employment system is increasing, suggesting an enhanced role for companies in the structuring of employment systems and an increase in managerial discretion. An alternative institutional analysis to that of the standard internal labour-market system has yet to be fully developed and as a consequence the analysis of labour markets is once again being claimed by market theorists. This chapter addresses four interrelated questions:

– What are the changes that have taken place in labour-market systems; are they towards a greater or a reduced role for organization-specific employment practices?
– How can the theory of internal labour markets be reinterpreted and adjusted in order to account for and explain the current turbulence in labour-market systems?
– To what extent can the changes be interpreted as responses to changing market conditions, including globalization, or to changing production and labour-market systems, for which the traditional internal labour market is no longer an appropriate institutional form?
– What is the likely outcome of these changes for the dual objectives of equity and efficiency?

Changes in Internal Labour-Market Systems

Several significant changes in employment systems with relevance for the operation of internal labour markets can be identified. These developments are particularly evident within the UK but can also be found in many advanced countries, albeit to different degrees of intensity and from very different starting points. The most important among them include:

- decentralization of regulation and bargaining, potentially increasing the significance of the organization as the site of the construction of employment practices;
- fragmentation of organizational structures, through subcontracting and through the creation of profit centres, thereby reducing the scale of organization-specific labour markets;
- changes in the boundaries of who is regarded as inside or outside the internal labour-market system, or within the core or periphery sectors;
- changes in the nature of the employment contract and in particular in the degree of job security offered even to those at the heart of the 'core';
- moves towards flatter job structures, functional flexibility and team-work organization and increased importance of firm-specific skills;
- individualization of employment relations involving individualized bargaining, personalized contracts and performance-related pay;
- changes in the work ethos, towards more emphasis on individual and group accountability for budgets, customer care, quality provisions and less on professional ethics and autonomy or public service;
- changes to the composition of the employed workforce, including a higher share of women employed, a higher share of graduate recruitment and an increased use of early retirement, thereby concentrating the age structure of employees more within core working years of 25 to 50.

These trends appear to be pulling in two directions, towards and away from organization-specific labour markets. Decentralization of bargaining and the deregulation of the labour market have given organizations a great deal more scope to be the independent architects of employment structures and practices. The consequence of the removal of regulation at the national or industry level is not the atomistic markets of labour-market textbooks where organizations become price-takers instead of price-makers; instead the result is to leave more unchallenged the power enjoyed by organizations to set the terms and conditions of employment. Large organizations may exercise greater power than the small, but even the latter have discretion in the construction of employment systems. The assumption of interchangeable jobs and interchangeable people has little relevance to most labour-market situations; many people in work are unwilling or indeed unable to find another job easily, because of unemployment, prejudice relating to age, sex or race and to high invest-ments in firm-specific skills, strong social attachments at work and domestic restrictions on job choice. Through judiciously chosen em-ployment strategies, for example targeting the more disadvantaged workers, even small firms with low ability to pay can create an internal labour market (Rubery 1994), in the sense of creating a captured and committed workforce, locked in by their limited alternative employment opportunities.

Against these trends towards greater importance of the organization for employment practices and careers, there are a number of counter-acting trends reducing the significance of the employer for an individu-al's career. These include first the tendency towards fragmentation of organizations which shortens the possible internal career routes, except sometimes for a minority of higher management. Secondly, there has been an increasing awareness of the inability and/or lack of desire by organizations to guarantee even their core employees job security. The reputation of companies as offering firm-specific training and career ladders has been tarnished; even if senior management wish to re-estab-lish their traditional internal labour-market systems, they may be unable to do so because they cannot recreate trust in the company's ability and willingness to deliver job security. The consequence may be that com-panies have to provide well-qualified new recruits with access to trans-ferable skills and qualifications even if companies would prefer to adopt the internal training and career ladder structure. The increased use of subcontracting also narrows the organizational scope for careers and fosters the development of highly specialized activities offering limited career potential.

Subcontracting and other changes in employment relations are also part of the process of changing the boundaries of the internal labour market, thereby narrowing the share of the total workforce which is providing services to the company for which the company accepts responsibility. This change is also evident in the public sector, where the share of the workforce providing public services which is directly employed by the public sector, and which may therefore expect the protection of the 'good employer' reputation of the public sector, has diminished in many countries (a problem in addition to any weakening of good employer practice towards the workers remaining within public employment). Other devices for narrowing the core include the use of temporary contracts, agency staff and part-timers, where these are excluded from rights and benefits accorded to full-timers. Segmentation of internal employment systems has been a persistent feature of internal labour-market systems, but while the initial emphasis in the 1970s was on explaining the durability of these divisions (Doeringer and Piore 1971), subsequent emphasis has been on how the renewed interest in flexibility has led to changes in the boundaries between the protected and the unprotected or between the core and the periphery. (Rosenberg 1989)

The move away from bureaucratic hierarchies to flatter structures is seen by some as heralding a more egalitarian system of organization, where rewards are tailored more to actual performance than designated job status. However, the delayering of organizations may, in practice, create a wider divide between senior management and others (Coyle 1995; Cappelli 1995), with the additional responsibilities of senior management used as a justification to widen differentials despite a reduced supply of management jobs relative to demand.

The moves away from narrow job definitions towards more generic jobs, involving functional flexibility and team-working, have taken place at different rates and to different extents within organizations and across countries. Nevertheless there is a general trend away from transferable skills and transferable job titles or occupations. The creation and maintenance of occupational labour markets requires a strong level of labour-market regulation. (Marsden 1986) Yet the destabilization of internal labour-market systems has coincided with the deregulation of the external labour market, making a labour-market system based on general transferable skills more difficult to secure. These twin developments are creating potential major problems for the long-term viability of current labour-market systems and arrangements. Just as organizations need to invest more in firm-specific skills, there is some evidence, for example from the US, that they are investing less because the risk of loss of that investment has risen as individuals feel less attachment to the organization. (Cappelli 1995) There is thus a widespread risk that there will be underinvestment in work skills from a societal perspective. Individual organizations are not in a position to resolve these problems because of the breakdown of trust in internal labour-market systems.

A key element of internal labour-market theory has been the assumption that pay will be related to job ladders and seniority and not to individualized performance criteria. Recent trends towards the individualization of the employment relationship and the move to personal contracts has on the surface turned on its head Williamson's (1975) predictions of pay grading structures used to prevent opportunistic bargaining. Part of the explanation may lie in the interest that managers may have in such developments; personal contracts may make workers more difficult to manage but they may facilitate significant rises in the relative pay of managers. The assumption that avoidance of opportunistic bargaining is more profitable for employers than exploiting labour-market disadvantage has also become more difficult to maintain in the context of high levels of unemployment. (Grimshaw and Rubery 1995; 1998)

Moreover, there are increasingly fewer benchmarks against which to judge the fairness of pay levels and as a consequence there may be less to gain for employers in establishing open pay structures which conform to some notion of 'felt fair' practices. The job queue model of Lester Thurow (1975) predicted that firms would not take advantage of temporary disequilibria in the labour market to adjust wages and conditions as this would harm their long-term ability to recruit which was based on a known set of career and earnings opportunities, but when such conditions are neither known nor predictable, the incentive to manage pay structures for the long term diminishes. Where internal labour markets were situated within industries with established industry-level pay and grading structures, the pay and conditions offered within the organization could be 'benchmarked' against these conditions. Currently the public sector in the UK is developing organization-specific pay structures but which can still be compared to nationally set conditions and rates. This encourages the maintenance of job-graded pay structures but if these national agreements were to disappear, as has been the case in much of private industry in the UK, there would no longer be a standard against which to compare local rates to decide if the organization is paying above or below the going rate. The disappearance of effective knowledge concerning the going rate for particular jobs, brought about by the demise of national benchmarks and the creation of firm-specific job structures, has provided a basis for moving from job-related to personalized pay. (Rubery 1995a) Although the increase in personalized pay should not be exaggerated, it is notable that the recent growth of job evaluation in the UK has in fact coincided with the decline of the significance of the job evaluation for pay as the range of earnings per job band rises, and the degree of overlap increases. (IRS 1994) This fits with the trend towards so-called broad banding in the US.

Possibly the greatest change of all has been the spread of market-oriented performance criteria, even when not linked directly to pay rises, to a much wider range of organizations and job categories. For some this is a process of empowerment as responsibility for meeting targets relating to quality or quantity are devolved through the hierarchy. For others it is evidence of the attempt to re-establish employment relationships around a simplistic reward-effort relationship. The types of problems that have been encountered with the changes include firstly mis-specified performance targets which divert the attention of employees from the main or basic tasks; these problems may be evident to the employees concerned, but because of the simplistic assessment criteria, no remedial action is taken even when the faults become apparent. (Lewis 1991; Kessler and Purcell 1992) Thus by changing the nature of the employment relationship, the responsibility of employees to adjust to actual job needs rather than pre-specified conditions may be sacrificed by an overarching managerialist approach to workforce management. Other problems with the new employment relations relate to the absence of any recognition of the integrity and professionalism of occupational groups; the employment package that many people implicitly bought into when joining internal labour markets involved not only a trade-off between maximizing earnings and maximizing job and career security, but a trade-off between a highly competitive career and one where there might be the opportunity, protected against the vagaries of competitive product and labour markets, to develop an interest in high standards for their own sake, not related to immediate pecuniary advantage. There is of course a counter argument that within bureaucratic structures standards may in fact fall below satisfactory norms precisely because of the absence of sanctions associated with more competitive systems. It is this latter perception of bureaucracies that has provided the basis for reforms to internal labour markets, particularly in public sector services. Yet replacing the professional ethos, based on high trust relations, with one of performance to specified targets runs the risk that the concept of the job holder's responsibilities may be narrowed rather than broadened, and standards of integrity may fall in the pursuit of targets. Moreover, once a professional ethos is destroyed or standards of personal integrity diminish, they may prove very difficult to rebuild, thereby providing further justification of the need for close monitoring of work effort.

The final significant change we have identified is the changing com-position of the workforce. There are a range of consequences for traditional internal labour markets following on from the changes in labour supply. First, as we discuss further below, changes in education and training systems impose new constraints on the age and seniority-related job ladders typically associated with internal labour markets. Second, internal labour markets are institutional constructs which are embedded not only in a production but also in a social reproduction system. One of the key historical achievements of trade-union organiza-tions has been to establish notions of fair wages linked to fair standards of living and not solely to product prices. The linking of wage increases to retail prices is symbolic of this embedding of the wage structure in the social structure. However, much of the trade-union activity around the notion of fair wages has been based on the assumption of a sole earner male breadwinner family. The breakdown of the single earner family and the emergence of dual and multi-earner families, together with the growth of atypical and part-time work, is undermining any simple link between wages and standards of living and provides a new basis on which to fragment the wage structure and to emphasize personal per-formance over notions of fair or living wages.

The cumulative effect of these changes is beginning to be evident within the UK labour market, and similar developments may follow elsewhere. The reductions in trade-union power found in the UK have gone hand in hand with a deterioration in pay and conditions in the external periphery. Thus instead of a process of equalization of risk in the labour market, the outcome has been to maintain or even increase the inequality of risk around a higher average level of employment insecurity for all. It tends to be the least advantaged parts of the core that are ejected from insider to outsider status, with the dismantlement, for example, of internal labour markets for manual workers in public transport, the steel industry, the post office and other areas of protected working-class careers. In the UK the undermining of job security and internal labour markets has reached quite a way up the occupation and industry hierarchy but those at the top have been compensated at least in part by significant increases in their real and relative pay, even if at the cost of longer hours of work. (Gregg 1994; OECD 1996) While much of the destabilization of the middle and lower parts of the labour market has been justified by reference to reducing the monopoly rents enjoyed by insiders, those extracted at the top of the labour market have been allowed to rise, on grounds of higher risks and responsibilities. Thus the emphasis on redistribution in the insider/outsider analysis tends to be on those closest to the outsiders, that is the most marginal insiders, giving up their employment protection and pay in the cause of greater equality at the bottom of the employment and income distribution. Greater flexibility at the bottom end of the market has coincided with further rises in pay for those at the top. These changes are often justified by the need to match market rates, but there is little evidence that recruitment and retention is the main factor[1]; instead the weakening of internal comparability associated with the fragmentation of the internal labour market has allowed managers discretion to adjust pay structures in line with their own interests and value systems.

Revising the Theory of Internal Labour Markets

To what extent can internal labour-market theory or segmentation theory be adjusted or reinterpreted to explain and account for the changes observed in current labour-market systems; or does the destabilization of labour-market structures suggest that we need to move away from institutional explanations of labour markets and return to the market-based models of labour organization?

There are of course a range of different interpretations of the role of internal labour markets in the employment system. For some working within the neo-classical tradition, the destabilization of internal labour markets and the associated increased flexibility enables more workers to 'price themselves into jobs' and reduces social exclusion. While in the initial phases this increased use of flexible employment may increase divisions between the core and the periphery, the argument is that any reduction in regulation and rigidity in the longer term must be good. This approach attributes problems of exclusion to the actions of workers and other institutions in creating barriers to entry and fits with the distinction which some neo-classical economists have tried to draw between 'justified' and 'unjustified' internal labour-market systems; the former are those where firm-specific skills require internalization from the perspective of employers, and the latter those where trade unions have tried to impose internal labour-market systems for jobs where high turnover rates cause few economic problems. (Addison and Siebert 1991; Polachek and Siebert 1995; Lindbeck and Snower 1989) However, there is little historical evidence to support this distinction as case studies of the development of internal labour-market systems have found these by and large to have been imposed against the perceived short-term interests of firms. (Jacoby 1984; Elbaum 1984; Osterman 1987; Rubery 1978) It is only later that organizations came to see bureaucratic structures based on job security and promotion by seniority as an economic benefit. This is not because employee commitment and firm-specific skills lack significance for organizations, but because employers could often secure a stable and productive workforce without the development of elaborate internal labour-market structures, at least in the short term. (Rubery 1994; Grimshaw and Rubery 1995)

One of the problems with initial formulations of the institutional segmentation theory was that it assumed too harmonious a relation between the interests of workers and the interests of capital, such that internal labour-market systems were seen to reflect a 'happy coincidence of wants'. (Doeringer and Piore 1971) This approach failed ultimately to distinguish itself from the neo-classical transactions cost approach to internal labour markets where institutions were constructed solely to serve the interests of capital. Once it is recognized that labour-market institutions evolve out of the struggle and divisions between capital and workers as well as from their mutual interests, it becomes much easier to develop a dynamic analysis of internal labour-market systems where the form and extent of bureaucratic structures depends on internal and external power relations as well as on the technical need to incorporate and internalize the labour force. (Osterman 1994; Grimshaw and Rubery 1998) Indeed once the balance of power between workers and capital change, then the institutions which emerged to maintain and reinforce a compromise between the interests of both sides may be undermined and a new power struggle can be anticipated. Such an approach provides a useful handle on the changes currently taking place within labour-market systems where it may be power relations rather than either companies' technical needs or even indeed companies' ability to deliver a stable employment contract that have been subject to most change. Those that believe in the division between 'justified' and 'unjustified' internal labour markets might subscribe to the view that it is the 'unjustified', those set up through the power of unions, which are being dismantled as a result of the power change and that markets are returning to efficient structures. However, from an institutional or segmentation perspective, the process of change may also destabilize internal labour markets which are appropriate to meet technical and organizational requirements, but which cannot be maintained because changing conditions both inside and outside the organization have undermined the conditions for an effective internal labour market.

A general problem with internal labour-market theory as developed by segmentation theorists and neo-institutionalists alike has been the overconcentration on internal conditions and a neglect of the influence of the external labour market and broader society in structuring the form of the internal labour market. The significance of the external labour market and social norms in influencing the design of internal labour markets has become evident primarily through comparative research which has identified the influence of different institutional arrangements including education and training systems, trade-union organization, gender relations and legal systems (see for example Maurice *et al.* 1986; Marsden 1992; Rubery 1988; Rubery *et al.* 1997; Deakin and Muckenberger 1992; Sengenberger 1981) on the structuring of internal labour markets. It is the failure to embed internal labour-market analysis within historical time and space, and specifically within its social environment (Granovetter 1985; Morishima 1995; Marginson 1993), which has in fact left it vulnerable to current trends in employment systems which seem to be unpicking most of the main tenets of internal labour-market models. These trends instead should be situated within an historical analysis in which the changes taking place within organizations would be identified both as reflections of and as causes of change in the external labour market, and indeed the broader society and economy.

Many of the accepted social norms based on both trade-union power and traditional class configurations are fragmenting, leaving organizations facing fewer constraints on the form of the internal labour market. However, while in principle employers are now freer to use a range of different systems without risk of labour turnover or skill shortage, the reality may be less favourable for employers. Bureaucratic internal labour-market systems were built around the notion of developing high trust relations within a secure environment (Fox 1974), so that although employers now have greater power to determine employment conditions without reference to internal or external power they may in fact be in a much weaker position to build up either high trust relations or the prerequisite, belief in a stable and secure environment. This may mean that they retain the form but not necessarily the substance of a skilled committed workforce. (Cappelli 1995) Here we confront perhaps the central weakness of much internal labour-market theory; by seeking to explain why apparently social and institutional practices within organizations can be explained by economic imperatives, the non-economic aspects of employment relations – such as notions of trust, belief in professional ethics or public service – have been considered outcomes of institutional arrangements set in place by economic necessity. Yet this *ex post* rationalization of non competitive labour-market institutions does not help with the more difficult task of rebuilding, reforming or establishing anew these non-market relationships.

From these current developments in labour-market structures we find a range of different transformations of internal labour markets which are changing the nature of the employment relationship and undermining the characteristics primarily associated with institutionally-constructed employment systems. Most of the changes we have identified appear to be moving employment systems away from explicitly bureaucratic and hierarchical structures, and this may appear at first sight to offer an opportunity for labour to escape the rigid hierarchical systems associated both with Fordism and internal labour markets. Indeed most of the debate in the past from a left perspective has been over why internal labour markets and hierarchies were used to control and restrict labour. (Williamson 1985; Marglin 1974) Yet what is at issue here is the significance of the role of collective and societal-based institutions in the establishment of 'felt fair' employment systems. Here we are contrasting the advantages to labour of hierarchical over individualized performance-related systems and not compared to forms of worker control. Bureaucratic systems are not socially desirable in themselves but were established within a context of stronger class organization and incorporated some checks and balances, providing some degree of autonomy to work groups and codifying social norms and values. The virtues of the hierarchical employment form, embedded admittedly in an imperfect social contract, are clear relative to the greater uncertainties of the personalized employment contract offered within a social climate where both the state and the unions impose much weaker checks on the discretion of management. (Jacoby 1994; Cappelli 1995) Further problems arise from current trends from an efficiency perspective. If work relations are seen either as entirely exploitative or as entirely instrumental then controls and monitoring may be the main and perhaps best methods of ensuring work is performed in line with business objectives. However, from, for example, the communitarian perspective that citizens seek more than individualized pecuniary advantage from work, alternative modes of organizing workforce relations involving mutual trust between parties may result in higher long-term levels of productivity. These integrative benefits from alternative organizational modes are not necessarily achievable at the individual organizational level and instead need to be embedded in broader social relations. (Streeck 1992,

p. 61) Thus the destabilization of employment relations may be interpreted as a breaking of the implicit social contract between classes which cannot be re-established through the actions of individual employers and may thus result in a loss of efficiency impacting on both employees and employers.

Explaining Changes in Internal Labour Markets

So far we have considered the main changes taking place in internal labour markets and how we can interpret them within a broader perspective in which external institutional arrangements impact upon internal labour markets and vice versa. While this provides a more adequate theoretical approach to understanding change in institutional labour markets we need still to address the issue of whether the emerging changes in labour markets can be attributed directly or indirectly to changes in the world order – to globalization and new forms of competitiveness. This leads to a second and related question of whether the traditional internal labour-market systems had in practice reached the end of their useful institutional life. Thus while the particular form of change that is taking place might not be fully in the right direction, the fragmentation of existing systems may be considered a necessary step towards the re-establishment of a new working order. The emerging new labour-market systems may be even less well adjusted to the needs of Europe within a globalizing economic system than the systems they are replacing, even if the process of employment destabilization is itself linked to economic destabilization and trends in world trade. This raises the question addressed in the conclusions, of the implications of these changes for both equity and efficiency, defined in the wider sense to include the creation of appropriate conditions for long-term growth and development.

The case that there is a strong link between current changes in pay structures in the West and the process of globalization and new competitive conditions has been made most forcibly by Wood (1994) who attributes widening earnings dispersion to the relocation of manufacturing activities and the West losing out on activities with a high demand for manual labour, resulting in widening earnings disparities reflecting changes in relative demand for unskilled labour. These structural arguments are seen to be the main reason also for the apparent inevitable collapse of labour-market regulatory systems, that is, the dark forces of the market have, in line with the predictions of Marshall (1890) and

Hicks (1932), been the prime cause of the destabilization of institutions. These arguments can be criticized on a number of levels; first the work of Freeman (1997) and others has cast doubt on the trade argument, because of the small share of the labour market actually affected by these trade patterns, and because the argument failed to distinguish earnings trends for male and for female unskilled labour. Female unskilled labour has been affected by globalization trends as much if not more than male unskilled labour but the argument has been developed largely related to male manual workers. In any case there has been little evidence of a decline in demand for female manual workers until recently once service work is taken into account. Perhaps an even more fundamental problem is the assumption that globalization requires an increase in inequality in all countries, yet without consideration of how different societies function with different levels of inequality and recent trends have been as much towards divergence as convergence in income inequality between countries. (OECD 1996)

While an argument can perhaps be made that the observed changes in income distribution are the result of globalization, there is little substance to the claim that widening earnings distribution is essential for competitiveness. In fact the opposite could be argued to hold. Lowering wages for unskilled workers to maintain competitiveness in world trade appears to be a lost cause and the argument that pay for the higher skilled has to rise for competitiveness is even more difficult to sustain. There is still only a very small number of people who operate within an international labour market, and there is little reason for the high earnings commanded by this group to spread all the way down the management hierarchy. Moreover, there is a much stronger argument that those countries which can contain wage levels for the more educated and skilled would in fact develop a comparative advantage over their rivals. (Dølvik and Steen 1997; Ellingsæter and Rubery 1997) A counter argument that high wages help competitiveness only makes sense if one posits both a strong world trade in high skills and a need for high wage differentials to induce effective performance of skilled labour. Yet there is little evidence that collective performance of skilled labour is positively correlated with high levels of inequality, particularly as most economic studies cannot overcome the circular argument that high wages are supposed to both induce high performance and also be a measure of high performance. Globalization thus seems to provide a relatively weak explanation for widening pay dispersion.

It may be more plausible to see the widening pay dispersion as in part the indirect effect of a more general move towards more flexible markets, required by firms to meet changing competition needs across a range of dimensions, not primarily related to pay. Yet even here the link with the concept of globalization is tenuous. Many of the sectors using flexible labour are not in the major traded sectors and it is the form of national competition and national regulation, for example relating to service opening hours, which influences the use of flexible labour. Where globalization has most impact is through the globalization or homogenization of lifestyles and consumption and leisure demands, rather than directly through the global system of production. It is still less apparent why the public sector has to change its employment system in the interests of globalization, except as a response to the pressure on public sector budgets which has been put into place by the new world order. Many of the changes in the public sector, made in the apparent interests of better and more flexible management, may perhaps be more attributable to the need to meet new budget targets and take cost out of the system.

However, while globalization and new forms of competition may not be said to have required the particular form of restructuring of labour markets currently in train, there is another related argument that needs to be addressed. Namely had the old order of formal internal labour-markets and bureaucratic structures passed its sell by date; and was a radical restructuring necessary in order for a new institutional order to develop more in tune with current labour-market and social conditions? One of the problems with institutions and regulations is that they tend to codify and reinforce arrangements appropriate to a particular social and economic order (OECD 1994; Boyer 1979) and may not be flexible enough to respond and restructure themselves to meet new challenges. The process of fragmentation currently observed may be a necessary phase, setting the basis for a new institutional order. There are three main arguments that can be made in this vein. The first is that these systems institutionalized power relations in the wider labour-market and social system, and specifically imposed and reinforced a white male hierarchy on both the external and the internal labour market. These reinforcement mechanisms included the selective recruitment processes into the entry points of the internal labour markets, the so-called extended internal labour market, whereby new recruits were selected through a series of informal networks with existing employees; the reinforcement of gender pay inequalities through their codification within formal and even job-evaluated pay structures; the emphasis on seniority and continuity for promotion and the hierarchical power structures which reproduced societal values of patriarchy, and white superiority. Justifications for fragmentation can thus be made on the basis both of the management literature stressing 'managing diversity', where companies are argued to gain in business performance by opening up their employment systems (Kandola *et al.* 1995) to a wider diversity of groups, and from the more radical feminist literature which rejects the liberal objective of increasing the share of women within the white male hierarchy in favour of the more transformational approach, where equality of opportunity would require a rethinking of internal labour-market structures towards a more open, democratic and egalitarian structure. (Cockburn 1991)

The second argument is that internal labour-market systems need to change to take into account the changing patterns of transition from school to work of the youth population. There has been a proliferation of patterns of transition, instead of the old divide, at least within the UK, between those leaving school and those leaving universities. Age-related entry points followed by hierarchical structures based on seniority fail to take into account the diversity of education and training among recruits, but to allow multiple entry points according to qualifications, complicates the role of internal training, raising all sorts of issues of comparability between education and work experience. The decline in the number of young people with good school records leaving education at early ages has coincided with the decline of entry grade jobs offering training opportunities and promotion up an internal labour market. Even within non-manual career hierarchies there have been problems in maintaining simple hierarchies (Rubery 1995b), given the range of qualifications from degree to basic school leaving qualifications found in many clerical areas, once all the generations are looked at together. Thus the ideal type internal labour market appears designed for a period when there was a small elite group who acquired higher education leaving a majority for whom the main source of differentiation in level of skill arose out of work-related experience and seniority.

The third and related argument is that job structures based around long career ladders and hierarchies are more suited to the Fordist than to the post-Fordist mode of labour organization, and that internal labour markets needed to be flattened and reconstructed to bring in new forms of work organization based around notions of devolution of responsibility, team-work and functional flexibility. (Cappelli 1995) Hierarchical pay structures based on seniority are not compatible with these new flexible forms of work.

While there is of course some validity in all three arguments, there is less evidence that the changes taking place within internal labour markets are designed to meet these problems, even when apparently justified in these terms. For example, changes to pay structure may be justified in terms of improving gender equality or the evils of social exclusion invoked to justify opening up public sector employment to competition, to prevent it being the bastion of the white population. Opening up opportunities to the previously excluded is given precedence over constructing stable and sheltered labour-market environments where people feel sufficiently secure both to work effectively and to plan their lives. Abolition of seniority pay and its replacement by performance criteria can be justified as more in keeping with the new flexible organization and also more equitable as it rewards performance rather than status, even though it allows greater managerial discretion over pay levels. To some extent the institutions of organized labour, the trade unions, have left themselves open to these pressures for change, by doing too little too late to adjust to new needs in the labour market and to bring within the framework of organized labour the new sources of labour supply, including many women, part-timers and ethnic minorities. Some are trying now to remedy this limited vision of an organized labour force consisting solely of the white male full-time continuous participant, but progress in some countries is still very slow, with even issues of equal pay hardly reaching the trade unions' agendas. Yet there is also a danger that those pressing for excluded interests to be put on the trade-union agenda, for example those of women, ethnic minorities or indeed young people, may fail to see the ways in which their arguments can be manipulated and used to justify fragmentation. For example, while the transition from a male breadwinner system to a dual earner family must involve redistribution between male and female wage-earners it is important to ensure that it does not also result in a reduction in the wage share of national income even at the same time as more labour is supplied to the labour market. The possibility that inter-gender struggles over resources could be used to increase inequalities in class distribution needs to be recognized, not to defend the existing order, but so that one distributional struggle does not serve to obscure and hide another.

Conclusions: Threats to Equity and Efficiency within the New Labour-Market Systems

The language of change and the language of modernization is a very persuasive form of rhetoric when confronted with the failures of the old systems to adjust to new conditions and to prevent social exclusion and the reinforcement of gender and race disadvantage. However, what is clear from the above discussion is that change without new forms of social regulation is likely to increase rather than reduce divergence between the advantaged and the disadvantaged, or the insiders and the outsiders, and at the same time to generate major problems at a macro and micro level in the efficiency of employment systems as producers of skilled and effective labour forces. The fragmentation of the internal labour-market system calls for imaginative development of new forms of regulation to plug the lacunae created by the dismantlement of the old institutional regularities and certainties. (Deakin and Muckenberger 1992; Deakin and Wilkinson 1996; Sengenberger and Campbell 1994)

There is a general problem of oversupply of labour relative to demand which cannot be solved through competition between groups to exclude the other or to open up areas to unfettered competition. In contrast to the standard neo-classical insider/outsider approach to labour markets where it is the actions of workers which create job shortage, the segment-ation theory perspective is that the search by workers to create shelters or segments within the labour market is a consequence of excessive competition in labour markets and the inherent tendency for capitalism to generate a jobs rather than a labour shortage. (Freedman 1976; Rubery 1978) A new form of solidarity needs to be developed around the notion that most adults would expect to be in work during their core or prime age years, unless absent for some specific purpose such as education, training or caring tasks. It is arguable that this notion has already passed the test of being consistent with social expectations and values, as more and more men as well as women expect men and women to wish to remain in the labour market except for short periods of absence. The new solidarity thus needs to be based on ending the distinction between those in and outside the labour force, and moving toward a citizenship ap-proach where all have the right to expect to be in work. Periods of leave from the labour market need to include some guarantee of rights to return, and indeed, not involve penalties in access to social protection. Such a new solidarity may be extremely difficult to bring about in the context of the fragmenting labour market, but the recognition of the need for an all embracing approach might at least place some clarity on the problems that derive from accepting the insider/outsider approach to current labour-market problems, where the emphasis is on breaking the monopoly power of the insiders and not on organizing and protecting the labour reserve to ensure both equity of access and minimum standards. Moreover, this approach provides a sound basis for the gradual transition from male to dual breadwinner families, where each adult is identified as having the same need for job security and for a basic income from employment, at least equivalent to adult subsistence.

The second problem is in the production of an adequately skilled labour force, including as Streeck (1989; 1992) identifies, the need for an over-skilled workforce with surplus capacity to adjust rapidly to new needs and new demands. The failure of firm-specific training suggests a new role for this training and education to be provided through the education system, possibly in partnership with companies, but with the objective of providing employees with transferable qualifications and skills to guarantee their employability in a wide sense, and to ensure that innovation and growth is not constrained by a lack of skill. The destabilization of internal labour-market systems means that there is now a renewed need for institutions at the labour-market level to ensure the appropriate reproduction of a skilled labour force.

Both these conditions for a new employment order appear highly unlikely to be realized within the current political debate except at the level of the individual state, and indeed usually small and homogeneous state[2]. Where fragmentation has already proceeded a long way, for example, in the UK and US, there is very little that organized labour can do other than fight specific issues at the individual organizational level. Here there is also a danger that short-term gains from, for example, decentralization, fragmentation and even performance pay will obscure the likely long-term effects and that trade unions may be happy to negotiate agreement to a more individualized employment system provided there is an initial gain for their members. Even where unions are operating within a strong regulatory framework they face major dilemmas: to defend the existing regulatory system may be to fall into the trap of defensive behaviour and reinforcement of moribund principles and institutions, yet to accept change may be to allow the fragmentation and dismantlement of a regulated labour market. Evolutionary change within a strong regulatory framework is what is required but is more difficult to achieve without the development of a political dialogue supportive of the need for an imaginative re-regulation of the labour market.

Notes

1. In a study for the Equal Opportunities Commission (IRS 1992) when employers who claimed that wages have been raised in line with market factors were challenged to explain how they had measured market rates or to specify precisely the problems they were having in recruitment and retention most could not provide concrete evidence of how the market impinged on their organization.
2. See for example the recent experience of Norway where egalitarianism and employment access has been maintained alongside a new initiative to improve training and transferability of skill. (Bosch 1997)

References

Addison, J.T. and W.S. Siebert (1991), 'Internal labour-markets: causes and consequences', *Oxford Review of Economic Policy*, **7** (1), 76–92.

Bosch, G. (1997), 'Flexibility in the Norwegian labour market in comparative perspective', in J.E. Dølvik and A. Steen (eds), *Making Solidarity Work: The Norwegian Labour Market Model in Transition*, Oslo: Scandinavian University Press.

Boyer, R. (1979), 'Wage formation in historical perspective; the French experience', *Cambridge Journal of Economics*, **3** (2), 99-118.

Cappelli, P. (1995), 'Rethinking employment', *British Journal of Industrial Relations*, **33** (4), 563-595.

Cockburn, C. (1991), *In the Way of Women: Men's Resistance to Sex Equality in Organisations*, London: Macmillan.

Coyle, A. (1995), *Women and Organisational Change*, Manchester: Equal Opportunities Commission.

Deakin, S. and U. Muckenberger (1992), 'Deregulation and European labour markets', in A. Castro, P. Méhaut and J. Rubery (eds), *International Integration and Labour Market Organisation*, London: Academic.

Deakin, S. and F. Wilkinson (1996), *Labour Standards - Essential to Economic and Social Progress*, London: Institute of Employment Rights.

Doeringer, P.B. and M.J. Piore (1971), *Internal Labour Markets and Manpower Analysis,* Lexington: Heath.

Dølvik, J.E and A. Steen (1997), *Making Solidarity Work: The Norwegian Labour Market Model in Transition*, Oslo: Scandinavian University Press.

Elbaum, B. (1984), 'The making and shaping of job and pay structures in the iron and steel industry', in P. Osterman (ed), *Internal Labour Markets,* Cambridge (Ma.): The MIT Press.

Ellingsæter, A.L. and J. Rubery (1997), 'Gender relations and the Norwegian labour-market model', in J.E. Dølvik and A. Steen (eds), *Making Solidarity Work: The Norwegian Labour Market Model in Transition*, Oslo: Scandinavian University Press.

Fox, A. (1974), *Beyond Contract; Work, Power and Trust Relations*, London: Faber and Faber.

Freedman, M. (1976), *Labour Markets: Segments and Shelters*, New York/Allanhead: Oman/Universal Books.

Freeman, R. (1997), 'Are Norway's solidaristic and welfare state policies viable in the modern global economy', in J.E. Dølvik and A. Steen (eds), *Making Solidarity Work: The Norwegian Labour Market Model in Transition*, Oslo: Scandinavian University Press.

Granovetter, M. (1985), 'Economic action and social structure: The problem of embeddedness', *American Journal of Sociology*, **91**, 481-510.

Gregg, P. (1994), 'Share and share alike', *New Economy*, **1** (1), 13-19.

Grimshaw, D. and J. Rubery (1995), 'Gender and internal labour markets' in J. Humphries and J. Rubery (eds), *The Economics of Equal Opportunities*, Manchester: Equal Opportunities Commission.

Grimshaw, D. and J. Rubery (1998), 'Integrating the internal and external labour markets', *Cambridge Journal of Economics*.

Hicks, J. (1932), *The Theory of Wages*, London: Macmillan.

IRS (Industrial Relations Services) (1992), *Pay and Gender in Britain 2*, London: Equal Opportunities Commission and IRS.

IRS (Industrial Relations Services) (1994), 'Developments in job evaluation: shifting the emphasis', *IRS Employment Trends*, **551**, January 10-16.

Jacoby, S.M. (1984), 'The development of internal labour markets in American manufacturing firms', in P. Osterman (ed), *Internal Labour Markets*, Cambridge (Ma.): The MIT Press.

Jacoby, S.M. (1994), 'Managing the workplace: from markets to manors and beyond', in C. Kerr and P. Staudohar (eds), *Labor Economics and Industrial Relations*, Cambridge: Harvard University Press.

Kandola, R., J. Fullerton and Y. Ahmed (1995), 'Managing diversity: succeeding where equal opportunities has failed', *Equal Opportunities Review*, **59**, 31-37.

Kessler, I. and J. Purcell (1992), 'Performance-related pay: objectives and application', *Human Resource Management Journal*, **2** (3), 16–33.

Lewis, P. (1991), 'Performance-related pay; pretexts and pitfalls', *Employee Relations*, **13** (1), 13–16.

Lindbeck. A. and D. Snower (1989), *The Insider-Outsider Theory of Employment and Unemployment*, Cambridge: MIT Press.

Marginson, P. (1993), 'Power and efficiency in the firm: understanding the employment relationship', in C. Pitelis (ed), *Transaction Costs, Markets and Hierarchies*, Oxford: Blackwell.

Marglin, S. (1974), 'What do bosses do? The origins and functions of hierarchy in capitalist production', *Review of Radical Political Economy*, **6**, 60-112.

Marsden, D. (1986), *The End of Economic Man?*, Brighton: Wheatsheaf.

Marsden, D. (1992), 'Trade union action and labour-market structure', in A. Castro, P. Méhaut and J. Rubery (eds), *International Integration and Labour Market Organisation*, London: Academic Press.

Marshall, A. (1890), *Principles of Economics*, London: Macmillan.

Maurice, M., F. Sellier and J.-J. Silvestre (1986), *The Social Foundations of Industrial Power: A Comparison of France and Germany*, Cambridge (Ma.): The MIT Press.

Morishima, M. (1995), 'Embedding HRM in a social context', *British Journal of Industrial Relations*, **33** (4), 617-640.

OECD (1994), *Women and Structural Change*, Paris: OECD.

OECD (1996), *Employment Outlook*, Paris: OECD.

Osterman, P. (1987), 'Comments on: Hartmann, Heidi I. "Internal labour markets and gender: A case study of promotion"', in C. Brown and J.A. Pechman (eds), *Gender in the Workplace*, Washington, D.C.: The Brookings Institute.

Osterman, P. (1994), 'Internal labour markets: theory and change', in C. Kerr and P. Staudohar (eds), *Labour Economics and Industrial Relations*, Cambridge: Harvard University Press.

Polachek, S.W. and W.S. Siebert (1995), *The Economics of Earnings,* Cambridge: CUP.

Rosenberg, S. (1989), 'From segmentation to flexibility', *Labour and Society*, **14** (4), 383-409.

Rubery, J. (1978) 'Structured labour markets, worker organisation and low pay', *Cambridge Journal of Economics*, **2** (1), 17-37.

Rubery, J. (ed) (1988), *Women and Recession*, London: Routledge and Kegan Paul.

Rubery, J. (1994), 'Internal and external labour markets: towards an integrated framework', in J. Rubery and F. Wilkinson (eds), *Employer Strategy and the Labour Market*, Oxford: OUP.

Rubery, J. (1995a), 'Performance-related pay and the prospects for gender pay equity', *Journal of Management Studies*, **32** (5), 637-654.

Rubery, J. (1995b) 'Internal labour markets and equal opportunities: women's position in banks in European countries', *European Journal of Industrial Relations*, **1** (2), 203-227.

Rubery, J., F. Bettio, C. Fagan, F. Maier, S. Quack and P. Villa (1997), 'Payment structures and gender pay differentials: some societal effects', *International Journal of Human Resource Management*, **8** (3), 131-149.

Sengenberger, W. (1981), 'Labour market segmentation and the business cycle', in F. Wilkinson (ed), *The Dynamics of Labour Market Segmentation*, London: Academic.

Sengenberger, W. and D. Campbell (eds) (1994), *Creating Economic Opportunities: the Role of Labour Standards in Industrial Restructuring*, Geneva: International Institute for Labour Studies (ILO).

Streeck, W. (1989), 'Skills and the limits of neo-liberalism: the enterprise of the future as a place of learning', *Work, Employment and Society*, **3**, 90-104.

Streeck, W. (1992), *Social Institutions and Economic Performance*, London: Sage.

Thurow, L. (1975), *Generating Inequality*, London: Macmillan.

Williamson, O.E. (1975), *Markets and Hierarchies: Analysis and Antitrust Implications,* New York: The Free Press.

Williamson, O.E. (1985), *The Economic Institutions of Capitalism*, New York: The Free Press.

Wood, A. (1994), *North-South Trade Employment and Inequality*, Oxford: Clarendon.

7. Global Logistic Chains: the Increasing Importance of Local Labour Relations

Leni Beukema and Harry Coenen

Introduction

In 1992 the Dutch corporate magazine of Nedlloyd/P&O (then Nedlloyd) announced the building of its new, fourteenth and largest warehouse for IBM. Since the beginning of that year all of IBM's distribution activities have been handled by Nedlloyd. As a result of this co-operation new premises were built in the port of Amsterdam. The new Westpoort distribution centre receives all computer equipment and parts from IBM factories in other European countries, North America and the Far East. Nedlloyd Districenters receive the goods, administer stocks, install software on the correct computers and test the equipment. Finally, the goods are prepared for distribution in Europe, Africa and the Middle East. For carrying out these activities, Nedlloyd has taken over 108 employees from IBM, so that the total number of employees now stands at around 150. The management of door-to-door transport and the processing of orders remains in the hands of IBM. (*Parade*, May 1992)

In 1993 the same magazine announced:

> The Russian automobile company VAZ (makers of Lada cars) has to introduce more environmentally friendly technology in order to keep abreast of competition. General Motors is to supply the systems, more than twenty in all, electronic devices among them that will also improve the performance of VAZ cars. Nedlloyd has been contracted to handle the transport entailed by the transaction. Nedlloyd Districenters Hannover is to become the logistic hub where goods from all over the world are collected, warehoused, and grouped, to be sent by road to the VAZ works in Togliatti, 900 km south of Moscow. (*Parade*, August 1993)

These kinds of announcements are frequently made in Nedlloyd's magazine. The company (now called Nedlloyd/P&O and ranking 5th on the list of the world's largest carriers) is extending its activities for clients. From transport only, Nedlloyd/P&O increasingly offers complete package deals, in which the focus is on control of the flow of goods and information between manufacturers and their clients, irrespective of which part of the world producer and client are. World-wide logistic services are the products by means of which this carrier is trying to increase its market share.

The question is whether there is anything new about the activities of companies like Nedlloyd/P&O, and, if so, what that is. For centuries goods have been hauled all over the world by transport companies, there is nothing new in that.

Where physical distribution is concerned, the current demand for globalization is important on a number of counts:

– From a historical perspective, where traditional global transport is of importance, since it has transported goods from one part of the world to another ever since the invention of seaworthy ships.

– From the perspective of current developments in transport companies themselves. The scale of multinational and transnational distribution companies is increasing. These companies too are going global, in the sense that strategic decisions are considered from a global point of view. At the same time we conclude that the concrete implementation of such global decisions, in view of the physical nature of transport, often remains a regional or local question.

– From the perspective of the strategies of some industrial companies which buy parts world-wide for regional assembly, by means of new and cheap transport and information technologies. This concerns mostly high-grade products, and low-volume products which can be transported relatively cheaply by air.

– From the perspective of the growing importance of logistic chains in which the activities of industrial companies and transport companies are getting increasingly interrelated. Transport companies are taking over activities from industrial companies. For all the companies concerned, the position which they take up in their logistic chain(s) is of growing importance for strategic decision-making.

Our research focuses especially on this last perspective. We shall try to tie up our investigation to that of those people in social sciences who stress the importance of networks (or related terms that indicate the formation of networks) among companies. (Castells 1996: Ruigrok and Van Tulder 1995; Lash and Urry 1994, among others)

In this contribution to the debate on globalization we should like to work out the following questions in more detail: What is the place of logistic chains (as a specific form of network) in the process of globalization? When globalization takes place especially through networks (as is indicated by a number of authors; *cf.* Castells 1996; Klapwijk 1996) the importance of the control over the logistic chain gets bigger for the parties concerned. Who is claiming this control? Does this only concern large manufacturers, or do the distribution companies also play a role, and if so, which? And finally, what are the implications of the developments in economic power relations for social relations inside and between companies.

First of all, we shall determine our position in the debate on globalization: what do we understand by globalization and to what extent, in the context, can we really speak of a transformation of developments in society in general, and of developments inside and between companies in particular. We shall then give a short survey of a number of recent views on the increasing importance of (global) networks among companies. After that we shall indicate what developments there are in the positions which companies in physical distribution choose or pursue in such networks. In a practical case study we shall also indicate the possible consequences for labour relations of strategic options concerning logistic chains. In the final section we give a summary of our argument and make some conclusions on the consequences of globalization of logistic chains for local and regional labour relations.

Globalization

There are, of course, different points of view on the question of the existence and the extent of globalization. The rise and development of a world market is an important basis for the debate. But then the question arises whether there is gradual progress along the road to internationalization, or whether there is a process of globalization which implies a real transformation of developments in society. These differences are the result of differing conceptions of the notion of globalization itself. Sometimes the focus is especially on traditional economic criteria (trade figures, investments, the operations of transnational companies, and so on). Those who take this approach have their doubts on the question whether there is globalization at all (*cf.* Hirst and Thompson 1996; *cf.* also Ruigrok and Van Tulder, who prefer to speak of triadization, 'interrelation of the economies in the three richest parts of the world, Japan, Europe and the USA', instead of globalization, 1995, p. 151).

Others take information technology as their point of departure for the analysis of globalization. (Castells 1996; Lash and Urry 1994) Castells refers to the global economy as follows: 'it is an economy with the capacity to work as a unit in real time on a planetary scale'. (1996, p. 92) This approach is connected with Giddens, who defines globalization as the 'intensification of worldwide social relations which link distant localities in such a way that local happenings are shaped by events occurring many miles away and vice versa'. (Giddens, 1990, p. 64)

Castells strongly stresses the development of information technology, not in a determinist way, but as the (temporary) result of a long-term development with far-reaching implications. In our view, this is an approach that creates openings for the adequate conceptualization of current developments. Castells connects globalization to the origin of information networks, which link up financial and economic centres directly. Thus it becomes possible that events or decisions in one part of the world have immediate effects in other parts of the world. Globalization in no sense detracts from the importance of local events, but it does place them in a world-wide context.

Globalization can be taken as the result of technological developments, which have arisen through human action and reflection on this action. The approach, then, is not primarily economic, but primarily social. This does not go to say that economic processes do not play an extremely important role in the process of globalization. Thus, Klapwijk points to the fact that for producers, in view of the level of the investments in technology design, it is essential to develop this technology for as many products and as many markets as possible. (1996, p. 54) In his view this process is an important incentive in the development towards companies with global dimensions.

According to Adam, it is important to realize that this transformation towards globalization has not dropped from the sky. Essential processes, basic to the current process of globalization, took place late in the last century, and early in this one: the development of the wireless telegraph and the standardization of time. (1995, pp. 111ff.) This addition places the interrelationship of economic, technological and social processes in a dynamic perspective.

Viewed in this manner, globalization could even have the effect of a decrease, instead of an increase in international trade: it could be decided to produce more on local markets, whereas management and strategic decisions will take place on a global scale. In principle, the new technology offers good possibilities for doing so. An important element that is currently hampering such a development is the low price of transport, and the failure to include environmental costs in the price of goods. This development would even be desirable, when the concept of the risk society, as developed by Beck (1986), is taken into account. For technology not only offers simultaneousness of information and a growing importance of knowledge, but it also entails risks; risks that are not bound to a certain place or time, nor to specific groups. They cross geographical and social boundaries. These risks affect all of us in various circumstances and there is no insurance that can cover them. Even those who cause these risks may fall victim to them.

On the basis of this conception of globalization, a new relationship between the local/regional and the global level arises. Companies (also divisions of companies operating on a global scale) included in networks have an altered relation to their surroundings. Players on the world market are also in the paradoxical situation that, in order to reinforce their position, they have to seek co-operation with others on the local level and relinquish part of their autonomy at that level. This means that global management is partly implemented through various local/regional situations and relations. We shall return to this question in our analysis of developments in logistic chains.

Logistic Chains as Networks in the Globalization Process

In this section we shall work out what the importance is of logistic chains in the process of globalization. We shall do this by means of literature about networks and their role in the current process of globalization. Important authors in this field are Lash and Urry, Ruigrok and Van Tulder, and Castells, and we shall discuss their work in more detail here. Before doing so, however, we want to indicate why we stress the importance of the connection between logistic chains and networks.

Logistic chains and networks

A generally accepted definition of logistics is 'the planning, execution, and control of the flow of goods from purchase up to and including distribution to end-users'. (Striekwold 1990, p. 57) In this definition logistics include both material management (from purchase to assembly) and physical distribution.

In current operating management, increasing importance is given to the passage of products from raw material to the consumer. Time-based competition presupposes that all stages of this process are finely tuned. For the analysis of developments in companies and sectors, then, this logistical process is essential, more important than the various separate stages of production and distribution. This brings us to the concept of the logistic chain, defined by the Nehem as 'all activities that are carried out in making raw materials into marketable products, and bringing them onto the market... Every chain is made up of links. One link comprises one or more consecutive activities in the chain. These activities are carried out by one or more companies'. (Nehem 1993, p. 18)

Logistic chains can be considered, then, as a specific form of network. According to Ruigrok and Van Tulder (1995, p. 64), a network has the following characteristics:

1. It is relatively stable: the actors do not meet accidentally; and the interaction is aimed;
2. at the exchange of goods, capital, technology, information, skills and/ or people; and
3. at the allocation of values (for instance on how the interaction should occur).

Logistic chains link these characteristics of networks to a specific content, a specific meaning: chemicals, computers, health, and so on. For a better understanding of this kind of network, it is necessary to understand its material basis, in other words the product or service. This reinforces the knowledge component in the network, a phenomenon that corresponds with the development towards a society in which information and knowledge are of growing importance.

Networks and globalization
In the last section we have indicated how networks are at the basis of the formation of the current process of globalization. The next question is what the nature of these networks is: what do they look like, who are the important players in these networks and what are their mutual relations?

A problem that is often mentioned in the debate on international restructuring is that company strategies are too often lumped together. Either all companies are supposed to be specializing in a flexible manner, in the way indicated by Piore and Sabel, or all hierarchies are disappearing and dissolving into horizontal co-operative conglomerates based on market forces, as Lash and Urry suggested in *The End of Organized Capitalism*, or other generally valid variations of restructuring that have been proposed.

Such sweeping generalizations entirely overlook the complexity and contextuality of social reality, and so the importance of the local to the global. For when locality is left out of the picture, the overall image that arises is incomplete, as we have pointed out in the above. Attention to contextuality is all the more relevant to the problem tackled in this contribution, since different strategies of restructuring can also yield different forms of logistic chains and different relations between production and distribution.

The generalizations we have mentioned thus need to be qualified. A number of authors have recently tried to work out some qualifications.

Ruigrok and Van Tulder, in their book *The Logic of International Restructuring*, have indicated three competitive systems of industrial restructuring: flexible specialization, (neo-)Fordism and Toyotism. These systems are characterizations of the organization not only within companies, but also between companies.

The dynamics of the different systems can be understood by means of the concept of industrial complexes. Industrial complexes are a specific type of network: 'a bargaining configuration organised around a core firm, consisting of (groups of) actors which are directly or indirectly engaged in the production and distribution of a given product'. (1995, p. 66)

Their central thesis is: Neither individual enterprises, nor states, but industrial complexes form the centre of the international restructuring (p. 164). The three competitive systems each entail a typical form of network, distinguished by the degree to which power is distributed among the participants in the network.

Castells (1996, p. 153) also opposes an evolutionist, general approach to company strategies. He proposes to distinguish between a number of types of organizational developments, each a specific arrangement for constructing meaning, aimed at greater productivity and competitive power in the new technological paradigm and the global economy. He distinguishes a number of trends, which have come about at different times and places, relatively independently. The basic foundation of the development of these trends is the crisis of the old, powerful but extremely rigid model of 'vertical, rational bureaucracies, characteristic of the large corporation under the conditions of standardized mass production and oligopolistic markets' (p. 167). The alternatives to these bureaucracies are different forms of networks. The trends distinguished by Castells all have the formation of networks in common. This formation of networks can take place among separate companies, but also within enterprises. In the latter case Castells refers to 'network enterprise'.

In order to clarify the concept of 'network enterprise', Castells distinguishes between two types of organization: bureaucracies for whom reproduction of their own existence is (or has become) the main aim of the organization, and enterprises in which the aims and the changes made to them continually create the structure of the organization in a new form. Network enterprises are then defined as: 'that specific form of enterprise whose system of means is constituted by the intersection of segments of autonomous systems of goals'. (p. 171) These network enterprises 'make material the culture of the informational/global economy: it transforms signals into commodities by processing knowledge'. (p. 172) In this conception, network enterprises function in a global economy, can take knowledge out of it and add knowledge to it, but do not necessarily need to be globally organized themselves.

The two last-mentioned authors focus on the relationship between enterprises in the current process of globalization. The question is how this process affects the individual enterprise at the local level. Lash and Urry, in our view, have contributed a number of insights worthy of consideration. They also place globalization in the perspective of networks among enterprises, which can function as networks by means of physical and electronic transport of products and information. (1994, p. 25) Just like Castells, they have greatly emphasized the influence of information technology on the current process of restructuring. They analyse not only the formation of networks among organizations, but also the developments within organizations. They introduce the term 'reflexive accumulation'. By this term they wish to indicate that economic processes of the construction of meaning are interrelated, and affect each other not least by means of technological developments. In particular the use of information technology in organizations has the effect that actions in labour organizations are not dominantly or exclusively guided by considerations of efficiency and effectiveness. Cultural processes have penetrated the economic structure itself.

Why speak of reflexive accumulation? Lash and Urry offer a number of arguments: First, the term emphasizes the importance of knowledge and information to current economic developments. Knowledge is not just a question of larger information-density for handling the turbulent economic environment. Knowledge is also used for debating fixed procedures and rules in the production process, and for orienting the organization in the (global) environment, and, in turn, for influencing that environment.

Secondly, reflexivity is seen as the capacity not only to use information, but also to giving meaning. Some products have specific symbolic functions (for example clothing, furnishing). An important factor in competition is finding the right forms for these symbols.

Thirdly, reflexivity not only refers to reflexive production, but also to reflexive consumption, as a result of *Enttraditionalisierung*, the process of individualization in which traditional structures no longer determine personal choice.

Reflexivity has arisen over the years through a growing complexity of the division of labour, which led to reflection on the labour process itself: the labour process of some people became the object of the labour process of others. Taylorism itself was also part of this process of increasing reflexivity. Through ongoing use of information technology, reflexivity in turn increases, and concomitant control also increases: computer systems control production systems.

Reflexive economy is more and more about non-material products (services, communication and information). Communication structures, both inside the enterprise and regarding the product supplied, are becoming of increasing importance.

It is not surprising that Lash and Urry make ideal types of organizations on the basis of a strongly cultural point of view. They distinguish:
– Collective reflexivity, which originates in Japanese culture, in the sense of the sharing of information, risks and decision-taking. This takes place in autonomous teams, between production units, between shareholders and enterprise, and between employees and enterprise.
– Practical reflexivity, which originated in German-speaking countries. The concept of *Beruf* plays a central role, in which individual performance is considered important and network ties are weak. Great importance is attached to the system of training and education.
– Discursive reflexivity, which was developed in the English-speaking part of the world, especially in highly-computerized sectors, sophisticated production and services. Expert systems play an important role, management are highly trained professionals. Other features are a strong division of labour, small networks with weak ties, and great mobility on the labour market.

Logistic chains and globalization
In our opinion, the authors we have discussed have contributed important insights into the nature of the current process of globalization, not only by their analysis of the growing importance of networks, but also by the

way they analyse them. Ruigrok and Van Tulder have contributed especially by paying attention in their typology to the relations as they are built up between enterprises (*cf.* our earlier plea for more attention for the politics of logistics, Beukema and Coenen 1997, p. 12). Castells is enlightening by his attention for, on the one hand, general tendencies like the increasing importance of the production of knowledge and information, and on the other hand, his emphasis on the contextuality of the materialization of such developments. Lash and Urry make an important contribution to the translation of technological developments into the reflection on the organization of the primary process inside the enterprise.

But from our point of departure, logistic chains and the position of distribution in them, we wish to point out a number of issues that need supplementation.

First of all, where the analysis of networks is concerned, we should like to link up the concrete content of the products in the network. Where networks exist between enterprises, several logistic chains can be involved, or enterprises can participate in several networks, each with their own chains. The relations between enterprises are thus not only determined by the nature of the network (for example Fordism, Toyotism or flexible specialization) and by their position in the network, but also by the product which they are working on. Thus, products of which the raw materials are physically determined will entail other options than products where this is the case to a lesser degree. The relations between the enterprises in the chain will also be different because of this.

A first qualification of the relation between the nature of the activities and the position of the enterprise concerned can be found in Gereffy (1994), who distinguishes two co-ordinating mechanisms of logistic chains. First, co-ordination can take place by the transnational industrial companies, modelling globalization by means of strategic investment decisions (producer-driven commodity chains). The automobile industry is a good example of such a chain. A second co-ordination mechanism can arise from the buyers (retailers), who use their large orders to mobilize world-wide export networks, consisting of a number of overseas factories and traders (buyer-driven commodity chains). Such chains are especially found in labour intensive industries, producing consumer goods like toys, household appliances, clothing, and so on. (pp. 215ff.)

A second addition to the authors under discussion concerns the relation between production and distribution companies in the network. They have in common that distribution is always derived from production.

Ruigrok and Van Tulder group their network typology around various types of assemblers and place distribution (just like, for instance, suppliers, trade unions, and so on) in a position that is derived from them. Castells also discusses trends, mainly as they occur in the production sector. Lash and Urry place transport of goods and information at the centre of the development towards globalization of the economy, but they, too, base their typology of reflexive accumulation mainly on production sectors. It is a question whether such approaches do not remain too much rooted in the past. With the development of chains in the era of information technology, it is very possible that the relations between production and distribution enterprises themselves are shifting. This is certainly what the strategy of distribution companies hopes to achieve.

In this connection investigation into 'chain management', as suggested by Klapwijk (1996, pp. 60ff.), is of importance. '...The chain manager will ideally be able to run the entire chain as if it were a single extensive process, despite the fact that the various sub-processes and operations may be carried out by different companies in different countries.' (p. 65) .... 'Generally the role of the chain manager is played by the company whose contribution to the chain product "makes the difference" from the perspective of the consumer'. (p. 66) This differentiating value attribute gives companies the power to control the chain. Increasingly, this factor is fulfilled by distribution companies because of their more direct contacts with end-users. In this way they gain power over the chain, according to Klapwijk. What the parameters of the changing position of distribution companies are, will be worked out in the next section.

A final point we wish to make in comment on the authors under discussion, is that when risks produced by technology are taken into account in the analysis of globalization, the image tends to change. (Beck 1986) This is true when the control of logistic chains is involved (how strong is the control, and for whom), or when the ecological effects of growing global transport come under consideration.

In the following section we shall discuss in more detail the gaps in the formulation of the theory of networks. We shall tackle this by taking developments in distribution as the point of departure of our analysis, and from there we shall consider what further problems this yields for the formulation of the theory just mentioned.

Distribution in Logistic Chains

Distribution companies focus on logistic services
The central feature of logistics as defined in what has gone before, is the control of the flow of goods. This control has two components, namely the bridging of time and distance in the total process from raw materials to the delivery of the finished product to the customer. (Veldkamp 1989, p. 7) Distribution is a central element in logistics. For the aim of distribution is, traditionally, to cover distance in a minimum of time. When the organization of transport is also involved, we may speak of logistics.

This is to imply that not every transport company is involved in logistics. On the contrary, in transport, planning and execution have traditionally been carried out in separate companies for dispatch and transport. But through the developments in information technology and the concomitant increase of scale, which has also taken place in distribution, we are seeing an increasing number of enterprises carrying out both planning and execution of transport.

A reconsideration is taking place of the question of what constitutes the product offered by physical distribution, or what it should be. Is it to be limited to transporting products from A to B? Are distribution activities to be linked to this transport, like, for instance, warehousing, transhipment or groupage? Or will physical distribution also take over part of the organization of distribution? Or, going even further, will physical distribution give information to the producer about the customers for the product and their wishes as to quality and quantity of the product?

A development in the direction of logistic services can be distinguished: large transport companies in particular are deploying other activities beside transport. They also wish to warrant the so-called 'continuity of transport', and take over the clients' worries about logistics at a low price. The form taken by this logistic service can be very diverse, in practice. The examples at the beginning of this chapter are just a few out of a great number. In all cases the logistic services provider takes care of an important part of the information management. The carrying out of this function by physical distribution is facilitated by the new information technology. This is becoming an important principle of competition in physical distribution: whoever is able to manage the flow of information is very valuable to the client. (Nehem 1993, pp. 41-2) The rise of logistic services means that the concept of chain management is being filled in from the side of distribution companies, as Klapwijk indicates.

Logistic services is a fast-growing sector. In the United States it is estimated that total turnover for 1996 was $25 billion (though a few comments need to be made on this figure). In Europe, a more secure estimate says that logistic services is a sector turning over between 10 and 15 billion Dutch guilders ($5 to $7.5 billion), and the sector is expected to grow by as much as 25 per cent annually. The contracted European Distribution Centres alone already have about 20,000 employees. (Van Laarhoven 1997, p. 10)

Thinking in terms of logistic chains and of logistic services means a major turnaround by the distribution sector in their thinking about desirable forms of organization. It is true that formerly the packing of goods constituted the organizational criterion: packed goods, bulk goods or container transport constituted transport from A to B. Nowadays, it is not just the cargo that has to move, the knowledge about what is transported has to be available.

Not all companies will be able to meet this requirement. In the transport sector, the following tendency can be distinguished: contracting-out of transport to smaller companies is growing, management and planning remains in the hands of larger companies. This means that a division in the world of transport is becoming visible. As transport is specialized and higher standards have to be met, this will come into the hands of companies who can deliver these services. The large number of small companies in this sector will not be able to make the change and so will become satellites of the big shippers and hauliers. They will be forced to transport from A to B, but in a completely dependent position, dependent on those who manage the transport. Thus, in distribution we see the rise of networks in which the large distributor manages the activities of a number of smaller transport companies.

Distribution as part of (global) logistic chains
The rise of logistic services makes it necessary for companies to look for new balances in their mutual relations in the logistic chain. Logistic services increase the organizational power of enterprises in physical distribution, and so their dominance relative to manufacturers and other distributors. Large transport companies in particular are able to control a large part of the chain. Specialized companies are able to consolidate their monopoly over a part of the chain (or in the case of product specialization, a large part of a small chain), and so maintain their

position of power, or even extend it. Whether production companies are prepared to relinquish not only their activities, but also their position of power in the chain, is open to doubt. Thus the tension between companies from the production sector and those in distribution is a fact.

In extension of Gereffy's distinction between producer-driven and buyer-driven commodity chains, it would certainly be worthwhile to think further about types of logistic chains, their co-ordination mechanisms, and the forms of networks which this entails. In our view, an important element in such a typology would be the nature of the product concerned. For products with a low value and a long life-cycle (for instance a raw material like iron ore), stockpiling is much cheaper than for high-grade products with a short life-cycle (for instance computers). In the latter case logistic services play a far greater role in the formation of networks in the logistic chain than in the former case. In chains of high-grade goods, distribution companies which concentrate on logistic services will try to reinforce their position.

Klapwijk (1996) is an author who takes into consideration the position of both manufacturers and distributors in his analysis of the development of chains. A central question in his analysis is that of the power over the chain: chain management is based on power, that is his thesis. (p. 90) He claims that globally operating manufacturers see to the management of production on the chain, whereas regional distributors do the same for the distribution in their area. Whenever distributors maintain contacts with clients, their power on the chain increases, certainly when a distributor gets larger as well. This power struggle between producer and distributor is linked to the nature of the product, and the contact with the client yields the division of power as outlined in Figure 7.1.

This analysis, in connection with the debate about globalization, contains points of departure for conceptualizing the power struggle between manufacturers and distributors, but the relationship between global and regional/local developments also plays a role. Chain management is traditionally the reserve of globally operating companies who develop and organize the production of goods and services. This control varies with time, however, and more and more often comes into the hands of the company who maintains contacts with the customers, the distributor. This client contact, and so the essential role of the distributor is, in principle, regionally limited, even though the company is part of a global concern. Regional embedding of globally operating companies turns out to be an essential mechanism in competitive relations.

On the basis of the above analysis, it is possible to study the shifts in power relations between production and distribution companies on several logistic chains.

In addition, for global networks study can be made of what sort of chains are contained in the networks, in which concrete contexts (localities/regions) developments are taking place on those chains, and what the consequences are for the central/global management. This includes the question of a typology by content or trend towards the formation of networks, in which both production and distribution, or logistic services take up a recognizable position.

Figure 7.1
Distributors and Producers Fight for Power

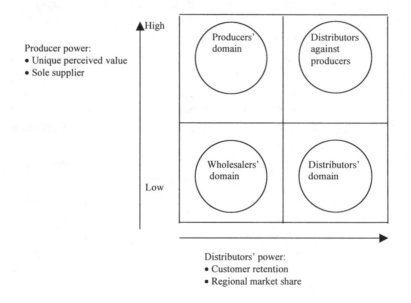

Power struggles on logistic chains and the consequences for labour relations: a case study

The importance of client contacts for the position of a distribution company on a logistic chain came to light in research we carried out into the development of a transport enterprise which is part of a transnational transport company. (Beukema and Coenen 1997; Beukema and Van der Vlist 1997)[1] We looked not only at developments in logistic chains on which the company was active, but also at the consequences of these developments for the situation of the workers concerned. We should like to highlight two elements of the research results.

First it should be noted that we are concerned with the transformation of a transport company (NedlloydRoadCargo) into a logistic services company. The company first concerned itself with the transport of various goods from A to B. After an intervention by the concern, it was decided to focus activities on the logistic chain of the chemical industry, and to concentrate on logistic services. Both global and local considerations played an important role in this: a chemical multinational company with a large establishment in the same region was one of the traditional customers. The Nedlloyd concern saw possibilities for extending activities for Road Cargo to other ways of transport than only by road (multi-modal transport). In addition, the two regional enterprises already had frequent contacts, where Nedlloyd aimed to develop logistic services: to carry out transhipment without delays, in other words, to optimize the continuity of the process.

These strategies had several consequences for the workers concerned. For a large number of the drivers (about 250), the decisions meant a change of employer. All transport activities that did not concern the chemical industry were contracted-out or sold, including the drivers. For a number of drivers, who had worked in the chemical industry until then, the concern had not been able to provide employment in view of the new requirements that chemicals drivers would have to meet. These drivers were aided in finding other jobs.

For the drivers who could no longer remain with the enterprise, this meant a deterioration of their position. The researched enterprise is one of the few firms in our country who are known to adhere to the collective labour agreements. Moreover, although in a very formal way only, it is a firm where the legal rules concerning employee participation are fully operational. The enterprises to which the drivers went do not, as a rule, benefit from either of these phenomena. This means that people were accepting jobs on an individual contract basis and without participation rights. At the time of the changeover there was a labour shortage for drivers. This meant that the drivers could make favourable agreements about their wages with their new employers. To what extent these agreements will be honoured when the labour shortage is over, or when the drivers concerned should succumb to one of the many occupational diseases typical of this sector, remains an open question.

About a hundred drivers continued with their original employers and are now deployed as operator-drivers. This term is used to indicate that an extension of their duties is to be introduced, but how and to what extent is as yet unclear. The term means that management wants the drivers to play an active role in logistic services. Here too, the direct contact with clients plays an important role:

> A transport company always operates in-between two enterprises: the client and the client's client. While relations between companies are increasingly charac- terised by the exchange of information, it is characteristic of the carrier that physical presence is always involved. Drivers and materials are physically present to the client, and to the client's client. (Beukema and Van der Vlist 1997, p. 8)

The knowledge gained by drivers in the course of these contacts is essential to their company. That is why, in the course of research, we proposed setting up an experiment to extend the function of operator- driver by setting up transport teams, in which planners, drivers and operational management attempt to set up logistic services by means of client analysis.

For the drivers remaining in the service of the company things ap- peared to change for the good, not only in the field of work conditions (extension and enrichment of duties will also bring higher remunera- tion), but also through the appreciation of qualifications and participa- tion in the formation of logistic services.

The unions reacted in different ways to the new management strategy. The unions which are affiliated to the FNV and CNV negotiated a social contract for those who had to leave the company. This contract mainly contained regulations on the amount of money drivers could take with them when they left. This strategy is quite common for the traditional unions in our country, although one can occasionally recognize efforts to do more than just take care of the social consequences of management policies.

The VLD seized the opportunity of the Nedlloyd situation to experi- ment with modernizing policy: at first a group of active members of the union made proposals to maintain jobs through flexibilization of work organization, combined with shorter working hours. These proposals turned out to be feasible for only a small part of the company. Then individual interests of members who were told they could not remain with the company were stressed: most of them got another treatment after the union had interfered.

Through and by means of this protection of individual interests, realistic modern policy was formulated on two main points: in the first place a so-called 'charter-agreement' was devised to prevent employees who went to a charter from suffering too much from bad conditions and relations which are frequently found in the transport sector. In part these proposals led to renouncement of contracts with mala fide companies by the management of Nedlloyd. The union succeeded in its efforts to prevent a division between employees. Through the charter-agreement the company which engages charters also takes responsibility for employees of these charters. Union policy extends to part of the logistic chain concerned.

Secondly it was proposed to conduct experiments with teams of drivers and planners who would keep their jobs in the company. The Union for Transport, Logistics and Services (VLD) tried to make clear with these proposals that the company should put a higher value on the knowledge of drivers about customers and (even more important) about customers of the customers. The union stresses the fact that local/regional knowledge of the company can be made concrete when knowledge of executives, those who have direct contact with the customers, can be used effectively. This requires a social interpretation of logistic services, in addition to which new social relations are at stake. By playing a part as a union in forming teams, the VLD tried to participate and shape a logistic service which has not only economic but also social goals. In principle, management reacted positively to these proposals, but at the same time indicated to be giving priority to the settlement of the reorganization. Whether an experiment with teams will become reality is not clear at the time of writing this chapter.

A second element in our research results also shows the interrelations of the local and the global level. During the reorganization we have mentioned above, a contract was concluded at the European level by the concern with a large car producer. Under the terms of the contract, the distribution company was to become chain manager for the entire distribution package of the car manufacturer. This concerned a multimodal transport package. One of the manufacturer's conditions was that the transport would not be contracted-out, but that everything (people and material) would be handled by the distributor. Although the local company was concentrating on the activities on the logistic chain of the chemical industry, it was still commissioned to carry out the road haulage for this large customer.

This caused problems for the local enterprise, because they had just hived off employees and material. Enthusiasm for returning to their old employer was not very great among the drivers. And the operation involved the formation of two groups of drivers, each driving for a different chain. Management is now doing its utmost, and the attempts appear to be successful, to keep these activities within the concern but to place them outside the local enterprise. The question of economies of scale is of paramount importance in these attempts.

Summary and Conclusions

In this contribution we have placed the development of logistic chains within the debate on globalization. Two matters were of crucial importance. In the first place this concerned the part played by computerization in the rise of global networks and logistic chains, in the second place there is the relationship between global and regional/local developments.

We have indicated that the primacy of manufacturers in managing these chains cannot be taken for granted, but that there is an on-going severe power struggle concerning chain management between manufacturers and distributors. In particular the increasing importance of client contacts in competitive relations reinforces the position of distributors, who have regional roots. Logistic services, as an up-and-coming branch of industry, must be placed in this context.

The effects of these developments on labour relations in enterprises, and on the position of employees are characterized by several developments. On the one hand there is the increasing importance of strategic decisions on a global and European level, the consequences of which are felt by employees at the local level. People are sold like so much cattle. The trouble this causes people is again determined at the local level, by the regional labour-market situation. On the other hand there is the fact that logistic services translate into the local knowledge of employees about the client's situation. Just like a concern needs to make use of knowledge of local enterprises, so local enterprises need to make use of the knowledge of their employees. This means that the position of this group of employees is fundamentally strengthened. This also means that unions who want to organize this strength can find a new, less defensive, position. For the workers concerned, and for their representatives, the challenge is to realize this strength and to extend it to those employees who are active on weaker links in the chain.

Notes

1. The VLD (Union for Transport, Logistics and Services) separated from the traditional Transport Union (Vervoersbond FNV). The main cause of this sepa-

ration was that members and executives of the VLD no longer saw possibilities in the traditional trade unions to develop modern policy on the basis of democratic discussions. The VLD has broadened its sphere of activity, not only in traditional transport but also in logistics and services, included in its name.

References

Adam, B. (1995), *Timewatch*, Cambridge: Polity Press.

Beck, U. (1986), *Risikogesellschaft. Auf dem Weg in eine andere Moderne*, Frankfurt: Suhrkamp.

Beukema, L. and H. Coenen (1997), *Just-in-Time-Distribution. Over de opkomst van logistieke dienstverlening in de fysieke distributie en de consequenties daarvan voor de arbeidssituatie van werknemers*, Utrecht: AWSB.

Beukema, L. and A. Van der Vlist (1997), *Wachturen als logistiek probleem*, Utrecht: Utrecht University.

Castells, M. (1996), *The Rise of the Network Society*, Oxford: Blackwell Publishers.

Gereffy G. (1994), 'Capitalism, Development and Global Commodity Chains', in L. Sklair, *Capitalism and Development*, London: Routledge, pp. 211-32.

Giddens, A. (1990), *The Consequences of Modernity*, Cambridge: Polity Press.

Hirst, P. and G. Thompson (1996), *Globalization in Question*, Cambridge: Polity Press.

Klapwijk, P. (1996), *Global Economic Networks. How Deregulation leads to a New Economic Landscape*, Amsterdam: ATKearney.

Laarhoven, P.J.M. Van (1997), *Distributielogistiek: kunst en vliegwerk*, Eindhoven: TUE.

Lash, S. and J. Urry (1994), *Economies of Signs and Space*, London/Thousand Oaks/New Delhi: Sage.

Nehem, *Meer doen met lading*, August 1993.

Ruigrok, W. and R. Van Tulder (1995), *The Logic of International Restructuring*, London/ New York: Routledge.

Striekwold, M.E.A. (ed.) (1990), *Logistiek. Begrippenlijst*, Deventer: Kluwer Bedrijfswetenschappen.

Veldkamp, A.A. (1989), *Inleiding integrale logistiek, Handboek Logistiek*, Alphen a/d Rijn: Samsom, pp. A0100-1-A0100-27.

8. The International Restructuring of the Media Industries

Peter Leisink

Introduction

The media industries[1] are involved in a process of restructuring which is transforming the ways in which their goods and services are developed, designed, produced and distributed, and which is accompanied by a convergence of these industries. Although these processes occasion the rise of global multi-media conglomerates, the information and communication technologies (ICT) also leave room for small and medium-size businesses, the strong presence of which has been a traditional feature of the media industries.

This restructuring has an enormous quantitative and qualitative impact on employment in the media industries, thus affecting the position of the workers and the trade unions. Their position is also affected by the neo-liberal policies of governments which have a special bearing on the media industries, for instance through the ending of state monopolies in broadcasting and telecommunications. Traditional routines of regulation, as well as the high standards of regulation, that have long prevailed in sections of the media industries have been effectively uprooted. In reaction, the media unions are divided amongst themselves between traditionally oriented adaptive and innovative policies (*cf.* Leisink, Van Leemput and Vilrokx 1996), whereas employers' associations do not always appear convinced of the benefits of regulation.

This chapter aims to explore the restructuring of the media industries, the employment effects, and the prospects for regulation of this process and its effects. Firstly, in line with the overall theme of this volume, the globalization of the media industries will be examined. In this connection the convergence of traditionally separate media industries will then be analysed as well as the role which information and communication technologies play. Thirdly, the quantitative and qualitative effects on employment of the restructuring process will be sketched, leading on to the question of what trade unions have done and can do to cope with these effects. Finally, the future of labour relations in the media industries will be discussed on the basis of the restructuring processes, in conjunction with responses and policies of collective actors.

Globalization

The most visible aspect of globalization in the media industries is probably global TV news, as served by CNN International and BBC World TV. A less well known example is European Business News which is owned by the US firm of Dow Jones, which also exploits TV stations with financial and business information for the US and Asia. This latter example illustrates that global news is seldom global but rather regional news. And even the regional scope appears too broad in some situations, for the American based global music station MTV has lost its leading position in Europe to national music stations (for example the Music Factory in Holland and Viva and Onyx in Germany). This is a sobering fact for those who are full of the globalization of culture, and it seems an appropriate point to start this section on the economic globalization in the media industries.

With a view to assessing the thesis that there is a globalization process in the media industries, it is necessary to be clear about the meaning of the term as it is used here, because globalization has several conceptualizations, even if we restrict ourselves to economic globalization.

Ruigrok and Van Tulder (1995) categorize a number of approaches to globalization, some of which concern the globalization of finances (capital flows), of competition and of the firm, of technology and of regulatory capabilities. In their study of company strategies, globalization is regarded as one strategy among a variety of internationalization strategies entailing a world-wide intra-firm division of labour. Another strategy is *glocalization* which characterizes firms seeking a geographically concentrated, inter-firm division of labour.

Hirst and Thompson (1996) distinguish between two versions of globalization. The strong version of globalization entails the development of a new economic structure, in which distinct national economies are subsumed and rearticulated into the global system by international processes and transactions. Transnational firms are the principal actors in a globalized economy. The other version involves an open internationalized economy that is still fundamentally characterized by exchange between relatively distinct national economies and in which many outcomes are substantially determined by processes occurring at the national level. These two versions are ideal types, the function of which is to assess degrees of internationalization of national economies. (Hirst and Thompson 1996, p. 7)

Thus, Ruigrok and Van Tulder as well as Hirst and Thompson regard globalization as a specific type of internationalization. Both conclude that international trade and direct investment flows take place largely within and between the regional blocks of the Triad, consisting of the EU, the USA and Japan as well as East and South Asia, rather than on a global scale. Therefore, this analysis of media industries will start in terms of internationalization, and after reviewing some indicators about which empirical information is available, will examine whether these indicate a type of internationalization that may be called globalization. The available data only warrant an empirical analysis of the sectors of publishing, printing and the reproduction of recorded media, from the point of view of the EU member states.[2]

The total turnover of enterprises in publishing, printing and the reproduction of recorded media rose between 1985 and 1996 from 57,004 million ECU to 129,980 million ECU. For the EU as a whole, extra-EU exports represent only a minor percentage of the total turnover: 3.6 per cent in 1988 and 4.1 per cent in 1995. Throughout this period the value of extra-EU exports was about double the value of extra-EU imports in publishing, printing and recorded media. However, there are considerable differences between the EU member states. Italy, Germany, Spain, the UK, the Netherlands and Denmark (and Finland since 1995) export more than they import while France, Belgium, Luxembourg, Ireland, Greece and Portugal (and Austria and Sweden since 1995) import more than they export.[3]

The trade data indicate only a very modest trend towards increasing internationalization of trade in these sectors. The value of total exports as a percentage of total turnover of the EU member states rose only slightly from 10.5 per cent in 1988 to 10.7 per cent in 1995. Over the same period the value of total imports as a percentage of apparent consumption declined slightly from 8.5 per cent in 1988 to 8.3 per cent in 1995. See Figure 8.1.

Figure 8.1

EU Exports and Imports as a Proportion of Turnover and Apparent Consumption

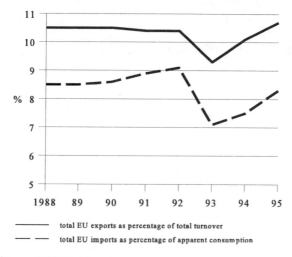

Source: DEBA database

The share of intra-EU exports (that is, between the member states) declined slightly from 63.4 per cent of total exports in 1988 to 62.0 per cent in 1995, while during the same period the share of extra-EU exports rose from 34.1 per cent to 38.0 per cent. See Figure 8.2.

Figure 8.2

Intra- and Extra-EU Exports as a Proportion of Total Exports

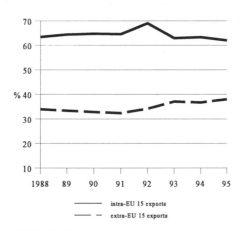

Source: DEBA database

The share of intra-EU imports declined from 78.3 per cent of total imports in 1988 to 74.2 per cent in 1995, while the share of extra-EU imports rose from 21.6 per cent to 25.8 per cent. See Figure 8.3.

Figure 8.3
Intra- and Extra-EU Imports as a Proportion of Total Imports

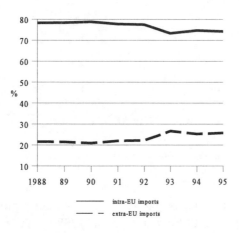

Source: DEBA database

These data certainly do not point towards strongly increasing internationalization of trade. Indeed, the main export markets have traditionally been other European countries (including non-EU member states, of whom Austria, Finland and Sweden joined the EU in 1995). Table 8.1 shows the destinations of extra-EU exports.

Table 8.1
Destination of Extra-EU Exports in Printing and Publishing

	1989	1994
Austria	12.8	12.9
Sweden	6.4	4.4
Switzerland	18.3	16.7
USA	16.6	13.5
Australia	4.7	4.0
Rest of the world	41.2	48.5
	100 %	100 %

Source: European Commission 1997, section 6, p. 22

The USA is the most important source of extra-EU imports, as Table 8.2 shows.

Table 8.2
Origin of Extra-EU Imports in Printing and Publishing

	1989	1994
Austria	10.1	10.1
Switzerland	18.1	15.2
USA	37.5	35.5
Japan	6.4	n.a.
Hongkong	5.9	6.6
Singapore	n.a.	4.2
Rest of the world	22.0	28.4
	100 %	100 %

n.a.= not available

Source: European Commission 1997, section 6, p. 23

Trade intensities, particularly of extra-EU trade, are low as far as the sectors of publishing and printing are concerned. This is related to the fact that publications on paper,[4] such as newspapers and magazines are very often language-bound and thus nationally specific, and they are of a time-critical nature. In parallel with this observation the European Commission (1997, pp. 6-26) notes that 'in sectors where time is not one of the critical factors, where economies of scale are important and transport costs form a relatively low proportion of output value, EU companies have been searching production, or parts of production elsewhere.' Mail order catalogues are an example of paper products for which time is not one of the critical factors and this type of printing is done in locations like Hong Kong and Singapore, and also in Central and Eastern Europe (for example Poland).

Thus the pattern of trade conforms to the *Triadization* pattern, noted by Ruigrok and Van Tulder, Hirst and Thompson. Trade within the EU and with other European countries is the most substantial, next comes trade with the USA, with Japan and East and South Asia (unfortunately, more specific data about the rest of the world are not available).

These aggregate data suggest that globalization takes place far away from the media industries. Yet, as early as 1990, early in the sense that it was well before the globalization hype, MacDonald (1990) made an interesting study of global multi-media conglomerates[5]. Focusing on 26 media companies that appeared in the 1989 *Fortune* listing of the 500 largest companies, he evoked the idea of a far stronger dynamic of internationalization than the aggregate industry data do. However, his data also conform to the Triadization pattern, as the following characteristics illustrate:

– Of the 26 media companies 18 were American-based (including 2 in Canada), 6 were based in Western Europe, 1 in Japan and 1 in Australia (MacDonald 1990, p. 9);

– the 13 top media companies made 77 acquisitions between 1983 and 1987, and the major flows of foreign investment by these top media companies were between North America and the European Union (MacDonald 1990, p. 13);

– the largest 15 publishing firms had a total of 749 foreign affiliates, 82 per cent of which were located in developed market economies; of all foreign affiliates 29 per cent were in the US and Canada, 48 per cent in Western Europe and 1 per cent in Japan. (MacDonald 1990, p. 21)

The aggregate data of the printing and publishing industry and MacDonald's data on the world's 26 largest media companies present a paradoxical picture of internationalization. This can be explained, however, by taking into account the differentiation between various segments of the media industries and the division between large and small companies. In fact, the media industry is polarized (*cf.* EC 1997, section 6, p. 26) between, on the one hand, the largest media conglomerates, and, on the other hand, the traditionally large number of small companies, mostly serving local and national markets. What should be added to this division, are company strategies of specialization in particular product-market segments. Within publishing there is a distinction between the segments of:

- scientific information (medicine, natural sciences, and so on);
- professional information (such as information used by lawyers, fiscalists and in education);
- business information (travel information, magazines on IT or for particular sectors such as advertising, nursing, and so on);
- general public information (newspapers, TV magazines, magazines and books on gardening, cooking, and so on).

These segments form a pyramid. (*cf.* Jagersma 1994) The top serves specific segments of the scientific community, where competition is based on quality and scientific networks, and where subscriptions are hardly dependent on the price and the overall economic situation. The broad base of the information pyramid consists of general public information, where the price is an important factor in competition and where economic circumstances are also important because of revenues from advertising. In addition, this pyramid has relevance for the general observation which was made earlier, about the language-bound and nationally specific character of printed publications, in the sense that this specific character holds least for the top and most for the base of the pyramid. Thus, the more a publishing company is specialized in the top segments of the pyramid, the more it will be internationalized in terms of sales and production. It should be emphasized that this thesis relates to information publications; for entertainment the situation is different.[6]

This analysis can be illustrated by examining the internationalization profile of publishing companies which specialize in one or more of these segments. For reasons of available company information, the three Dutch multinational publishing firms which generate more than a third of their sales abroad will be analysed; these are Reed Elsevier, Wolters Kluwer and VNU[7]. Interestingly, both Reed Elsevier under its former Chief Executive Officer, Pierre Vinken, and Wolters Kluwer (Kist 1992) have explicitly used the information pyramid as a basis for their international publishing strategies.

Table 8.3
Dutch Publishing Multinationals: 1996 Sales in Percentages Related to Information Segments

	Reed Elsevier	Wolters Kluwer	VNU
Scientific information	16 %	12 %	--
Professional information	31 %	62 %	3 %
Business information	38 %	23 %	35 %
General public information	15 %	3 %	62 %

Source: Annual Reports 1996

The distribution of sales over the various segments (Table 8.3) clearly shows that Reed Elsevier is stronger in the segment of scientific information, whereas VNU is completely absent in the scientific segment and has the strongest presence in the segment of general public information. Therefore, it may be expected that Reed Elsevier's sales and production are comparatively most strongly, and VNU's least strongly internationalized. Table 8.4 confirms these expectations in terms of the geographical distribution of sales and of the number of people employed.[8]

Table 8.4
Dutch Publishing Multinationals: 1996 Geographical Distribution of Sales and Employment

	Reed Elsevier		Wolters Kluwer		VNU	
	sales	employment	sales	employment	sales	employment
Netherlands	6 %	10 %	23 %	20 %	55 %	54 %
UK	23 %	29 %	6 %	6 %	7 %	8 %
rest of Europe	13 %	8 %	36 %	33 %	14 %	9 %
North America	46 %	44 %	32 %	37 %	24 %	29 %
Asia/Australia	12 %	9 %	3 %	4 %	--	0 %

Source: Annual Reports 1996, additional information concerning VNU

Table 8.4 shows that Reed Elsevier's distribution of sales and employment is the most internationalized, if we take as a measure the extent to which sales and employment are more or less equally distributed over the three regional blocks. By the same measure, VNU is least internationalized.

When Reed Elsevier and Wolters Kluwer are compared more closely their respective patterns of internationalization can be determined.

Wolters Kluwer employs substantial numbers of employees in most European countries and in the USA. This is related to the fact that Wolters Kluwer is dominant in professional information, particularly for lawyers and fiscalists, and this type of information is more nationally specific, which is reflected in Wolters Kluwer's mosaic of publishers in 12 West European states. In terms of the various internationalization strategies which Ruigrok and Van Tulder (1995, ch. 8) distinguish, Wolters Kluwer's strategy in the segment of professional information represents the multi-domestic strategy. The national subsidiaries serve mainly national markets and there is a weakly developed international division of labour.

Reed Elsevier has a far bigger proportion of employees than Wolters Kluwer in the UK and USA (73 per cent versus 43 per cent). Reed Elsevier is stronger in scientific information and English is the dominant language in the scientific community. Elsevier Science, which is Reed Elsevier's main publisher of scientific information, is organizing production and sales in a globally co-ordinated way. Elsevier Science has its head-office in Amsterdam; it has one marketing and sales organization, whose regional activities are carried out through offices in Amsterdam, New York, Rio de Janeiro, Singapore and Tokyo; delivery and distribution are fully centralized in Oxford (UK), in order to serve customers efficiently (Reed Elsevier, *Annual Report 1996*, p. 10). When it comes to printing production, information is less exhaustive. This is partly related to the fact that Reed Elsevier, as other publishing firms, decided some years ago to disinvest their printing facilities because return on investment was considered too low. Nevertheless, Reed Elsevier still had Northprint, a technologically advanced pre-press facility in the Netherlands, whose services include data conversion and digitized graphics for Elsevier Science. However, this work can be done by firms in the Philippines at a quarter of the cost in the Netherlands. So, since 1994 Northprint has subcontracted part of its pre-press work to SPI Technologies in the Philippines, as a consequence of which 60 jobs were lost in the Netherlands. In 1997 Reed Elsevier decided to contract out all pre-press work and has sold Northprint to SPI Technologies, which has decided to cut another eighty jobs since Northprint's activities will be restricted to operating a marketing, sales and pre-press co-ordination centre for Europe, while production will be concentrated in the Philippines.

Interpreting these features of Reed Elsevier's internationalization strategy in the segment of scientific information, one can discover a globalization strategy as regards publishing, marketing, sales and distribution – a regional intra-firm division of labour with a high level of global co-ordination. This is combined with a Toyotism-type of inter-firm division of labour when it comes to printing production; at least, so much can be concluded if the example has a more general bearing: Reed Elsevier has contracted out pre-press work to SPI Technologies, which in turn appears to contract out part of the work to China where labour is still cheaper.

While the publishing and printing industry has a polarized structure, the world market of music recording is dominated by seven major international players. Three of these are based in the EU: Polygram (until 1999 Philips, the Netherlands), Thorn EMI (UK) and Sonopress (Bertelsmann, Germany). Together they account for 44 per cent of the world music market. (European Commission 1997, section 6, p. 34)

The music publishing companies tend to centralize the reproduction of sound recordings in a few large production facilities in each trading area, *EU Panorama 97* observes. (European Commission 1997, section 6, p. 36) This type of production, which fits the globalization type distinguished by Ruigrok and Van Tulder (1995), is explained, first, by the global market positions which these music publishing companies have and, second, by the fact that transport costs are low.

A situation similar to the music industry appears to hold for the reproduction of software programs and data on floppy disks or CD-ROMs, which is dominated by USA-based companies which have reproduction facilities in the EU, notably in Ireland. By contrast the reproduction of video recordings is more fragmented. Although there are some big video distributors, duplication facilities are located in many countries because of the importance of being close to one's market and because of differences in the coding of visual signals across the world. (European Commission 1997, section 6, pp. 34-40)

To conclude this analysis, it must be noted that it has not been possible to present a comprehensive picture of all segments of the media industry. However, those sectors that have been discussed, and the implications

which these have by analogy for other segments, underpin the conclusion that there is a differentiated development in the media industries:
- Some segments – scientific information, electronic information services, record and film industry, multimedia entertainment products – are tending towards a situation of a globalized economy in the sense of both the global distribution of sales and an oligopolistic type of market control by a few multi-/transnational companies;
- some segments – professional and business information, broadcasting and audiovisual production, general interest magazines – are an example of limited internationalization in the sense of a regional block/national production structure which is serving a regional block/national market which is controlled by national or multinational media companies;
- other segments are examples of purely national control and production – local radio and TV stations, non-English language educational publishers.

Convergence in the Media Industries

The restructuring of the media industries is driven to a large extent by major developments in information and communication technologies. These are also an important dynamic in the globalization potential of the media industries, at least that is what this section will attempt to argue.

The term convergence is widely used in relation to information and communication technologies. (*cf.* Castells 1996; Freeman and Soete 1994; Van Dijk 1994) This convergence of technologies is based on technological innovations in microelectronics, computers and telecommunications. Through the digitalization of all sorts of data, these data, irrespective of their origin, can be manipulated and integrated on the basis of their common informational structure. In addition, the development of optical fibre and satellite technology creates the possibility of rapid transmission of increasing amounts of bits per second. In this respect the development of the integrated circuit and the exponentially increasing capacity of microchips were very important for data communication, and also for the integration of data-, mass- and telecommunication.

The growing convergence of these technologies into a highly integrated system is referred to by the term network society. (Castells 1996; Van Dijk 1994)[9] The attractiveness of this term is that it indicates that the convergence and the integration of information technologies into information systems, and a convergence and integration of economic activities go together. An example given by Castells, which is directly relevant to the case of the media industries, is the ending of the separation and even the distinction between audiovisual media and printed media, entertainment and information. Castells (1996, p. 372) attributes this convergence to the advent of multimedia, a term which he uses to indicate the Information Superhighway or the Internet. (Castells 1996, p. 364)

This analysis of the converging set of information and communication technologies explains why convergence in the media industries is now qualitatively different from the more or less arbitrary conglomerates of entertainment and media activities which emerged in the 1980s. An example of this arbitrary type of conglomerate is Time Warner, the world's leading media and entertainment company which grew out of the merger of Time and Warner in 1989, which serves customers for magazines, books, music and film products. The media in which such media conglomerates are engaged, are mainly separate activities. Now, however, digital technology facilitates the generation, storage, retrieval, processing and transmission of any sort of information: text, data, sound, still images and video. Therefore, there will be an increase of multiple media companies, by which term companies are designated that engage in activities which used to belong to traditionally different sectors of the media industry, and there will be an entirely new range of multimedia companies, which term is used to indicate companies that specialize in off-line products (such as CD-ROM and DVD) and on-line information services (for instance Websites, electronic commerce), that fully integrate text, data, sound, still images and video, and that allow interactive use.

The convergence process and the emergence of multimedia companies do not simply add up to an increase of big firms operating globally, however. In fact, the structure of the printing and audiovisual sectors which have always been known for their above-average share of small and medium-size companies will probably not be changed by ICT. The polarization of the publishing and printing industries, that is, the combination of a small number of big firms and a large number of small firms, is likely to continue. This pattern also emerges from the forecasts by research institutes which are related to the American and European printing industries. This is what they expect for some segments of the information and entertainment industry:

- As regards digital information processing it is expected that a large collection of specialized small businesses and a smaller number of larger, more integrated businesses will deal with digital manipulation activities; these digital processing firms are likely to provide global or near-global service, interconnected with customers and allied firms through the high-bandwidth data highways of the future (PIA 1994, pp. VII-3/4; PIRA 1994, p. ix);
- Ownership and management of the most valuable information and entertainment libraries, those with mass and global market appeal, will probably be concentrated in a few large firms – today's media conglomerates; but at least tens of millions of smaller databases will also exist, many owned by households and individuals (PIA 1994, p. VII-4);
- Production, including print, for very large (typically global) markets is expected to be concentrated in very large companies, but many smaller specialist manufacturing firms as well as small neighbourhood products will also survive. Printing and production of other packaged media will be both global and local. (PIA 1994, p. VII-4)

For each of these segments it is not difficult to find examples of big firms, which the research institutes call global. For the segment of digital information processing, SPI, the Philippines' database conversion company, is an example. SPI, which currently employs about 2000 workers in Manila, has a network of marketing/sales offices and agents in the US, in Europe (France, Germany, the Netherlands and the UK), Australia and Hong Kong and serves international publishers such as Bertelsmann, Elsevier Science and Wolters Kluwer. SPI aims at generating half of the global sales in this segment by the year 2000, and as part of this global expansion strategy it has acquired the former Reed Elsevier pre-press facility Northprint. A feature of SPI's global production strategy is that the Northprint facility has on-line connections with the Manila site and the main clients, so that files of text and images can be transferred to any production facility depending on considerations regarding technological expertise and labour costs.

For the segment of information and entertainment libraries, Microsoft and Leo Kirch's library, which contains all movies produced by Colombia Tristar, MCA, Paramount, Walt Disney and Warner Bros, are examples of global media companies.

Production of print on a global scale was no unknown phenomenon in the 1980s with some international newspaper publishers making use of overseas printing plants, such as the International Herald Tribune which had ten printing plants outside the US. (McArthur 1990) However, global printing is now a qualitatively different phenomenon which is based on the co-operation of telecom companies such as AT&T and manufacturers of digital colour printing machines such as Indigo (Israel) and Agfa (US). The latter have digital printing equipment all over the globe which can be fed by any client through the telecom network with printing-on-demand orders. (*Pers*: 12 October 1995, 7 May 1997)

Whether the firms which are mentioned here as examples of global firms are economically globalized must be assessed by indicators such as were used in the previous section. However, another feature emerges from these examples. With these firms the reach of sales and production is global because information is their raw material and because digitalized information can be transported to any place without loss of time through the global information and communication network. Indeed, all these examples have in common that they are based on the globalization of information transfer, for which the universality of digital language and the pure networking logic of the communication system have created the technological conditions. (*cf.* Castells 1996) For getting involved in electronic media operations on a global scale it is, therefore, not necessary to be a large media corporation. This effect is not reflected by authors whose analyses of globalization and multinational enterprises take the manufacturing industries as their frame of reference (for instance, Dunning 1993). A striking illustration is provided by the Dutch electronic publisher AND.

AND started in 1984 as a software house and entered the publishing sector only in 1995 with publications on CD-ROM and the Internet. (AND International Publishers 1996) In 1996 AND International Publishers still generated most of its turnover in the Netherlands (53 per cent in 1996 versus 61 per cent in 1995). However, an increasing share of turnover is generated in the rest of Europe (38 per cent in 1996) and in the USA (9 per cent in 1996); offices have been opened in the USA, UK, Germany, Spain and Hungary, with Italy and France to follow. Another feature of AND's rapid internationalization strategy is its relocation of production. For instance, in the case of the production of the Dictionary of the Dutch Language on CD-ROM, key-in was done in India by 60 keyboard operators whose job took six months, six days per week. (*Volkskrant*, 24 September 1994) While in 1996 about 80 per cent of all employees were located in the Netherlands, this proportion is now decreasing and will decrease more rapidly when a new data factory opens in Ireland in 1998 offering employment to at least a hundred employees.[10]

In addition to these conventional economic data, which show the growing internationalization of AND, information about AND's electronic publications conveys a sense of its globalization potential. AND's strategic competence is the development and maintenance of databases using infra-structural information (that is, information giving access to other information), and the development of compressing and indexing technology. On this basis an increasing number of electronic publications have been generated. CD-ROM and on-line publications include the Airline Flight database with flight information of some 600 airlines, a world wide database encompassing more than half a million cities and towns, thus setting an international standard for the way in which their names are presented, and a database of geographical information on a world wide scale. These global information services serve private consumers as well as business, for instance transport companies. Only some competition exists in the areas in which AND operates, for instance from Reed Elsevier, and from on-line flight reservation systems in the area of flight information. Some of these information services involve AND's alliance with globalized companies in the information and communication industry. The world-wide database of city names was established in conjunction with Microsoft and late 1996 AND signed a contract with Elsevier Science for a three year project of publishing 150 scientific dictionaries on CD-ROM. (AND International Publishers 1996)

What the example of the electronic publisher AND illustrates, is that because of global information networks and the international business networks which these facilitate, it is not necessary for a firm in the media industry to become a transnational enterprise in order to participate successfully in the globalization of the informational economy. (*cf.* Castells 1996, pp. 190-5) This means that the prominence given to transnational companies in analyses of globalization is less self-evident in the case of the media industries.

This analysis also has a bearing on the importance of ICT for globalization, which is a topic of some debate. Hirst and Thompson (1996) observe that, in respect of financial trade, submarine telegraph cables, which from the 1860s onwards connected intercontinental markets, were a far greater innovation than the advent of electronic trading today. This observation may be correct in a qualitative sense, but it may be doubted whether this evaluation appreciates adequately the acceleration of globalization which the media industries are witnessing. It is true, the British and French news agencies Reuters and Havas established an effective global cartel for fast news, based on these telegraph networks. (Tunstall and Palmer 1991) Yet what telegraph networks did for news agencies in the second half of the 19th century, global information and communication networks are doing for the media (and culture) industries in a broader sense today, precisely because their non-material commodities are so mobile. (Lash and Urry 1994; Waters 1995)

In addition, those media companies that invest heavily in ICT and electronic databases also have an internationalization/globalization strategy and vice versa. To some extent this is a contingent relationship. Before the emergence of information networks, there were global media corporations, such as Murdoch's News Corp. and Reed Elsevier, which had a dominant international position in the segment of scientific information before it started investing in ICT and electronic databases. However, media companies which operate in certain segments which are in the process of internationalizing, such as the scientific information and the general entertainment segments, can only serve their increasingly international clients by providing globally accessible services. In general, leaving aside specialized niches, this requires investments in ICT and electronic databases which cost huge sums of money. Only multinationals/transnationals and international business networks can afford those. This stimulates the search for strategic alliances, mergers and acquisitions as well as the search for ever expanding global markets to generate return on investment. Thus the intended merger of Reed Elsevier and Wolters Kluwer was argued by the two chief executive officers on the ground that each of the partners was too small to survive in the digital arena by itself. (*Volkskrant*, 14 October 1997) And, similarly, Reed Elsevier argued its intention to sell its general interest magazines by saying that it needed the money to invest in the further development of its core activities, that is, the scientific, professional and business information services. (*Volkskrant*, 28 October 1997) What is also true, of course, is that this merger, if it had come about, and this further concentration on (electronic) publishing activities in the top segments of the information pyramid, further strengthen the dominant position of Reed Elsevier and Wolters Kluwer which enables them to raise subscription charges by 15 per cent per year, and to increase annual profits by a roughly similar percentage.

Employment Effects of Globalization and Convergence

The processes of globalization and convergence which the previous sections examined, have a strong impact on employment in the media industries. This impact occurs in connection with political processes such as liberalization, privatization and deregulation. The effects are varied and concern numbers of employees, the qualitative structure of employment, the organization and quality of work, skill requirements and labour relations. As an initial indication of winners and losers this section will first examine the quantitative and qualitative employment effects. However, since the shifts in employment affect the position of trade unions in a more general sense, the restructuring of the media industries has a broader impact on the position of workers and their employment conditions than just those of the workers who are directly affected.

The European Commission (1993) expects European employment to grow by five to ten million new jobs by the year 2010 as a result of investments in ICT. These forecasts are highly speculative and depend on particular assumptions concerning the effects of legal-political, economic and technological conditions. By focusing employment forecasts on particular sectors of industry, more reliable forecasts can be obtained. Thus Seufert (1996) predicts for the German media and communication industry that employment in the printed media industry will decline between 1992 and 2010 by 12 per cent, while employment in the electronic media, which includes 'traditional' electronic media such as broadcasting as well as the new multimedia, will rise by 62 per cent. Employment in the communication services, which includes telecommunication and computer hard- and software services, will also grow (by 12 per cent), but, as far as telecommunications is concerned, this growth is in new private telecom firms, whereas public or formerly public telecom companies are in the process of shedding jobs by the thousands.

For lack of adequate data for the EU member states it is impossible to test these predictions. It is quite clear, however, that employment in the printed media is declining. Until 1991 employment in the printing and publishing sectors grew steadily in the 12 EU member states, from 801,632 in 1985 to 882,654 in 1991, but in 1995 employment was down to 817,318, which is 7.4 per cent less than in 1991. (European Commission 1997, section 6, p. 20)

These data indicate that the restructuring of the media industries has negative effects for some industries and positive effects for others. The printing industry is most badly hit and suffers from substantial job losses. Particularly the pre-press sector has suffered from ICT. For instance, as a result of the introduction of DeskTop Publishing many composition and litho shops closed. Employment has shifted partly to new DTP shops and to in-house DTP departments. (European Commission 1997, section 25, pp. 66-8) One can also observe a global relocation of work in this area. Research by Mitter and Pearson (1992, p. 22) estimates that in 1992 about 8000 workers, particularly women, in Latin America, Africa and Asia were involved in data-entry on behalf of Western multinationals. That number will certainly be higher now, if only because three known firms (SPI in Manila, plants of Thomson Press and Macmillan in India) employ more than half that number of workers.

Typesetters and compositors are the categories which have seen their numbers decline substantially. Some have been retrained to work as DTP operators, but there is much doubt whether compositors will be in a position to benefit from the expected job growth in the new electronic media, even as regards jobs which are most related to print composition jobs such as that of website screen designer. Research of employment in Southern California's multimedia industry (Scott 1977) and in the emerging multimedia industry in Austria (Hummel 1997), Sweden (Sandberg 1998) and the Netherlands (Leisink 1998) indicates that qualification requirements are generally higher than in the printed media. Many workers in the multimedia industry have higher professional training or university degrees, whereas technical jobs in the printing industry usually require secondary vocational training. Workers from the printing industry have an addi-tional handicap for getting jobs in the multimedia industry, since apart from the technical qualifications which they usually have, other skills are required such as creativity, flexibility, client orientation, communication skills and teamwork skills. (Hummel 1997; Leisink 1998; Michel 1997)

Other occupational categories will benefit in terms of job numbers from the restructuring of the media industries. The fastest growing occupations are, generally speaking, highly skilled jobs. For the Netherlands these are expected to include during the 1990s (CED-SER 1996, p. 51):

– journalists, authors and announcers (+ 19.9 per cent)
– system analysts, programmers, system supervisors (+ 16.5 per cent)
– information service and media specialists (+ 14.2 per cent)

– photographers, film-makers, designers (+ 13.1 per cent)
– visual and performing artists (+ 12.0 per cent).
However, some of these jobs are affected by the restructuring process in another way, as an interesting study of the British book publishing industry shows. (Stanworth and Stanworth 1995) The book publishing industry has undergone a process of restructuring, resulting in concentration, internationalization, developing new products and cost savings. In conjunction with the concentration of ownership, there has been a shift away from literary or cultural goals towards financial and business goals, which in turn have also led to new labour-use strategies. A survey of the UK book publishing industry shows that publishing houses have increasingly externalized jobs with low task interdependency, that use relatively inexpensive equipment and are cerebral rather than manual in nature. Notably, proof-readers and editors have been externalized and are now self-employed. They work as home-based teleworkers. These self-employed teleworkers are to be regarded as casualized workers, rather than as the ideal-typical self-employed, owning their means of production and having a high degree of self-direction and autonomy in the process of work. To substantiate this view, Stanworth and Stanworth (1995) give a number of indicators of their casualized status:
– their heavy dependence on one client for over half their work, which makes them vulnerable to changes in demands;
– their low hourly pay (10 pounds) below the minimum free-lance rate that the union of journalists has set (11.50 pounds), which does not even include provision of paid holidays, sick leave or retirement;
– the isolation of working at home, with little or no face-to-face interaction with publishers or colleagues.
Only a small minority of 10 per cent of some 800 members of the British Society of Freelance Editors and Proofreaders had voluntarily chosen self-employment, and most entered self-employment as a result of industry mergers, relocations and redundancies. What these indicators illustrate, is that these workers may belong to job categories that are expected to grow (see above) but that their employment position is severely affected by the restructuring of the media industries.

Similar examples of flexibility at the expense of the employment position of workers have been documented for the culture industries, including film production, TV production and the record industry, for instance in Australia (Markey 1996), the Netherlands (Van Klaveren and Posthuma 1992; Ter Steeg 1994), the UK (Campling 1995; Lash and Urry 1994) and the US (Storper 1994).

There are also job categories whose labour-market position has un-equivocally become stronger. Prominent among these are the information technology specialists. Despite the constant growth of employment in software houses, the proportion of job vacancies remains high – in the Netherlands: + 85 per cent in 1995, + 55 per cent in 1996, + 26 per cent in 1997 (Van der Linde 1997) while the number of graduates is more or less constant. As a result, average earnings are relatively high and rising annually, and include extras such as a company car. (De Jong and Rippen 1997) There is also a growing need for IT specialists in the media industries. For instance, printing and publishing firms that change to database publishing need IT specialists for building datawarehouses and multimedia firms need software devel-opers and user interface designers to take care of the interactivity of CD-ROM and on-line applications.

Overall, one of the effects of the restructuring of the media industries is that relative positions in the labour market change. For some this may be quite dramatic, as in the case of the typographers who have long been a labour aristocracy, and who now see themselves pushed aside and being overtaken by information engineers. An interesting issue is in what way the groups who used to have a priviliged position have responded to these changes through their associations. This will be the topic of the next section.

Regulating the Effects of the Restructuring Process

Regulating the employment effects of the restructuring process is not restricted to collective bargaining between employers and trade unions. Theoretically the state could also play a role in regulating the effects. However, government policies in most countries involve deregulation measures (privatization and liberalization) which cause employment effects which are negative from the point of view of the workers concerned. Only as regards the cultural industries such as the film industry do some states, notably Canada and France, have regulatory policies that aim to protect the national/regional culture industry from free trade (read: American dominance). In general, government policies involve more or less enthusiastic support of the information society (*cf.* Kahin and Wilson 1997), which, at best, is backed up by funds for training, from which companies and workers can benefit. Thus, it is mainly the trade unions which attempt to regulate the employment effects of the restructuring process. Therefore, this section will concen-trate on trade-union policies.

Looking at the employment effects of the restructuring of the media industries from the perspective of possibilities for regulation, one can observe that the negative effects have partly been concentrated in areas such as the printing industry where unions have traditionally been strong. However, in the case of the printing industry the constantly declining numbers of print workers have also caused continued substantial membership losses and the (unregulated) rise of DTP and photocopy shops outside the printing industry has further weakened the power of the unions. The same holds for other segments of the media industry such as broadcasting, where unions used to be strong when this was still a public service. With neo-liberal government policies of privatization and liberalization, employment and employment conditions in the public service have been under pressure of increasing competition from private audiovisual production and commercial broadcasting. These private firms have competitive advantages of lower labour costs which are partly gained at the cost of working conditions, but workers accept these for being part of the glamour and glitter of the show-world, or they are not in a position to dispute them because of the individualization of employment relations and the low rate of union membership. In addition, the convergence of the media industries contributes to the erosion of established patterns of employment regulation in the sense that these are often sectorally institutionalized but convergence causes 'holes in the regulatory fence' through which employers are happy to escape to a less regulated zone. Against this background union strategies will be examined, focusing first on the substantive employment aspects which unions address and then on the procedural aspect of inter-union relationships which have a special significance for sectoral unions when these sectors themselves converge.

For many years, unions in general concentrated their efforts on defending workers' interests in terms of pay and conditions, but an increasing number of them have begun to include occupational interests, for instance, quality of work, training and career policies in the agenda too. (Leisink 1993; 1996) As regards the employment effects, particularly the job losses in the printing, public broadcasting and telecommunications industries, the type of approach that concentrates on pay and conditions would involve unions' bargaining over, for instance, severance pay and the prevention of compulsory redundancies. The type of approach which concentrates on occupational interests would also involve bargaining over retraining for new jobs and preferential placement for workers who have taken retraining. This distinction will be used to analyse the policies of unions, particularly of the printing unions. The relevance of this distinction is more than merely analytical. In fact, given the decline of employment in the traditional printing industry and the rise in the electronic media, the first type of policy cannot offer much prospect of employment in the media industries to printing workers losing their job while the second can hope to offer prospects by retraining which extends acquired traditional qualifications.

Quite a few printing unions were quick to recognize the potentially disruptive effects of information and communication technologies. Perhaps they had been prepared for this by previous experiences with the introduction of photocomposition in the 1970s and automatic page make-up in the 1980s. Despite this common experience unions reacted in a different way.

American unions, the Communications Workers of America and the Newspaper Guild, were among the first to produce a booklet (1995) explaining what the Information Superhighway is and what it means for citizens and workers. The unions pay much attention to the threat of a widening gap between the haves and the have-nots in information. When it comes to workers' interests, attention concentrates on pay and conditions. The unions argue that writers and other media workers must be compensated for the multiple use of their work (intellectual property rights) and protest against the increase of non-union firms which pay lower hourly wages and no pensions, and which undercut permanent employment by contract labour, daily hires and agency temps.

At the same time the German unions in the telecommunications and printing and publishing sectors *Deutsche Postgewerkschaft* and *IG Medien* also began a series of joint conferences and publications about multimedia and their impact on employment. (Van Haaren and Hensche 1995, 1997) These deal with the same issues which the American unions examined, but in addition pay attention to workers' occupational interests. This can be illustrated by the proposal of the German printing union for a joint strategy of the employers' and workers' organizations in the printing and publishing industry. This strategy should include:

1. strengthening of workers' participation - participative development of new technologies;
2. offensive multimedia training policies, including training of pre-press workers, requalification of pre-press workers who have lost their job, a restructuring of the system of vocational training;
3. collective regulation of the employment conditions of teleworkers;

4. counselling and monitoring of multimedia activities and pilot projects by labour studies researchers;
5. intensification of the dialogue between the parties to the collective agreements about the industry policies. (Werneke 1995, p. 77)

These points for a joint strategy agenda draw their inspiration both from the traditional union function of protection of the workers with the weakest position in the labour market (in this case teleworkers), and from the pro-active orientation on training for a new multimedia industry. As regards the former issue, some examples now exist of collective agreements between companies and unions over the conditions of tele-working, one of which was concluded in 1995 between *Deutsche Tele-kom* and the German union of postal and communication workers[11]. The latter issue of training has been elaborated by the media union in job profiles and the content and structure for a curriculum for multimedia designers.

Unions in a number of other countries have developed initiatives along broadly similar lines to the German *IG Medien*. (EGF 1998) The Swiss printing union, which has a long tradition of training workers for the printing trade, prepared and started in April 1997 with a full year's training course of two days per week, which qualifies pre-press and graphical workers to work as multimedia designers. The Dutch printing union organized a series of national and regional conferences on the information society[12] and commissioned research as a basis for (multi)media-wide training and labour-market policies. In the case of the reorganization of Northprint and other pre-press companies, the union negotiated agreements according to which workers will get retraining and outplacement to another job, for the account of their former employers. In fact, the union prefers retraining and redeployment/outplacement to severance pay, and tries to implement this as part of employability policies.

The British Graphical Paper and Media Union (GPMU) was less quick in responding to the emerging multimedia industry. In 1995 it produced a special report on technology (GPMU 1995) and devoted less than one page to the electronic media, but now it has a task force to organize and service workers in electronic communications and electronic media. Attention for training is oriented towards the printing trades and as such training in DTP skills is included, but union policies do not reassess training and vocational profiles in the wider context of an integrated information and communication industry. In general GPMU policy conceives of workers' interests in terms of pay and conditions (Leisink

1993), and likewise its website for workers in the new media is 'dedicated to raising standards in new media operations and to assisting its members achieve the best possible terms and conditions of employment.' (CMS Online, update 3 February 1999) Better pay and better working conditions are cited as arguments to join the union. In addition, compensation against injustice at work, protection against health and safety hazards, redundancy advice, legal advice and financial services such as travel insurance and mortgage facilities are offered. Occupational interests and training in particular are not given much attention, however.

European and international federations of graphical unions, of media and entertainment unions, of communication workers, actors and journalists have also prepared publications (for instance, Pate and Werneke 1995) and organized conferences to discuss the implications of the multimedia revolution for international trade-union policy. These address not only issues of flexibility, homeworking and the regulation of pay and conditions, but also implications for work organization, worker participation in decision-making, VDU-related health and safety problems, comprehensive training and retraining as well as social and ethical questions concerning universal availability, public control of broadcasting and multimedia services and privacy of data and citizens.

In sum, union policies with regard to the substantive aspects of the effects of the restructuring of the media industries appear to have different foci. On the one hand, the American and British unions take an approach which concentrates on demands concerning pay and conditions. An orientation on the traditional trades predominates, and training is conceived within the framework of the traditional trades. On the other hand, several national unions on the European continent as well as the European and international federations focus not only on pay and conditions but also on occupational issues and the redesign of training in the wider framework of the multimedia industry. In particular, such initiatives as elaborating multimedia job profiles and curricula indicate a pro-active and innovative style of trade-union policy. (Leisink 1996)

The conditions of achieving the trade-union policy goals are related to the *procedural* aspect of which union(s) is (are) authorized to deal with the employment effects of the media restructuring and at what level(s). This issue is particularly relevant in view of the convergence of media industries. As has been observed before, the convergence process involves the dissolution of borders between what used to be sectors with their own traditions and institutions, including collective agreements. Workers originating from these different sectors may now be doing the same work under different employment conditions. In addition, the new information and communication technologies have created new businesses which have no tradition at all of collective organization and regulation. For this reason, there is good ground for unions which are traditionally active in different segments of the media industries, to join forces and work together if not to merge. Moreover, history provides relevant lessons on the destructive effects on employment conditions caused by competition between the printing unions and the unions of journalists over the introduction of automatic page make-up in the 1980s. (*cf.* Leisink 1993; Noon 1991; Ramondt and Scholten 1985; Smith and Morton 1990, 1991) In this respect the situation is again different from country to country.

In Germany *IG Medien* was in fact an early example of a union which organizes across the media industries. At present the emergence of information and communication networks and its specific implications for the media industries are one factor which has brought about a closer co-operation between *IG Medien* and *Deutsche Postgewerkschaft*, the union of postal and communications workers. In Italy and Spain single media and communication unions have been formed. In the Netherlands the unions in printing, publishing, broadcasting, the audiovisual industry and the union of artists have co-operated since early 1993 in a joint project aimed at workers in new media activities. This co-operation entered a new stage in 1998 with the merger of the graphical union and the union of artists and the creation of a platform of all unions in the media industries, including the communication workers and the union of journalists. The British GPMU is presently not involved in talks with other media unions which aim at closer co-operation and merger. In the summer of 1993 the GPMU General Secretary commented on a decision of the Irish Print Union to consult its members regarding the possibility of a merger with the Services, Industrial, Professional and Technical Union: 'I personally do not believe that such a merger would be seen as helpful overall for print workers (...) it is unprecedented for a print union anywhere in Europe to submerge its interests in what is, in effect, a conglomerate general union'. (*GPMU Journal*, July/August 1993, p. 3) In 1995 GPMU congress delegates decided that 'a single union for the media, telecommunications and entertainment industries is a long term objective'. (*GPMU Journal*, October 1995, p. 11)

Closer co-operation of various media unions is in itself no guarantee of more union influence, but certainly opens the door for coping more effectively with the effects of convergence. Rather than continuing a situation in which companies in the same business, but originating from different sectors, compete with each other under different conditions of employment, media-wide unions could attempt to introduce a media-wide collective agreement. Obviously, such an agreement can only set up a framework which regulates some basic common employment conditions and leaves it to the companies and the workers to work out further detail according to local circumstances. (Leisink 1997a) On the one hand, such a framework agreement will probably imply that privileges that were based on craft positions that have been undermined by new technologies, will gradually go. On the other hand, it offers an opportunity for modernizing the traditional union goal of solidarity in combination with the need for differentiation, which stems not only from companies operating in different local circumstances but also from workers who come from different cultural backgrounds and who prefer different styles of working and living. (Leisink 1997b)

Significant as these forms of union co-operation are, particularly in the sense of coping more effectively with the effects of convergence, they remain at the national level and thus do not provide an answer to the process of globalization. It is true, at the international level the establishment of the International Committee of Entertainment and Media Unions in 1995 signalled the beginning of a closer co-operation between six international federations.[13] The idea of a merger of the Communications International, the International Federation of Commercial, Clerical, Professional and Technical Employees (FIET), the International Graphical Federation and the Media and Entertainment International appears as a realistic possibility in the not too distant future. However, these federations have thus far never been authorized by affiliated national unions to enter into collective bargaining with multinationals/transnationals. In fact, it is still national unions which negotiate with multinationals over the collective agreement for the workforce in their own national state; there is no single international union body representing the entire workforce employed by a particular multinational which can negotiate their employment conditions irrespective of the place where they are doing their job.

This gap is not only due to slow trade-union recognition of internationalization processes. When the printing unions of Austria, Germany, the Netherlands and Switzerland inquired about the possibility of their forming an international union organization, they found that within the European Union the legal framework for setting up a European union body which could enter into supra-national EU-wide agreements with binding force does not exist. The so-called Davignon Group of Experts, set up by the European Commission to prepare a proposal for a European System of Worker Involvement in relation to the European Company Statute, does not suggest the possibility of such a European trade-union negotiating body. (Final Report, May 1997) This absence is curious, because the proposal for a European Company Statute springs from the wish by enterprises to adapt their structures to the increasingly transnational nature of their activities, but then this wish would seem to hold equal relevance for trade unions representing the workforce in these transnational activities.

Conclusion

Convergence and internationalization are major dimensions of the restructuring process of the media industries. Convergence entails the integration of all segments of the entertainment and media industries into one digitized information system. At the same time the entertainment and media business is internationalizing, judging by trade and production data, but its pattern conforms largely to Triadization. Globalization in the specific sense of the emergence of transnational entertainment and media corporations that operate a world-wide intra-firm division of labour seems to hold for only a small number of media corporations.

Both convergence and internationalization have serious impacts on employment and employment conditions. In some industries – printing, public broadcasting and telecommunications – specific job categories become obsolete because of technological change and jobs are lost, partly as a result of international relocation of production. Jobs in the new multimedia industry require higher education qualification levels and the qualitative structure of media employment in general is upgrading both in terms of specific knowledge (IT knowledge for instance) and in terms of personal qualifications such as communication skills, customer orientation, flexibility and ability to function in multidisciplinary teams.

Workers and unions in the media industries are largely unprepared for coping with these employment effects. The internationalization process requires strong international co-operation between unions, if not the formation of negotiating bodies, which are authorized to enter into binding supra-national agreements. However, platforms to co-ordinate policies of unions operating in industries in the same regional block have only just been formed and international co-operation between the federations of unions in the media industries is still in an embryonic stage. It is true that international co-operation between employers associations is even less developed, but this will not help the unions much. At present employers' representatives can refuse without damage to discuss a joint declaration, as they did at the end of an ILO symposium on multimedia convergence in January 1997, knowing that there is no strong international trade-union organization that could stage serious opposition if they continue to refuse to get involved in a bi- or tripartite dialogue.

Internationalization may not be a phenomenon that affects media companies generally, convergence based on new information and communication technologies certainly does. In this respect unions are better prepared to cope with its effects. Evidently, unions in the printing industry, in public broadcasting and telecommunication companies find themselves in a difficult position. An approach focusing on pay and conditions and on the traditional industry will not help those workers who lose their jobs. In addition, workers in the new media business, many of whom have had higher education and have a different cultural background, will not be attracted by this type of union policy which does not take much interest in the content of their work. (*cf.* Leisink 1996) However, unions in many countries are broadening the scope of their bargaining agenda, and are taking a serious interest in substantive training and labour-market issues of the (multi)media industry. Many unions are also convinced of the need of closer co-operation between unions operating in various segments of the media industries in order to develop a comprehensive policy.

The chances for union efforts to bring about new opportunities for those workers who could be the victims of the rapid transformation of the media industries, also depend on the willingness of employers and employers' organizations. However, although employers' organizations in the printing and publishing industries lose members and become less representative, they often remain institutionally geared to their traditional industry and do not want to engage in broader media platforms while collective organization is fragmented or completely lacking in the new media business. Thus, unions find themselves in a position of not only having to develop innovative policies but also of finding new ways of turning them into practice. In this respect states could, and should, do more than merely subsidize research, training and development. In fact, the recognition that the realization of positive effects of information and communication technologies depends on institutional adaptations, should persuade governments to take more insistent action in bringing unions and employers' organizations to discuss and undertake joint action programmes. If these would come about it will be of great interest to observe whether Europe's information society, built on technological as well as on social and political innovation, can emulate the success of Europe's welfare state in building an arrangement that replaces the social inequalities entailed by capitalist economies by a balanced combination of economic performance and social justice.

Notes

1. The term 'media industries' will be used because of the focus on the value chain which includes content creation, publishing, production and distribution. Other terms such as 'communication sector' or 'culture industries' are also in use. These have specific references, which are not directly relevant for this chapter. For instance, the communication sector also includes the manufacturers of telecommunication and computer hardware/software equipment and the operators of telecom infrastructure (for example Van Dijk 1994). The term 'culture industries' as used by Lash and Urry (1994, ch. 5) includes book publishing, cinema, the record industry and TV. They share the feature of communication through aesthetic symbols, images, sounds and narratives which entail a hermeneutic sensibility of creators and consumers. (Lash and Urry 1994, pp. 112, 123) I will also examine these industries but not concentrate on the aesthetic quality of their products, and, in addition, I will include publishers who specialize in scientific and professional publications which appeal primarily to cognitive knowledge.

2. Some of the data which are used come from the *Panorama of EU Industry 97* (European Commission 1997), and most of the time series cover the period until 1994 for the 12 member states. This means that the data for Austria, Finland and Sweden are not included. Some other data come from the DEBA database, whose 1997 version has data for the 15 EU member states. The DEBA database has been created by Eurostat and a number of European Trade Associations. It covers a number of manufacturing industries, including publishing, printing and the reproduction of recorded media.

    The Mercure database which relates to the service sectors, including motion picture and video activities and radio and television activities, has so many gaps that it is not useful for a comparative analysis.

3. An interesting question is whether there is a relationship between the export-import ratio ranking order of member states and their average labour costs per person employed. Conventional employer wisdom would have it that those who export most owe this to the lowest labour costs per person employed, while those countries which export less than they import owe this to their high labour costs. Some data are available for 1993, 1994 and 1995 to test this hypothesis. The first part of the thesis seems to be confirmed. The better the export-import ratio score the lower the average labour costs per person employed, with one very curious exception, namely Italy which has the best score but has average labour costs per

person employed that are higher than the next three or four member states in the rank order. The second part of the thesis is completely falsified: the lower the export-import ratio, the lower also the average labour costs per person employed, instead of the predicted higher labour costs. Thus, the thesis must be rejected. Obviously, labour costs are a factor in export performance but other factors are relevant as well, such as distance from consumer markets and language.

4.   It should be noted that the data in the tables do not include electronic publications! (EC 1997, section 6, p. 19)

5.   The study by MacDonald does not restrict itself to printing and publishing. Some of the media conglomerates also engage in TV/radio, music and film activities, but printing and publishing is the main set of activities. *Fortune*'s 1997 edition of the global 500 includes only ten companies in entertainment, printing and publishing.

6.   When general public *entertainment* is also included in the analysis - for instance, music and video recordings and games - it appears that this segment is less nationally specific.

7.   Ruigrok and Van Tulder (1995) assess the degree of internationalization of firms on the basis of assets, sales, workers, shares and management approach. Since information that is needed for a systematic comparative analysis of the geo-graphical distribution of assets and shares is lacking, this analysis of publishing multinationals will be based on sales and employment. Thus, the degree of internationalization of production will be assessed on the basis of employment only because relevant information concerning assets is lacking.

   Of the three multinationals which will be examined, Reed Elsevier and Wolters Kluwer announced their intention to merge on 13 October 1997 but on 9 March 1998 abandoned their plan because of objections by the European Commission. In December 1997 VNU took over the American owned ITT World Directories (publisher of Yellow Pages). This will change VNU's distribution of sales in the information segments as well as its geographical distribution of sales and em-ployment. For lack of exact information, these effects could not be included in this analysis.

8.   The point about the international distribution of sales by companies operating in different segments of the information pyramid can also be illustrated by data about some German firms. However, in the case of the German firms, of which the sales are presented in Table 8.5, data do not only pertain to the information segment of the media industries but also include entertainment, such as music recording, film and video production and broadcasting. For some of these entertainment segments, such as music and film production, a more internation-alized market exists while others such as broadcasting have a more national or even local character. What the table shows is that foreign trade as a proportion of total sales by companies operating in the segments of music, film and video production (the upper part of the table) is significantly higher than the proportion of foreign trade by companies operating mainly in segments that are national or provincial markets, such as newspaper publishing, general interest magazines and broadcasting (the lower part of the table).

Table 8.5
German Publishers' Foreign Sales as a Proportion of Total Sales

company	1990/1	91/2	92/3		93/4	94/5	95/6
Bertelsmann	63.0	62.1	61.5		63.7	65.2	65.6
Gruner+Jahr		47.5	44.4		45.8	51.1	51.7
		91	**92**		**93**	**94**	**95**
Springer Verlag					10.4	10.9	10.8
Bauer Verlag		18.4	13.9		17.2	22.1	23.3
Burda		12.6	11.5		9.5	13.9	13.7

Source: Röper (1997)

9. The term can of course be misleading, as Van Dijk (1994, p. 22) observes, when it is understood as suggesting that this infrastucture for information and communication would be the essential feature of our (future) society, thereby ignoring the material substratum and other infrastructures of our society.
10. AND's decision to open a new data factory in Ireland rather than in the Netherlands is based on a combination of reasons. Costs come in through Ireland's lower corporation tax and subsidies on wages, but in addition the supply of qualified employees has been an important factor. (*NRC Handelsblad*, 19 September 1997)
11. Another example is in *Telecom Italia* and a number of other companies (*cf. Notiziario del Lavoro*, no. 75, April 1996 and no. 81, November 1996).
12. Printed booklets (Van Tilborg 1996) and electronic media (a CD-Interactive and a website) accompany these activities.
13. Chris Pate, the General Secretary of the International Graphical Federation was also the Secretary of this International Committee. He played an important role in preparing a policy statement of the media unions about the information society in June 1995. His untimely death at the age of 37 in September 1997 was a severe loss for the Committee, and a setback for the efforts to bring about closer international co-operation within the graphical federation and between the various media and entertainment federations.

References

AND International Publishers, *Annual Report 1996*. Rotterdam: AND.

Campling, J. (1995), 'From rigid to flexible employment practices in UK commercial television: a case of government-led reform', *New Zealand Journal of Industrial Relations*, **20** (1), 1-22.

Castells, M. (1996), *The Rise of the Network Society*, Oxford: Blackwell.

CED-SER (Commissie van Economische Deskundigen SER) (1996), *Arbeidsmarkt, informatietechnologie en internationalisering*, The Hague: SER.

Communications Workers of America & The Newspaper Guild (1995), *The Information Superhighway: What it Means for Working Families*, Washington/Silver Spring: CWA/Newspaper Guild.

De Jong, S. and R. Rippen (1997), 'Naïeve onbezorgheid kenmerkt IT'ers', *Intermediair/Computable*, 19 September 1997, pp. 20-3.

Dijk, J. Van (1994), *De netwerkmaatschappij*, Houten/Zaventem: Bohn, Stafleu, van Loghum.

Dunning, J. (1993), *Multinational Enterprises in a Global Economy*, Wokingham: Addison-Wesley.

European Commission (1993), *Growth, Competitiveness, Employment*, (White Paper), Brussels.

European Commission (1997), *Panorama of EU Industry 97*, Luxembourg, Office for Official Publications of the European Communities.

European Graphical Federation (EGF) (1998), *New Media, New Challenge!* Brussels: EGF.

Freeman, C. and L. Soete (1994), *Work for all or mass unemployment?*, London/New York: Pinter Publishers.

GPMU (1995), *GPMU & Technology*, Bedford: GPMU.

Haaren, K. Van and D. Hensche (eds) (1995), *Multimedia; Die schöne neue Welt auf dem Prüfstand*, Hamburg: VSA-Verlag.

Haaren, K. Van and D. Hensche (eds) (1997), *Arbeit im Multimedia-Zeitalter*, Hamburg: VSA-Verlag.

Hirst, P. and G. Thompson (1996), *Globalization in Question*, Cambridge: Polity Press.

Hummel, R. (1997), 'Which multimedia jobs: some insights from an Austrian research project', Paper presented at the Multimedia Workshop (Utrecht University).

Jagersma, P. (1994), 'Multinationalisatie van het uitgeefwezen', *Economisch Statistische Berichten*, **79** (3953), 241-45.

Kahin, B. and E. Wilson (eds) (1997), *National Information Infrastructure Initiatives*. Cambridge, Mass./London: MIT Press.

Kist, J. (1992), 'The Netherlands in the European Community: A cultural area of modest properties with a few large publishing companies with international interests', in F. Kobrak and B. Luey (eds), *The Structure of International Publishing in the 1990s*, New Brunswick/London: Transaction Publishers, pp. 197-209.

Lash, S. and J. Urry (1994), *Economies of Signs and Space,* London: Sage.

Leisink, P. (1993), *Is innovation a management prerogative? Changing employment relationships, innovative unions.* Coventry: Warwick University, Industrial Relations Research Unit.

Leisink, P. (1996), 'The wavering innovation of trade union policy: the case of ecological and occupational issues', in P. Leisink, J. Van Leemput and J. Vilrokx (eds), *The Challenges to Trade Unions in Europe: Innovation or Adaptation*, Cheltenham/Brookfield: Edward Elgar.

Leisink, P. (1997a), 'Multimedia convergence and labour relations; effects, policies and prospects for economic and social innovation', in *Final Report Symposium on Multimedia Convergence*, Geneva: ILO, pp. 111-16.

Leisink, P. (1997b), 'New union constituencies call for differentiated agendas and democratic participation', *Transfer*, **3** (3), 534-50.

Leisink, P. (1998), 'Multimedia: bedrijven, werknemers en opleidingen', in P. Leisink, J. Boumans and J. Teunen, *De multimedia sector in beeld*, Veenendaal: GOC, pp. 27-56.

Leisink, P., J. Van Leemput, J. Vilrokx (1996), 'Introduction', in P. Leisink, J. Van Leemput and J. Vilrokx (eds), *The Challenges to Trade Unions in Europe: Innovation or Adaptation*, Cheltenham: Edward Elgar, pp. 1-27.

MacDonald, G. (1990), *The emergence of the global multi-media conglomerates*, Geneva: ILO.

Markey, R. (1996), 'Marginal workers in the big picture: unionization of visual artists', *Journal of Industrial Relations*, **38** (1), 22-41.

McArthur, R. (1990), *The internationalization of print: trends, socioeconomic impact and policy*, Geneva: ILO.

Michel, L. (1997), 'Qualifikationsanforderungen in der Multimediawirtschaft', in K. Van Haaren and D. Hensche (eds), *Arbeit im Multimedia-Zeitalter*, Hamburg: VSA Verlag, pp. 51-58.

Mitter, S. and R. Pearson (1992), *Global information processing: the emergence of software services and data entry jobs in selected developing countries*, Geneva: ILO.

Noon, M. (1991), 'Strategy and circumstance: the success of the NUJ's new technology policy', *British Journal of Industrial Relations*, **29** (2), 259-76.

Pate, C. and F. Werneke (1995), *Multimedia in the Printing and Publishing Sector; Opportunities, Dangers, Recommendations for Action*, Brussels/Stuttgart: IGF/IG Medien.

PIA (Printing Industries of America) (1994), *Bridging to a Digital Future*, Cannes: Comprint International conference.

PIRA (1994), *Communication 2000: Visions and Strategies for Printers and Publishers*, Cannes: Comprint International conference.

Ramondt, J. and G. Scholten (1985), *De stille voorhoede*, Leiden/Antwerpen: Stenfert Kroese.

Reed Elsevier, *Annual Report 1996*, Amsterdam: Reed Elsevier.

Röper, H. (1997), 'Formationen deutscher Medienmultis 1996', *Media Perspektiven*, 1997/**5**, 226-55.

Ruigrok, W. and R. Van Tulder (1995), *The logic of international restructuring*, London/New York: Routledge.

Sandberg, A. (1998), *New media in Sweden*, Solna: Arbetslivsinstitutet.

Scott, A. (1997), 'Patterns of employment in southern California's multimedia and digital visual effects industry', Paper at the Multimedia Workshop (Utrecht University).

Seufert, W. (1996), 'Beschäftigungswachtstum in der Informationgesellschaft?', *Media Perspektiven*, 9/96, 499-506.

Smith, P. and G. Morton (1990), 'A change of heart: union exclusion in the provincial newspaper sector', *Work, Employment and Society*, **4** (1), 105-24.

Smith, P. and G. Morton (1991), 'New Technology in the provincial newspaper sector: a comment', *British Journal of Industrial Relations*, **30** (2), 325-8.

Stanworth, C. and J. Stanworth (1995), 'The self-employed without employees - autonomous or atypical?', *Industrial Relations Journal*, **26** (3), 221-9.

Storper, M. (1994), 'The transition to flexible specialisation in the US film industry: external economies, the division of labour and the crossing of industrial divides', in A. Amin (ed), *Post-Fordism*, Oxford: Blackwell, pp. 195-226.

Ter Steeg, G. (1994), 'Flexibele binding: moderne arbeidsverhoudingen in de audiovisuele branche', *Tijdschrift voor Arbeid en Bewustzijn*, **18** (1), 27-33.

Tunstall, J. and M. Palmer (1991), *Media Moguls*, London/New York: Routledge.

Van der Linde, I. (1997), 'De hektiek op de arbeidsmarkt is nog niet voorbij', *Intermediair/Computable*, 19 September 1997, pp. 6-11.

Van Klaveren, M. and J. Posthuma (1992), *'Voor jou tien anderen'*, Woerden/Amsterdam: FNV Dienstenbond/Kunstenbond FNV.

Van Tilborg, R. (1996), *Drukker op de informatiesnelweg*, Amsterdam: Stichting FNV Pers.

VNU, *Annual Report 1996*, Haarlem: VNU.

Waters, M. (1995), *Globalization*, London/New York: Routledge.

Werneke, F. (1995), 'Zwischen Bangen und Hoffen', in K. Van Haaren and D. Hensche (eds), *Multimedia, Die schöne neue Welt auf dem Prüfstand*, Hamburg: VSA-Verlag, pp. 65-78.

Wolters Kluwer, *Annual Report 1996*, Amsterdam: Wolters Kluwer.

9. Work Reorganization in a Globalized Mining Industry; the Impact of Globalization on the Potash Industry

Stephen Heycock

Potash Mining as an Example of a Global Industry

Two empirical case studies are presently being carried out in Britain and Canada into the causes and the effects of the reorganization of work in Potash Mining upon labour relations.

The same product for the same global market is being produced using similar technologies and techniques, yet there are differences in how work is organized at different mines and also, it would appear, growing similarities too, both nationally and internationally. How much these have to do with the process of globalization in the industry is the purpose of the research. This will involve researching what managerial strategies have been adopted hitherto and what new global managerial paradigms are appearing if any and what the driving forces for them might be.

The present state of this research is that preliminary work has been completed on the global and national economic framework in which selected potash mines operate in Canada and Britain and a detailed survey has been made of contrasting managerial strategies and their impact upon work reorganization and therefore the labour process in Canada. This is now being compared to a later but similar process as it is occurring in Britain and to what extent this is being driven by similar global economic forces and the extent to which the managerial strategies being adopted owe anything to examples collected internationally by a globally aware management.

Majorco as a Global Mining Company

Majorco is a very good example of a global international mining company. It has what it terms operations, that is working mines, and projects, that is exploratory sites for mines in Europe, North America and South America, and more recently in Eastern Europe and South East Asia. Its Registered Head Office is in Luxembourg but many of its key personnel controlling the company work from its London Offices. Its ownership structure shows that it is owned 45 per cent by the Anglo American Group, 23 per cent by De Beers Centenary, 7 per cent by the Oppenheimer Family Interest and 25 per cent by Public Shareholdings. This makes it a truly global company as far as ownership is concerned, being spread across Europe, the USA, and South Africa principally.

It mines industrial minerals, base metals, gold, and has interests in paper and packaging and agribusiness. It is currently preparing to enter the international coal sector in a joint partnership with the Anglo American Coal Corporation (Amcoal).

It has a current market capitalization of US$ 5 billion a year and employs 23,000 people around the world.

Of its total operating earnings 33 per cent were derived from its European businesses, 12 per cent from its South-American businesses and of the total operating capital employed 40 per cent was attributable to European businesses and 32 per cent to South-American businesses.

Majorco divides itself up both by continent of operation and by product. Its management structure reflects this with the top management each being responsible for a continent and for some of its other activities like exploration added on. There is a separate manager for its Financial Operations.

To give some idea of its scale of international operations it has six goldmines in the USA, Argentina and Brazil. It has 12 base metal mines in Chile, Venezuela, Brazil, Canada and Ireland. It has ten industrial mineral mines in the UK, Germany, Spain and Brazil. It has three paper and packaging plants in Austria and the UK and one agribusiness plant in the USA.

The Dales Potash Company

The Dales Potash Company lies within the Industrial Minerals Division of this global company and is of course in the UK. However it is managed separately from the other industrial mineral operations in the UK and Europe being a separate entity in terms of its management. This signifies its importance to the company five years after it was bought by Majorco in 1993.

It produces potash principally and salt as a saleable by-product. Potash is used to make fertilizers for agriculture and the salt is used to keep roads free of ice in winter.

The main markets for its products are the UK, France, Spain and Scandinavia, though it is now looking for markets for its salt as far away as North America. In 1996 Ashby produced 1.03 million tonnes of potash and 662,000 tonnes of salt.

It opened in 1969 and therefore has been in production for almost 30 years. Only in its last five years has it been owned by Majorco. However these years have seen its most radical changes in management style and strategies and whether this is in part at least due to its new ownership and becoming part of the new and larger management structure of Majorco is an important aspect of the research.

The Geology of Production

The working environment in any mine is in large part determined by the type of mineral mined and the geological conditions of the strata in which it is found. The limits to the organization of work and therefore to managerial choice or strategies in the ways miners are put to work, are at the outset determined by these facts. That is not to say that there is not organizational choice, the very name of one of the earliest and best known studies of the reorganization of work and managerial strategies in coal-mining (Trist *et al.* 1963; Trist and Bamforth 1951) or that it is not possible to change the culture of management in mining. (Gouldner 1955a, 1955b)

But as these and other studies have found since, there are different ways in which a mineral can be mined in the same or very similar geological conditions in terms of the organization of work, and these can reach up as far as the industrial relations system at mine level affecting relations between unions and management (Heycock 1987, 1989; Heycock and Winterton 1989; Burns *et al.* 1983, 1985; Dix 1979; Yarrow 1979) and even the form and type of mining community that develops. (Warwick and Littlejohn 1992; Dennis *et al.* 1969; Allen 1981; Pitt 1979; Williamson 1982; Bulmer 1975) In this study we will be focusing on how much of this can also be driven by managerial strategies and in particular how these in turn are driven by the effects of globalization upon the mining industry.

The geology of the Dales Potash Mine at Ashby which lies on the North East coast of England, is a very important determining factor in how the potash and salt is mined.

To begin with the deposits of salt and potash found here off the coast lie beneath the sea, for the mine although built on the cliffs runs out under the North Sea to a distance of eight kilometres and forms the very edge of a very large deposit which stretches under the North Sea as far as Scandinavia. This was a former inland lake or sea, in which were laid down the deposits now being mined. However being at the very edge of that former sea, the deposits are almost akin to ripples at its edge. The strata are very buckled and twisted and difficult to follow when mining them. However this disadvantage is tempered by the fact that in global terms these deposits are very pure and carry a high potash content in the ore of about 38 per cent to 42 per cent which makes it worthwhile economically to mine them.

They also lie very deep and Ashby is the deepest mine in Europe at 1100 metres which makes for very hot working conditions for the miners and machines. Unusually for a potash mine there also occur irregular pockets of methane gas which also have an important effect upon how the mine can be worked.

The two mineral deposits worked are salt and potash. Although it could be seen as a byproduct salt is marketed as a product. The reason salt is mined at all is because the potash ore strata are too friable to support driving roadways into them as well as the fact that they are too twisted and it is difficult to predict their course enough to be able to drive straight roadways into them.

The roadways are therefore driven into the underlying strata of salt which is much thicker, more solid and therefore a more reliable seam to follow and drive roadways into, to a distance of eight kilometres out under the sea. Basically the method of work is to come up at intervals from the salt seam below into the potash seam and take bites out of it. The ore and salt is then transported along the roadways and up out of one of the two shafts at the mine dedicated to conveying material. The other is used to transport men and supplies.

The Technologies and Methods of Production

The technologies of production are, as can be seen from the above, largely determined by the geology of the mine. The potash and salt production areas or faces are known as panels which are reached from the salt seam along incline ramps using a stress relief system. This is a similar technique to that used in coal-mining in that taking a face forward sets up a pressure wave of stress as the mineral is undercut from the roof above which then presses down onto the undercut seam. This downward pressure is used to help break off the mineral from the seam.

This process must be a continuing one or eventually if left the face or panel will be crushed by the pressure from the weight of the roof above and the opened face of the seam will be closed up. In other words this is a continuous process of production which cannot be stopped and this is an important factor which determines the nature both of managerial strategies and labour relations. Both know that they cannot stop this process and both are driven by this need to continue it and to negotiate under this 'closing roof' of opportunity and production time.

The mining method is that which was used historically in the coal-industry before the introduction of longwall working and is known as pillar and stall working with strata control.

The potash ore is extracted using either mining machines which bore into the seam – but which are used mainly to drive the roadways through the salt and therefore are responsible for salt production – or by drill and blast techniques which bring the potash ore down. The exact method chosen for both minerals will depend upon the geological conditions met at any time. Partly this will be due to the state of the seam and partly to the likely danger of meeting pockets of methane gas. For example continuous miners as used in the coal-mining industry cannot always be used at Ashby as there is always the danger of unknown pockets of methane gas which could cause explosions if the continuous miner cut into them. Blasting reduces this pressure safely. This all increases the cost of production significantly in a number of ways. For example all machines and vehicles working close to the face must be flame proofed which in itself increases costs of production by four to six times.

Irrespective of the way it has been won, each panel has a heli-miner (a rotary borer) which either cuts directly or gathers up ore that has been blasted down from the face.

Two shuttle cars then transport the ore to the nearest belt which partly crushes it in an attached ration/feeder before loading it onto the belt.

Before this a driller has drilled holes forward into the seam and a shotfirer has blasted it down. After the ore has been removed a roof bolter drills and fixes long bolts into the roof with a special adhesive which holds the roadway up after the panel has been cut out and the ore removed. The roadway is then continued along in the salt seam until the next panel to extract is chosen in the potash seam. This pillar and stall method is so called because the extracted panels are called stalls and the area remaining between the cut out stalls are the pillars which help to keep the roof and the mine from subsiding.

The Organization of Work

The total complex of Dales Potash at Ashby employs about 950 people. Of this about 500 were until recently, production and maintenance workers. In the last year these workers have been cut by approximately 20 per cent, that is by just over 100 workers. This is obviously a very significant labour reduction which is part of a new managerial strategy. The question addressed here is why and how these cuts were made, and of what managerial strategy do they form a part.

These plans were in existence at least three years ago in 1995 which was two years after Dales Potash was bought by Majorco and are therefore possibly, though by no means at this stage can it be said to be so definitely, a result of a new managerial strategy being brought in now by the parent company which owns it 100 per cent. As already outlined Dales Potash is treated as a separate entity, separate from Majorco's other Industrial Minerals Division and it is therefore obviously seen as important within the global company.

The reduction in the labour force has been achieved without any lay-offs and there has been a stated commitment to employment stability. The reduction has been achieved through early retirement and agreed or voluntary redundancy.

To answer the present reorganization of work we must first understand what the organization of work was in the nearly 30 years prior to this.

Thirty years ago most miners were recruited from the local area and most had no prior experience of mining and this has continued up to the present day. A very small number came from coal-mining areas where they had lost their jobs due to the decline of coal-mining. However apart from these examples, miners generally had no experience to bring from other mining environments to place against the methods of work and organization of work demanded at Ashby. This is in contrast to the very strong and pervasive mining cultures built up in coal-mining which were always a significant factor in how they reacted to management's attempts to control or change the methods and organization of work. (Heycock 1987)

Nevertheless during the 1970s, that is in the first decade of the mine's life, the industrial relations record at Ashby was very poor with many strikes.

During the 1980s with increasing unemployment in the area during the recession and the changes in Employment Law, industrial conflict in line with the rest of industry in Britain declined.

In the 1990s there have been different pressures driving management of the mine and in turn the reaction of miners to them.

It is these pressures and changes of the 1990s and in particular those connected with globalization that we will be concerned with here.

The Reorganization of Work

There has been traditionally very little job turnover at Ashby. It has been a stable workforce and this has been a policy of the mine. This has always been an object of managerial strategy in mining generally because it takes time for a miner to become accustomed to the nature of the working environment so different from other working environments. Any new miner is more subject to the normal dangers of mining through inexperience and is indeed a danger to others who work with him. Stability of employment is an advantage to management and miners. Working with the same group also allows common knowledge and methods to increase the safety and productivity of a miner's work.

Training came with experience traditionally in mining and this was the case at Ashby too. Men would start working in the shaft area to begin with before entering the body of the mine. In coal-mining men would start as boys in the haulage work of the mine away from the face. At Ashby men would not graduate to facework for approximately five years.

Before the changes of the 1990s a job evaluation scheme had been introduced at Ashby in the 1980s in an attempt to reduce the conflict and disputes of the 1970s. This resulted in there being seven to eight job classes at the mine. There was a feeling even then amongst some of the management that it was a scheme which because it was developed and used for industry generally was not suitable for mining, and that it was sold to the mine by consultants who were brought in but who did not really understand mining conditions.

There were about seven miners working at each face. In global terms this is high when compared to Canadian potash mines. But this can partly be explained by the different geological conditions already mentioned, that is, the difficulty of following disturbed thin seams in contrast to the deep flat seams found in Western Canada. Also the unknown pockets of methane did not allow the use of the less labour intensive methods of production like continuous mining; there are only two continuous mining machines in the mine.

Nevertheless there are still many more job classifications at a typical Western Canadian Potash Mine than at Ashby and this may be explained in terms of the different union-management relationship and agreements reached there. This needs further comparative research in order to discover what the ranking of explanatory factors is.

The main underground production classes at Ashby were mine overseer, shot-firer, grade 1 miner (experienced miner), grade 2 miner (novice miner), electrician, fitter, assistant geologist (GCSE A level and trained on site).

However there has been a gradual erosion by management of job classes and demarcations as part of a conscious management strategy over the last five years, which coincides with Majorco's ownership of Dales Potash. So that now if miners are not occupied by their principal task then they are given other jobs to do. For example a skilled electrician may be put to ferrying men to and from the shaft in transport vehicles. As a result job demarcations now are far less firm than they were in the past at Ashby. All this has had to be agreed by the three unions representing workers at mine and district level.

Mine management referred to this in the past as multi-tasking and not multi-skilling which may give an indication as to the nature of the changes they had in mind as part of their then management strategy. In the last two years there seems to have been a subtle shift in their strategy with a genuine attempt to change the management culture which could be seen as a move from a Fordist to post-Fordist strategy. Now management stress that they are attempting to change the former management culture and to offer miners continuous improvement in their skills and competencies. This change began to be put into place from 1996 onwards, only three years after the mine was taken over by Majorco.

However by 1996 there was already a degree of job flexibility in place and job rotation for underground miners was quite common and was allowed to be determined by the individual crews themselves. It was for example common for miners to operate heli-miners (which bore holes into the salt seam), shuttle cars (to transport the salt and potash ore to the conveyor belts) as well as to operate rock bolters (to fix roof supports). All these were formerly separate jobs.

The only two jobs which were not subject to rotation were the shot-firer which can only be done by a miner who has passed the necessary examinations at the end of a course of study and whose work cannot legally be done by anyone else as set out in the Mines and Quarries Acts. The other restricted job was also linked to matters of health and safety and that was the assistant geologist's job.

These were experienced miners who had a desire or feeling for the job and were trained in-house by the company after gaining a GCSE A level in Geology but who did not have a University Degree in Geology, although they were under the direction of a manager who did.

The reason for their existence, quite uncommon in mining, was the peculiar nature of the seams at Ashby mine which as already stated contained, unusually for a potash mine, pockets of irregularly occurring methane gas. This was the health and safety aspect of their exclusivity from job rotation. However they had also to literally find the potash seams as they were difficult to follow being so twisted and buckled. This was particularly so as it was a relatively thin seam which was being worked from within the salt seam, so that if it moved away from the salt seam any distance it literally had to be found again, or at the least its probable continuing course along the salt seam had to be constantly charted to maximize its winning and removal and hence its productivity.

During each shift they drill into the seam to take ore samples and then leave precise instructions chalked onto the mine walls regarding the height and width at which heli-miners are to cut.

This also means therefore that the job discretion of the borer operators is thereby reduced and is for example less than that of their Western Canadian counterparts where the job of assistant geologist does not exist in their deep, flat, dependable seams. However the ore at Ashby is much richer than in Canada and therefore the extra miners employed to mine it is still economical.

There are approximately seven faces being worked at Ashby at any time and mining crews vary from four to nine depending upon conditions. Crews work three shifts at eight hours a shift, for five days a week. At weekends maintenance is done in the potash seam and salt is mined and taken to the surface. The rest of the week potash is conveyed to the surface.

Although a byproduct of potash extraction, salt is now treated as a separate production and profit centre and this is another example of global economic pressures in the international market for potash which is driving Dales Potash to increase profits from the sale of salt which they unlike other potash mines for example in Canada have to mine.

Ashby employed about 150 underground potash miners and 60 salt miners, but now they have an increasingly common cross-over between the two processes of production as part of the new managerial strategy driven by global pressures in the markets for both products.

The market for Ashby's potash is divided between 40 per cent domestic and 60 per cent for export principally to France. Salt is sold to the domestic market for spreading on roads in winter but here too export markets are now sought for example in North America in a bid to increase overall profitability in an increasingly tight global market. Up until now Ashby's advantage over other exporters like Western Canada has been its proximity to its main markets in Europe.

Global Pressures and the New Managerial Strategy and Initiatives

There are global pressures affecting Dales Potash which are driving the changes in their managerial strategies.

First costs of production are rising. The mine is now nearly 30 years old and it is not worked on the retreat system of mining whereby roadways are driven out to the edge of a field first and then return, working the mineral production faces back to the shaft. In the more usual mining method, which Ashby works, where mining begins at the bottom of the shaft and is worked outwards, then the older the mine gets the longer are the roads back to the shaft and the greater the costs of haulage and maintenance of them. The working faces are already eight kilometres out under the North Sea and there are now over 100 kilometres of roads to upkeep.

As Ashby globally is a relatively high cost producer of potash, their margin for profitability is relatively narrower compared with their competitors.

There are cyclical movements in the world prices for potash and at the moment there is a downturn in those prices. There are a number of short- and long-term factors responsible for this. For example North American farmers are trying to cheapen their costs of production by reducing the amount of fertilizers they use. The collapse of the South East Asian economies means that imported fertilizers will be much more expensive for them and they will cut back drastically in the future it is expected.

As regards salt, warming of the earth's climate will mean milder winters and therefore less salt being necessary for laying on roads.

More recently the relatively high exchange value of the pound sterling means that export prices of potash are now higher and this reduces Ashby's competitive position in the world market particularly with regard to the Canadian dollar whose value in relation to the pound is now almost what it was 30 years ago when Ashby mine was first opened.

Even if the pound were not so high, constant fluctuations in exchange rates, so much a feature of the global financial markets during the 1980s and into the 1990s, have constantly adversely affected the Dales Potash Company because their margins are less than some of their competitors due to their higher costs of production.

One important way of combating these global market driven forces is to increase production without increasing costs. They have found however that the maximum tonnage of production seems to have reached a ceiling at the mine as it is. Technological solutions to this problem of increasing production have also been found to be limited.

The only remaining solution has been seen by the company to lie in new methods of work and in new ways of organizing work to reduce relative labour costs. Linked to this has been the perceived need to reduce the size of the labour force to reduce absolute labour costs. In other words flexibility of work and of employment are seen as part of a new managerial strategy.

Aspects and Philosophy of the New Managerial Strategy and Initiatives

There was an early decision taken at least two years ago in 1996 to shed up to 150 employees through voluntary retirements and redundancies. Another decision was to introduce some form of continuous improvement programme and was associated with the new General Manager of the mine. This was begun when a climate survey of the workforce was initiated and geared towards health and safety in the first instance to test the feeling and attitudes of the miners on how this particular area might be improved before going on later to develop ways of continuously improving other areas of work and production.

However it was not just because health and safety might be seen as an area where miners might be expected to see the value of improved health and safety to themselves and therefore to co-operate with such a survey and any changes made to the working environment to improve it as a result, but because importantly for management of the company too, they would affect the product eventually as well as the miners themselves.

Basically, dust, heat, and water will affect the product eventually as well as the miners. This will to some extent depend on the required state of the product. Sometimes it is needed in a dry state sometimes not. Generally speaking, water for damping down dust is not a problem for the product itself materially in potash mining, but the introduction of water into such a deep hot mine as Ashby raises the humidity to very high levels and makes the heat much harder to bear for miners in the working environment. This in turn affects their working practices and this in turn can affect the quality of the product they produce. Conversely a healthy working environment is recognized now by management as necessary to produce an advantageously high-quality mineral product in the present tighter global market for potash.

Specifically in the case of using water to damp down dust as a result of the new managerial initiative on health and safety, air curtains have been developed to protect the operators from dust. However whilst this works for the immediate working environment, it displaces the dust elsewhere in the mine to others by recirculating it.

Before an attitudinal climate survey was initiated, management waited for the union's response at the mine before going ahead with it. So far they have received union co-operation at mine and district level.

When this was received the company employed a consultancy firm to undertake the survey and to draw up a plan for continuous improvement strategies at the mine.

However this was not seen by some top managers as all that there was to do. They identified a need for a change in the whole of the company culture and for there to be changes to the company and management structures and not just to the working practices of the miners and other production workers. It was felt by these managers that change in the company up to then had been insufficient to meet the problems Ashby mine was facing and would face in the future and most of these were linked to Ashby's global position in the potash market.

In the past various quality schemes had been introduced like Total Quality Management and British and European Quality Standards accreditation had been achieved, but these were not seen as enough for the new situation facing the mine by some managers. However there was a perceived need to make workers quality aware as contamination of the product is seen as a very important issue now, being, as already stated, one important competitive factor in a tighter global market.

'Doing more with less' sums up the guiding philosophy or principle of top management. Its rationale is forcing change by reducing or stripping out layers of management and supervisory staff as well as production workers and miners, yet expecting the same amount of work, or even more, to be done by forcing miners and management to look for new ways to organize work and adopt or adapt new methods. It is a way of forcing change under pressure. Some managers have expressed the view too that perhaps some level of insecurity is needed to spur workers and management on.

The practical visible result so far in this new strategy has been by 1997 to reduce the workforce by just over 100, or 20 per cent of the production personnel, and although this has been done voluntarily through early retirement or voluntary redundancy and with the co-operation of the unions it is a clear testimony to the determination of the top management at Ashby to proceed with a radical programme of change.

The Changed Initiative Project

Top managers like to see this as a transparent way of working and words like empowerment, change, initiative, improvement, a new working platform, are also used frequently in conversations with them.

A number of teams, and committees have been set up to carry forward these new initiatives.

Departmental Task Teams

These look at problems from the bottom up and include junior management as well as production workers or miners and trade-union representatives. Their philosophy is summed up by management in the phrase 'who knows best?' which means that in looking at any problem of production for example the people who are given the job of deciding how to tackle it and suggest changes if necessary to sort it out, are those who know most about the area irrespective of their position in the managerial, supervisory, or occupational skill hierarchy.

These Departmental Task Teams meet when necessary and are given problems to solve when and where they arise and not on a regular basis, as say teams would in the Japanese team-working systems who might meet at the beginning of each shift. (Elger and Smith 1994)

Change Workshops

These have been set up under a scheme where 15 to 20 employees are taken out of the process of production and put through courses of instruction which attempt to explain the need for change and new methods by which this can be achieved. As part of this scheme employees are also told about the company's problems and prospects. This is part of what management refer to as their policy of transparency. These are run by a consulting company for the company.

Management Information System

A Management Information System has been adopted by management consisting of a new computerized system which makes information about the company and its running instantly available to the different departments of the company in an attempt to produce the same feelings of openness and inclusivity as has been attempted in the change workshops. Not all the information which is available on this system however is necessarily available to the employees generally or to those who take part in the Change Workshops who do not have access to it and have to rely on their managers in their own department for such information.

Company Steering Committee

This oversees the whole of this Changed Initiative Project and is made up exclusively of top management which controls the general direction of it and was responsible for setting it up in the first place and obviously keeps control of its present and future direction. It was this committee which decided to call in a consulting company and which picks the training and development courses for employees which are run by local universities and colleges.

Joint Consultative Committees

These already existed for surface and underground workers and these still run alongside the Change Initiative Project and it is here where there is the most trade-union input still, although the three unions at the mine have not objected to or obstructed the Change Initiative Project so far and in fact the trade unions up to the level of full-time officers have been involved in it from the beginning according to management.

General Conclusions, Comments and Comparisons

There are both advantages and disadvantages in Ashby Mine now being part of a global mining company. The technological, work organization and product market problems would be there anyway given global factors now affecting potash production. But the methods chosen to meet them will almost inevitably also be affected in some way by the fact that they are part now of a global company.

There is already clear evidence that this is the case. For example, top managers from Ashby are at present travelling to mines in both North America and Europe for the very purpose of studying how they tackle problems of work organization with a view to seeing how these might be incorporated into the Change Initiative Project at Ashby. These mines are either part of Majorco or are chosen through the contacts Majorco has with them.

Majorco itself as a global mining conglomerate has a wealth of international experience and information which can be drawn upon from its running of many different types of mines around the world and this must have an effect upon the particular managerial strategies adopted at Ashby. This is borne out by comments made by top management to the effect that certain segments of the ownership of Majorco like the Anglo American Company carry more weight than others in their influence upon the global company's philosophy and practice.

There is however also evidence of some disadvantages to Ashby being part of a global mining company now, and interestingly enough it is because there is a conflict with an earlier and different form of globalization culture typical of the mining industry historically.

This is the fact that mining engineers typically during their careers work all over the world in many different types of mineral mines and are themselves as individuals repositories of practical experience and knowledge which defines their understanding and chosen ways of tackling mining problems, be they technical, organizational or managerial. These ways of doing things may conflict with the ways of working which any company they work for may want. As younger mining engineers they may not resist but accept and move on. But later in their careers as they begin to achieve higher positions which involve management more and engineering less, they may resist more.

Of course this may be looked at from the positive angle too in that this wealth of global experience can be made available to a company in providing alternative options and solutions to present problems, and this is what Dales Potash is attempting to do.

However if it is adopting a completely different philosophy of management practice to that subscribed to by its present mining engineers and managers then resistance to it may be expected.

This is the situation which prevails to some extent at Ashby today. Managers who have been at Ashby for a long period of time, who have long formed and practised ways of managing the mine based upon their past experiences abroad and at Ashby are reluctant to change and adopt new methods and a new philosophy. Global economic pressures and global managerial experience are not necessarily symbiotic, even in a global company.

This situation gives a different meaning to the phrase 'the global and the local'. For while some managers expressed the feeling that while Ashby might seem to be in an isolated corner of England, in reality it was very much part of the globe, others may prefer to retain their local methods to meet the problems associated with a growing globalization.

This emerging pattern of work reorganization is following quite closely in some respects that adopted already in the 1990s in the potash mines of Western Canada. At this stage it is not possible to say whether this is as a result of observation and knowledge of their practices or whether it is simply a parallel response to the same pressures in the industry found globally.

Of course the general awareness of the post-Fordist organization of work is already quite widespread in industry generally and it may not be surprising that it is now being tried out in the mining industry.

In a study by Russell (1995) of two potash mines in Western Canada he compared one 'Fordist' mine and one 'post-Fordist' mine.

It is interesting to note the similarities between the reorganization plans of the post-Fordist mine and those of Ashby. He also identified past poor industrial relations records and global competition as the motive for management of these Canadian mines to look for alternative forms of workplace organization.

The post-Fordist mine also adopted a form of work reorganization which as at Ashby included natural task work teams; problem solving work teams; joint problem solving forums; payment for knowledge systems and gainsharing; broad banding of jobs; and a quest for Continuous Improvement (Russell 1995, p. 4), overseen by a union/management Joint Steering Committee. (Russell 1995, p. 12)

All these aspects of work reorganization are part of the process of change now also being undertaken at Ashby.

As Russell also notes however critics of these same factors describe them alternatively as, hyper-Taylorism; management by stress; peer pressure; deskilling; planned labour shortages to maximize work intensity; and a diminished union presence. (1996, p. 6)

The key to these very similar changes in Canada and Britain was declared by managements in both countries to be a cultural shift, in which

'... every employee is both committed and motivated continuously to improve all aspects of operational performance...' (Russell 1995, pp. 11-12) Very nearly the same statement, though one which expressly included management too, was made by management at Ashby. Also the motivating force was stated by both to be the same, to increase company profitability.

Other aspects of work reorganization at both mines were also similar. For example early problems tackled by task teams were to do with health and safety issues presumably to make them more acceptable to the miners. Also courses were set up for managers and miners in continuous improvement and were linked to the dissemination of management information about the viability of the company and the need for collective knowledge and commitment to improvement.

Perhaps more to the point is that this process is reported as being very uneven and became little more than a plan in Canada due to union resistance. The resistance at Ashby seems to be more general and to include management as well. Perhaps as a recognition of this both the post-Fordist mine in Canada and Ashby in Britain used consulting companies to help bring in these changes. The issue that halted any further move towards work reorganization in Canada was that of reduction of the labour force. However at Ashby this has already been achieved and the reorganization of work still continues.

Russell's conclusion is that the Fordist and post-Fordist mines still shared many common organizational factors. At both, reductions in the workforce had occurred along with job enlargement or multi-tasking, though both workforces still felt that they had not been significantly deskilled or that work tempo had been significantly increased.

On the other hand at the Fordist mine joint problem solving did not translate into real power sharing according to Burgess and worker control could not be said to be greater at one mine than the other.

What this suggests is that apart from the need to continue further research in both Canada and Britain, which is planned, it is difficult though we feel important to pursue the premise that globalization in this mining industry is producing the pressures and driving forces to work reorganization and that these are taking on patterns which are recognizably similar. The object of further research is to investigate how much of this is a conscious global search by mining companies to copy or develop the 'best practices' of those mining companies which have been most successful in this.

References

Allen,V.L. (1981), *The Militancy of British Miners,* Shipley: The Moor Press.

Bulmer, M. (1975), 'Sociological Models of the Mining Community', *Sociological Review,* **23** (1), 61-92.

Burns, A., D. Feickert, M. Newby and J. Winterton (1983), 'The Miners and New Technology', *Industrial Relations Journal,* **14** (4), 7-20.

Burns, A., M. Newby and J. Winterton (1985), 'The restructuring of the British coal industry', *Cambridge Journal of Economics,* **9** (1), 93-110.

Dennis, N., F. Henriques and C. Slaughter (1969), *Coal Is Our Life.* London: Tavistock Publications.

Dix, K. (1979), 'Work relations in the coal industry', in Zimbalist, A. (ed.), *Case Studies in the Labour Process,* London/New York: Monthly Review Press, pp. 156-69.

Elger, T. and C. Smith (1994), *Global Japanization? The Transnational Transformation of the Labour Process.* London: Routledge.

Gouldner, A.W. (1955a), *Patterns of Industrial Bureaucracy,* London: Routledge and Kegan Paul.

Gouldner, A.W. (1955b), *Wildcat Strike,* London: Routledge and Kegan Paul.

Heycock, S. (1987), 'The Effect of Changes in Technology and Techniques of Production upon the Organisation of Labour and Work in Coal Mining', *The British Sociological Association Annual Conference,* University of Leeds, March 1987.

Heycock, S. (1989), 'New Technology in the Coal Industry and its Effects upon the Redesign of Working Time', in S. Heycock and J. Buber-Agassi (eds), *The Redesign of Working Time: Promise or Threat?,* Berlin: Sigma, pp. 84-95.

Heycock, S. and J. Winterton (1989), 'The Labour Process at the Coalface', Paper for the 7th Annual International Labour Process Conference, University of Manchester Institute of Science and Technology, March 1989.

Pitt, M. (1979), *The World on our Backs,* London: Lawrence and Wishart.

Russell, R. (1995), Rival paradigms at Work: Work Reorganisation and Labour Force Impacts in a Staple Industry, University of Saskatchewan, Department of Sociology. Unpublished paper.

Russell, R. (1996), The Subtle Labour Process and the Great Skill Debate: Evidence from a Potash Mine Mill Operation, University of Saskatchewan, Department of Sociology. Unpublished paper.

Trist, E.L. and K.W. Bamforth (1951), 'Some Social and Psychological Consequences of the Longwall Method of Coal Getting', *Human Relations,* **4** (1), 3-38.

Trist, E.L., G.W. Higgin, H. Murray and A.B. Pollock (1963) *Organisational Choice,* London: Tavistock Publications.

Warwick, D. and G. Littlejohn (1992), *Coal, Capital and Culture*, London: Routledge.

Williamson, B. (1982), *Class, Culture and Community. A Biographical Study of Social Change in Mining*, London: Routledge and Kegan Paul.

Yarrow, M. (1979), 'The labor process in coalmining', in A. Zimbalist (ed.), *Case Studies in the Labour Process*, London/New York: Monthly Review Press, pp. 170-192.

10. Australia's Historic Industrial Relations Transition

Rob Lambert

As the bitter maritime and shearers' strikes of the 1890s led to Australia's 20th Century labour arbitration and import protection, so today's farmer inspired battle on the docks will define whether the country can work out how to earn a quid in the globalised economy .

The Australian Financial Review (editorial, 9 April 1998)

In the modern globalised economy, wage rates and labour market practices cannot be insulated from market conditions.

Michel Camdessus (*The Australian*, 6 May 1998)

End Game

In the dead of night on Tuesday 7 April 1998, Patrick, one of Australia's two major stevedoring companies made a decisive move with direct government support: the company dismissed its entire 2000 strong unionized workforce. Workers were replaced by non-union labour that included persons previously employed by the Australian Defense Force. The action was decisive because the confrontation marked a definitive moment in the transition of the Australian industrial relations system from its democratic form to a more authoritarian one, similar in certain respects to Asian systems. This event highlights the redefinition of the role of the Australian State set in place by the passage of the new Workplace Relations Act in 1996. The state is no longer a mediator in capital/labour conflicts, moving instead to a far less ambiguous representative of the interests of capital against labour.

The conservative federal government was intimately involved in this corporate strategy from the outset, promising the company unlimited financial and legal support in the confrontation with the Maritime Union of Australia (MUA). The government has become organically involved, in a manner unprecedented in Australian history, because it views breaking the MUA as critical to cleansing Australia of the inefficiencies of regulated labour markets. This is an accurate assessment in that the demise of the MUA would severely weaken organized labour at a time of great adversity following labour-market deregulation. The MUA, which to this point, controlled labour supply, is fighting hard. Mass · pickets surround all Patrick's terminals to prevent container movement; unionized tug-boat operators are delaying the berthing of ships wherever possible. Internationally, the International Transport Federation (ITF) and the International Confederation of Free Trade Unions (ICFTU) are organizing a world-wide boycott of any shipping company trading through Patrick.

These dramatic events have been described as an 'endgame', as the 'final conflict' and as 'an old style' union movement's 'last gasp' by commentators in the Australian financial media. (*The Australian Financial Review*, 9 April 1998) Without doubt, this conflict is a defining moment; one that will determine the future character of Australian society. The ICFTU has stated that this dispute is one of the most important ever to face the international trade-union movement. The confrontation has a significance beyond the dispute itself because the events capture the contradictions of globalization and signal a critical phase in Australian trade-union history. A defeat of the MUA would accelerate trade-union decline as companies in other sectors adopt similar militant tactics to cut unionism from their workforce in the cause of global efficiency and the further advancement of the frontier of economic deregulation. Alternatively, a defeat of the company would signal that globalization may also provide a window of opportunity for the emergence of a new style of global social movement unionism that may begin to counter the erosion of employment conditions produced by global change.

This chapter will highlight these contradictions and strategic choices in a manner that may provide a useful basis for comparing the logic and social consequence of this radical brand of labour-market restructuring. This aggressive strategy contrasts markedly from the present course of the European Union where worker rights are integral to the social fabric of European societies. For this contrast with the European trajectory of industrial relations to be meaningful, the following argument will be substantiated: the political drive to fully deregulate Australian labour markets reflects both the impact of globalization and the geographic proximity of Australia to the Asian region. The latter is significant because of the authoritarian character of Asia's labour-market institutions. The argument will be structured in five sections. Firstly, key conceptual issues underlying the argument will be clarified. Secondly, a brief exposition of the historic form of labour regulation in Australia will be presented. Thirdly, the external pressures to reform this system will be highlighted through an analysis of labour-relations change in China. Fourthly, the organic linkages of Chinese labour-market reforms to the Australian system will be illustrated through a corporate case study. Fifthly, the reform process deriving from these global pressures will be analysed. Finally, future prospects are considered through an assessment of the current maritime dispute.

Globalization and Industrial Relations Systems

The forces propelling Australia's industrial relations system towards a more authoritarian form are unregulated trade and investment flows in a more fully globalized economy, characterized by marked regional differences in industrial relations systems. This industrial relations transformation has grave consequences for the future of independent trade unionism in Australia. What do I mean by 'more fully globalized economy'? The understanding that informs this analysis is that whilst globalization is distinctive from the early phase of internationalization, a fully globalized economy is yet to be realized.[1] This contrasts with Hirst and Thompson (1996) who argue that globalization is a myth, or Strange (1996) who argues that a fully globalized economy has already been accomplished. The ideal typical models developed by Hirst and Thompson and summarized in Table 10.1 are a useful way of giving greater precision to the notion of a transition stage in the process of global restructuring.

The purpose of drawing attention to these features is not to engage in a wide ranging debate on the nature of globalization, but rather to clarify understanding of those aspects that have the most direct bearing on industrial relations change in Australia. As the European Union's policy in this arena shows, national states, supported by a strong regionalism, do determine policy. They are not simply squeezed by international markets to reform industrial relations. So a region like Europe provides evidence supporting the views of Hirst and Thompson (1996) and Zysman (1996) that nation states determine policy. In contrast to this, the Australian state, now part of the Asian region through the APEC structures yet not fully accepted by Asian states has chosen to subordinate its policies to international market forces to a much greater degree, viewing industrial relations reform as essential to its global competitiveness. While the Australians claim that they have been forced into this by the pressures of international markets, they have in fact chosen one particular path of global engagement from a range of options in the labour sphere.

Table 10.1
Ideal Type Models of the Global Economy

Features	International	Fully Globalized
Principal entity	National economy. Continuing relative separation of national and international systems.	Distinct national economies subsumed by the international economic system. Atomized, socially dismembered markets truly global.
Corporate Sector	MNC - dominant operations within a particular national location.	TNC - genuinely footloose companies.
Finance Capital	Restricted flows due to national regulation.	Genuinely unrestricted flows between nation states.
Governance and the role of the state	Nation still has the power to determine policy and intervene in markets.	Nation state increasingly subordinate to international market forces.
Technology	Long history of technological advance and international-ization of economies (Intercontinenal telegraph cables).	Technological breakthroughs in micro-electronics and communications systems adds significant new dynamic to the system.
Labour market	Nationally determined industrial relations systems.	Global markets dominate. Union power in decline.

Global restructuring can therefore be seen to be uneven, characterized by marked differences in state responses, rendering the notion of a transition phase more credible.

The contrasting responses of the European Union and the Australian State to global pressures on democratic industrial relations systems confirm that national states do have power to shape policy in this sphere. Hence the debate over whether or not national governance in the new circumstances is possible, is somewhat misplaced when industrial relations is being considered. Rather, the question that should be asked is what are the strategic choices that states are making and why are they taking particular reform routes rather than others. Choice in this regard is indicative of the form of engagement of particular states with global forces. This chapter attempts to explain why the Australian State has chosen the authoritarian pathway.

Before proceeding with this analysis, it is important to clarify what is meant by authoritarian and democratic labour-market institutions. Establishing criteria for evaluating and comparing labour-market institutions is vital in assessing these changes. Here it is argued that ILO Conventions 87 and 98 on freedom of association and collective bargaining rights are the basis for any such assessment. Central to conformity with these Conventions is the state conceding the right of citizens to establish trade unions 'of their own choosing without previous authorization' by either the state or employers. (Article Two of Convention 87, adopted at the Thirty First Session of the ILO in June 1948) Convention 98 stipulates that collective bargaining is only effective when trade unions are allowed to operate free of employer interference. Article Two of this Convention states that 'acts which are designed to promote the establishment of workers' organizations under the domination of employers' organizations' are a contradiction of this Convention. Clearly, these Conventions provide a basis for a broad characterization of labour-market institutions. In accepting these norms one could argue that labour markets marked by a unilateral regulation of the employment relationship which organizes and consolidates employer power whilst simultaneously disorganizing workers, may be characterized as authoritarianism. A notable feature of these markets is the high degree of state coercion, particularly during phases when workers resist the unilateral imposition of wages and conditions. Alternatively, labour markets that institutionalize freedom of association and collective bargaining rights as defined by the ILO may be characterized as democratic. While the absolute rule of the former resides in a range of sanctions that require unquestioning obedience, the latter's emphasis on liberty, independence and representation seeks to secure its goals through consent. Such systems are never frozen in these pure forms over time. They are the terrain of struggle. So for example, newly emergent unions in Asia are demanding the democratization of labour-market institutions, whilst conservative forces in certain industrialized nations push for the dismantling of democratic labour markets.

This distinction is no mere theoretical construct, but is evident in the architecture of Asian industrial relations systems. Notwithstanding the diverse histories that have given rise to distinctive institutional arrangements, the essential features of authoritarianism are readily discernible.

As a state apparatus, industrial relations systems are constructed around a contradictory balance between coercion and consent. Democratic systems secure consent through the participation of free and independent trade unionism, which have legitimacy precisely because they are independent of the state. Legal frameworks set the rules, which all parties consent to. The authoritarianism of Asian systems resides in their use of repressive laws to weaken and marginalize independent trade unionism. Malaysia's Internal Security Act has been used against independent leadership. In Indonesia, the state's National Security Agency is the instrumentality used to detain and interrogate the leaderships of the independent trade unions. This has been used to intimidate new recruits in the factories and has been central to the process of imprisoning the leaderships of the new unions. Eight key national leaders of these unions are presently serving long prison terms. In the past, the Philippine state has relied on direct violence against union leaders through special counter-insurgency cells that the military had established in workplaces and in communities. When the military imposed martial law in South Korea in May 1980, the laws were used to crack down on the emerging independent labour movement. The purification campaign that followed decimated the independent union leadership. Similar repression followed the 1987 strike wave.

This direct repression closely articulates with another key feature of Asian authoritarianism: legal restrictions on the right to freely associate and bargain collectively as defined by the ILO Conventions. These restrictions have been reinforced through either the direct state construction of official unionism, or through rendering already existing independent unionism weak and pliant. The latter was achieved in the Philippines through entrenching company unionism that made it difficult for the new unions to gain access to workers. In Malaysia, pliant unionism was secured when the application of the Internal Security Laws led to militant leaders being replaced by weak ones which has resulted in the growth of weak, bureaucratized unionism with little active presence in workplaces. In Indonesia, the state established military styled unionism after the 1966 coup. In all these circumstances, workers who wish to have their interests represented collectively, find themselves caught within a web of these ineffectual structures. This has proven to be an effective form of control. These systems contrast markedly with Australia's democratic tradition.

Australia's Democratic Industrial Relations System

Recognition of the role and the rights of trade unionism and protection of their power to bargain collectively were significant features of the social character of the new federal state formed in 1901. This was a state that defined itself in terms of a particular relationship to the working class. Alfred Deakin, a founding father of the Australian federal state, commented in 1890: 'Instead of the state being regarded any longer as an object of hostility to the labourer, it should now become identified with an interest in his works, and in all workers, extending to them its sympathy and protection, and watching over their welfare and prosperity.' (quoted in Pusey, 1991)

Recognition of worker rights was to usher in the age of the common man (Ward, 1958), and the beginning of a new phase of civilization. (Deakin quoted in Kelly, 1992) The industrial relations system that was to play a central role in making Australia the social lighthouse of the world was founded on the Conciliation and Arbitration Act of 1904. The Act forced employers to recognize unions registered under the Act, and empowered these unions to represent the interests of all workers within an industry. Under the Act, unions could force employers into an industrial court even if they were unwilling to negotiate. Courts were empowered to make an award, that is, a legally binding ruling on wages and conditions. Employers eventually came to support the arbitration and award system because the government promised them tariff protection if they could prove that they had met their responsibility to pay fair and reasonable wages.

Some 70 years after the introduction of the first moderate levels of tariff protection in 1902, the highest tariff levels of any industrialized nation, barring New Zealand, shielded Australian manufacturing. (Garnaut 1987, p. 6) This interventionism was seen to assert the positive social value of egalitarianism. Wage justice through arbitration became the means which marked the beginning of a new phase of civilization. A regulated minimum wage structure grounded in the principle of human need and welfare, not profit and productivity, was enshrined through the famous Harvester judgement. In this the state set minimum wages by judicial decree rather than abandoning workers in the turbulent waters of market forces. The notion of the cost of living became the basis for wage movements. The then President of the Arbitration Commission, Justice Higgins was ruthless in his enforcement of these principles. In a case involving one of the large mining companies, BHP in 1909, he argued that if the company could not pay the minimum rate it was preferable that it shut down. He commented, 'If it is a calamity that this historic mine should close down, it would still be a greater calamity that men should be underfed or degraded'. (Rickard 1984, pp. 173-5) Hence the industrial relations system came to be viewed as the greatest institutional monument to Australian egalitarianism. (Kelly 1992, p. 9) Trade unions were a recognized, integral component of this system and came to play a key role in securing a steady, uninterrupted improvement in wages and conditions. Between 1939 and 1974, workers' real wages rose by an annual average of 2 per cent and the 40-hour working week was common by the late 1930s. (Gruen 1985, p. 4)

The industrial relations system, which achieved these social outcomes, is one in which compulsory arbitration plays a central role. Arbitration is compulsory in two senses. Firstly, once the parties submit to arbitration, they have to submit to a mandatory procedure for presenting their case. Secondly, the outcome of arbitration, awards, are legally binding. Awards specify minimum standards of remuneration and conditions, which have to be met or else legal sanctions will be applied. Davis and Lansbury (1993, p. 108) point out that it is important to distinguish between the formal provisions of the arbitration system and the way it actually works. The system does not preclude direct negotiation between the parties. Agreements directly negotiated between employers and unions may co-exist with or take the place of arbitrated awards. These agreements are known as 'consent awards'.

This democratic industrial relations system contrasts markedly with authoritarian systems in the Asian region. The essentials of the Chinese system are analysed so as to illustrate the processes through which authoritarian norms and values are transmitted into the industrial relations processes of other nations. These processes are also at work through Asia's other industrializing nations such as Indonesia, Malaysia, Thailand, Vietnam and the Philippines. China has been selected because of its dominance in the region as a whole.

Labour Relations Change in China

Labour relations change is perhaps the most dramatic feature of China's ambitious programme of economic reform ushered in under Deng Xiaoping from 1979. The Special Economic Zones (SEZ) which first took root in the Pearl River Delta (PRD) region were also the vanguard of

labour relations reform which is now impacting on China more generally.

The PRD comprises eight municipalities and is equivalent in size to
the Netherlands with a population of 23 million. (Leong 1997, p. 231)
As part of the open door policies to establish market socialism SEZs
were first established in four south eastern coastal towns, the most
important being Shenzhen. These were consciously designed to engineer
international competitive advantage. In this regard, public policy has
secured the PRD as the locus of Asia's cheapest industrial labour force,
several times lower than the competing cheap labour locations of South
East Asia. Since the Asian region has itself attained a global competitive
advantage in labour costs, the PRD thus ranks as a world competitive
labour centre, providing impetus to the unfolding of an international
cheap labour economy. This has vast consequences for the structure of
manufacturing in the established industrialized nations. Labour-market
policies combined with other SEZ incentives have stimulated stunning
rates of foreign investment. The PRD has grown at a rate of more than
15 per cent for the past 15 years, attracting investments in electronics,
textiles, clothing, footwear and other light industries, building materials,
petrochemicals, machine building and food.

These post-Mao economic reforms have had a dramatic impact on the
character of the Chinese labour market. Agricultural reform has displaced peasants and rural workers on a massive scale. Estimates of this
floating workforce eager to secure work in the SEZs and in other
industrial districts range from 80 to 100 million. This surplus labour-
market situation is being further exacerbated by state enterprise restructuring which has classified as redundant an estimated further 50 million.
Neo-classical labour-market theory underpins these changes. Workers
need to be released from the existing bureaucratized labour market where
work is allocated and controlled by the state and where the wages system
is regulated to achieve social ends. A free labour market would create
an incentive to work, thereby enhancing productivity. Du Haiyan, a
leading exponent of the free labour market in China has asserted that by
'giving people a completely free hand in choosing their own jobs, an
environment of equal opportunity and fair competition will be created,
with labourers bearing the economic risks for their own decisions on
labour inputs'. (Greenfield and Leong 1997; P. and R. Howard 1995)
This necessitates the reform of labour-market institutions and resulting
practices that have created systems of job security and egalitarian wages
(the iron rice bowl and eating from the one big pot).

The most significant policy measure to free the labour market was the decision to further formalize, deepen and extend a labour contract system through the passage of the 1986 Labour Contract Law. This law has institutionalized individual employment contracts and a labour migratory system similar in many respects to apartheid South Africa's much despised influx control system. This displaced the comprehensive labour-market allocation system that had been established in the 1950s. This system allocated work to all China's urban citizens, who on completion of their schooling, waited for labour bureau officials to distribute work, having notified the officials of their work and geographic preferences which most often could not be met. Once assigned a job, workers received their citizenship registration or *hukou* which was identified with their work unit, the *danwei*. (Leung Wing-yue 1988, p. 55) This process assured them of life-time employment. The work unit then took charge of the workers' welfare needs through the provision of wages, housing, living subsidies, medical benefits, education, family affairs and pensions. Under this system children usually inherited their parents' jobs when they retired. Dismissal was virtually unheard of.

The contract system that displaced life-time employment was introduced nationally for all new workers in state enterprises in July 1982. Further modifications through the 1986 laws brought all workers under a system of individual, fixed term, renewable contracts. This institutionalized a migratory labour system in the SEZs in a manner that enhanced the global competitiveness of Chinese labour. Under these arrangements, workers are rigorously controlled through institutions that regulate their labour-market entry. This operates as follows. Workers are required to apply for a special permit from the local state authority granting permission to leave their village. At the border, they require a further permit to enter the SEZ. When they are offered employment in the zone, an employment contract is drawn up which then has to be approved at the local labour bureau. This office then issues a work permit which is in effect a temporary residence permit that assumes the status of an ID card. Workers have to carry this permit with them at all times or else they will be in trouble. (Interview with GEW production manager, May 1994) Periodically, police conduct raids and arrest those without the necessary documentation. They are placed in detention centres and then deported. There is evidence that migrants in this situation are often harassed, humiliated and mistreated, revealing a precarious and marginalized existence. (Chan 1997; Gao 1997; Solinger 1997) Most often they are forced to live in crowded dormitories provided by the factories or in shanties. Migrants are not entitled to any of the benefits enjoyed by local residents such as the right to bring their families, social welfare, schooling and employment for their children. Hence they assume the status of non-resident guest workers within their own country. (Chan, 1997; see also *Chinese Sociology and Anthropology*, **20** (1), 1996) The competitive logic of global labour markets underpins these denials. As was the case in Apartheid South Africa, wages can be set at the individual workers' subsistence level rather than in terms of the subsistence needs of the family thereby securing comparative labour advantage over states where labour markets are not structured around these denials.

The coercive character of China's SEZ labour markets is further reinforced through the creation of a bonded labour system. On taking up employment, migrant workers are required to pay for their temporary work permit in full. Since these workers have not the means to meet this financial requirement, the factory pays on the workers' behalf. This is then deducted from the worker's wage over the first 12 month period. Some companies also require a deposit of around 50 per cent of the first month's wage. Should the worker decide to leave his or her employment they are, in many instances, required to repay the balance owing. There is evidence that some companies even retain their workers' residency permits for safe-keeping even though such practices are illegal. Without a permit, workers cannot even venture onto the surrounding streets. They are effectively imprisoned between workplace and factory dormitory. Clearly, bonded labour gives employers enormous power over the workforce. Under such circumstances, migrants have little option but to accept the given working conditions and wage rates. The production manager of a Shenzhen home appliance company commented, 'If they are not suitable and we dismiss them, they have to pay us for the permit. This guarantees that the workers do not run away'. (Chan 1997)

A second vital dimension of this coercive labour-market system is the denial of freedom of association and collective bargaining rights in a bid to pre-empt resistance. In this regard, the intent if not the form of China's labour-market institutions are similar in many respects to those of other Asian nations where officially recognized trade unions are structured to control and discipline the workforce, whilst independent labour unions are repressed. The All China Federation of Trade Unions (ACFTU) is the only organization sanctioned to represent workers' interests. The Federation is an organization whose history is closely interwoven with the immense social upheavals that have characterized 20th century China.[2] However, after 1949, the ACFTU became the transmission belt of the state, the vehicle for communicating the will of the state to a widespread, diverse workforce. This was achieved through the Trade Union Law of 1950 which clearly designated the trade-union role. Under the law, unions were subordinate to the CCP and soon became completely controlled by the party. Trade-union leadership, in particular at national and provincial levels, is exclusively appointed by the CCP. In 1995 the ACFTU President stated that 'The unions must better obey and serve the overall task of the Party....union organizations should not act independently'. (quoted in *China Labour Bulletin*, special issue, November 1995) The primary role of the union became the construction of a culture of self-sacrifice in the cause of increased production.[3] After 1979, the role of the ACFTU in the SEZs was tightly defined. Here it is argued that China now exhibits a mature form of unionism that strives to ensure that foreign venture production is in no way disrupted. Hence the ACFTU's pre-eminent role is to educate workers on the need for disciplined co-operation with management. In 1994 the General Secretary of the ACFTU Xiao Zhen-bang asserted, 'Unions must try by all means to eliminate instability' and ensure that 'unexpected incidents' are prevented. (quoted in Greenfield and Leong 1997, p. 31) At the 12th Congress of the ACFTU it was stated that trade-union activities should not conflict with the 'legitimate rights of investors'. (Greenfield and Leong 1997)

A recent paper has argued that the image of stability propagated by the Chinese government and the ACFTU is in fact contradicted by a rising tide of labour resistance outside the formal structures. (Greenfield and Leong 1997) News that labour-market reforms have met with considerable resistance from below has generally been hidden from the public arena through state censorship. In 1994 there were 135,000 reported labour disputes followed by a further 150,000 during the first six months of 1995. The Chinese Labour Ministry itself reports that 'labour disputes' have escalated by 73 per cent during 1995 and by a further 73 per cent during 1996. (*Far Eastern Economic Review*, 26 June 1997)

The majority of strikes in foreign factories in the zones were over forced overtime, beatings, and sexual harassment.[4] The situation of workers in many state-owned enterprises has become critical. In March 1997, in the inland province of Sichuan, workers at a silk factory in the city of Nanchong took their manager hostage and paraded him through the city centre demanding six months' unpaid wages. More than 20,000 besieged the city hall for 30 hours, forcing the government to meet the wage bill. Similar events occurred in Jialihua, another inland city where a textile factory manager was thrown into the back of a truck and forced into a demeaning 'aeroplane position'– bent at the waist, arms straight out at the sides – and paraded through the city. (*Far Eastern Economic Review*, 26 June 1997) In most instances, the response of the ACFTU to these strikes, especially in the SEZs, has been to try to end the action as swiftly as possible.

A third characteristic of the way in which labour-market institutions operate in the zones is through direct repression of independent union activity and workers' attempts to bargain collectively. The seeds of independent unionism were planted with the brief appearance of the Workers Autonomous Federation (WAF) during the Tiananmen events of 1989. Following the crackdown, 14 leaders of the Federation were executed, two sentenced to life imprisonment and hundreds more were detained. (Hong Kong Trade Union Education Centre 1990, p. 19) Post-Tiananmen, the list of persons imprisoned for any form of independent activity has lengthened. In China, brutal forms of physical and psychological punishments are metered out to signal to the workforce in general: any form of independent action, however innocuous, will be ruthlessly dealt with. Han Dongfang, a leader of the WAF in Beijing, was detained without trial for 22 months after 4 June 1989. Han was deliberately and maliciously admitted to a contagious prison ward where he contracted tuberculosis. He was released from prison when the authorities feared the international reaction his death might arouse. Wang Miao-gen was sentenced to a three year re-education through labour *(laojiao)* punishment for being chairperson of the WAF in Shanghai. In 1993 he was placed in custody in a psychiatric hospital and has not been seen since. A special ICFTU report details the names, date of arrest, sentence, place of detention, health status and union activities of 67 victims. The report exposes a chilling pattern of repression.[5]

These mutually reinforcing policies are aimed at maintaining a disciplined, controlled work force, individualized, lacking security and therefore weak with little apparent bargaining power. As the following case illustrates, foreign companies structure their operations to maximize the competitive advantage these authoritarian labour-market conditions offer – cheap, highly controlled labour. This brings pressure to bear on the uncompetitive democratic labour markets of the industrialized nations.

The Global Impact of Authoritarian Labour Relations: The Sunbeam Case

The shift towards a more fully globalized economy has meant that authoritarian labour markets in Asia have a significant impact on the terms of global competition, forcing change in the strategy of companies in the industrialized world. This can be best illustrated by research into the restructuring of the Australian home appliances industry following the reduction of tariff protection from 30 per cent to 5 per cent. Three corporations dominated the sector in Australia: the multinationals Black and Decker, Cambrook and the Australian owned Sunbeam Victa. When tariffs were lowered, three key dimensions of public policy in China shaped their corporate strategy. These were SEZ tax incentives; access to Asian markets and authoritarian labour-market conditions. All three companies established joint-ventures in China to gain international competitive advantage. However, the Australian based Sunbeam Victa also retained a production base in Australia. In the SEZs companies are zero taxed for the first two years with the tax gradually graded upward to 17 per cent. Companies constantly move their location in the zones to retain the zero rating (interviews with company managers in the Shenzhen SEZ, May 1993). Prohibitive tariffs were a motivation for the Australian based companies to establish Chinese joint-ventures to jump the tariff wall, access Asia's booming middle-class markets and escape Australia's highly unionized labour market.

The establishment of transnational joint-ventures effects an organic connection between national labour markets. That is, a new and direct relationship between national labour markets is embedded and structured within the joint-venture relationship itself. The Sunbeam Victa case illustrates this critical transformation. Wages, working hours and general conditions in the workplace in their joint-venture in the Shenzhen SEZ were a product of the institutionalization of labour migrancy, bonded labour and the absence of representative trade unions.[6] As a consequence, Shenzhen SEZ wage rates in the home appliances sector were a mere 2.5 per cent of the Australian rate. Australian trade unions had secured a 38-hour working week in home appliances whereas the Shenzhen migrants worked a 60-hour week.

The then democratic character of Australia's labour-market institutions that had enshrined free trade unions and collective bargaining rights secured these conditions. China's authoritarian labour-market institutions in maintaining vastly different conditions placed intense pressure

on Australian manufacturing which had to be responded to. The strategic
choice of two players was closure and relocation to take full advantage
of China's authoritarian labour market. The third factory which has tried
to maintain an Australian base presented its Sydney workforce with a
stark choice: intensify production to meet Chinese unit production costs
or face closure.

Thus far the assembly line workers have met the challenge. During the
1990s they increased productivity by 200 per cent through a three and a
third fold increase in the line speed, from one iron every 40 seconds to
one every 12. The line speed of the Shenzhen plant was 66 per cent
slower. These changes came at considerable personal cost to the Australian workers, many of whom now suffer RSI problems.

In this we see the impact of Chinese labour markets on Australia
reflected in plant closure, relocation and work intensification. Hence
whilst labour markets are embedded nationally, their effects now transcend physical boundaries more forcefully. These labour-market effects
are transmitted through corporate structures that have transnationalized.
Authoritarian labour markets provide corporations with new strategic
options in fiercely competitive global consumer markets. Corporations
are seeking to maximize their own individual advantage in this way.
Investment decisions are therefore strongly influenced by the public
policy of Asian states.

At one level, complacency has characterized the Australian
government's response to the increasing relocation rate of Australian
based corporations into Asia. Such restructuring is accepted as inevitable
– a sign of the maturity of Australian based corporations as they evolve
global strategies. However, the job losses accompanying this hollowing
out is now a central concern for complacency on this front is electorally
dangerous. The government's main answer is the achievement of international competitiveness through the reform of labour-market institutions. The contradictions inherent in this reform process are analysed in
the following section which focuses on a critical question: to what extent
are Australia's labour-market institutions and the deep historical legacy
of internationally recognized rights being remoulded into an image that
reflects certain aspects of Asia's authoritarian model? Are we witnessing
a gradual process of fusion where distinct, divergent, geographically
distant systems are being blended through the organic labour-market
linkage corporate restructuring has realized? Is this occurring in a
manner whereby certain democratic features of the one meld into a
degree of labour-market authoritarianism that may well remain distinct

from various Asian forms while differing markedly from its historical antecedents?

Australian Labour Relations Reform

There are three dimensions to this reform process that at least, to some degree, reflect the influence of Asian policy: labour-market institutional reform, the Australian government's flirtation with an EPZ strategy and finally, the government's concentration of all its resources, including the military, to break trade-union power. Of course, such a significant shift towards authoritarian industrial relations does open up contradictions. This raises a key question: how durable are Australia's democratic institutions, traditions and culture in the face of this concerted drive? These tensions are now considered.

The neo-liberal architects of labour-market reform assert that the 1996 Workplace Relations Act's promotion of a system of individual employment contracts in preference to union negotiated, collective agreements and awards is a positive step towards modernizing outdated institutional arrangements. This change reflects the evolution of Australian culture towards greater individualism. The flexible character of individual contracts best expresses individual aspirations and provides the greatest scope for the realization of the hopes and desires of individual Australians through securing freedom of choice. Individual talent is more fully developed and people are restored to the heart of the process. The gray mediocrity of collective agreements is transcended.[7]

An alternative perspective views this move as heralding a critical turning point as significant as the establishment of the first democratic labour-market institutions at the turn of the century. Emphasis on individual contracts ushers in a phase of hesitant, contradictory transitions to a particular form of labour-market authoritarianism that is quite distinctive. Initially, it seemed as if this softer version of authoritarianism would suffice and that Australia would not mirror the harsh, repressive rule of Asian labour-market institutions. As will be shown, the present attack on the MUA reflects a new stage in the march to authoritarian labour relations not dissimilar in intent to the Asian model. Initially, the government had hoped that the soft authoritarianism of individual contracts would secure the demise of independent trade unions. The institutional stress on individual contracts would reinforce the coercion inherent in modern labour markets. This derives from the fact that in modern industrial societies, historical development which strips the means of subsistence from the majority, creates relations of power-lessness and dependency.

Individual contracts, in reflecting this basic relation, will reproduce a certain spirit of authoritarianism through their unilateral regulation of the employment relationship. That is to say, a system of individual contracts reinforces relations of dominance and dependency; a consoli-dation of power and hierarchy; unilateral decision-making and the promotion of a culture of obedience that can only be transformed through labour-market institutions that promote checks and balances in em-ployment relations. Even though formal contracts of employment appear as 'a very Eden of the innate rights of man', workers enter this relation-ship timidly, holding back, 'like someone who has brought his own hide to the market and now has nothing else to expect but – a tanning'. (Marx 1976, p. 280) The theory is that workers who anxiously recognize their dependency will work more intensely to prove their worth, thereby improving productivity and Australia's competitive position. 'Employ-ees need stress to work well', commented an employers' association representative.[8]

These individual contracts are not the only way that Australian labour markets are being transformed. Just as Asian states impose limitations on independent trade unionism, so too does the new Act. Employers can now take punitive action against trade unions with greater ease through the Trade Practices Act. The primary and secondary boycott provisions of this Act are intended to constrain strike action outside of limited periods of protected action as well as any form of solidarity action. Fines of up to $750,000 can be imposed. Further new laws dubbed 'the Third Wave', introduced into the Western Australian state system in May 1997, extend the boundaries of punitive action against unions well beyond the Federal Act.[9] In its initial form the Federal Act also sought to constrain trade unionism through limiting the workplace access of union organizers. While this is the case in Western Australia, the federal government was forced to retreat on this issue.[10] The regulation of wages and conditions through the Australian Industrial Relations Commission (AIRC) and through industry-wide awards is another key area of reform. The government wishes to achieve greater flexibility in wages, working hours and general conditions through limiting the scope of both the AIRC and the award system. The reformers preferred position is a highly flexible individual contract system that can vary without reference to award standards and without being vetted by the AIRC.

This competitive pathway is constrained by Australia's democratic values and traditions. Hyman (1989) has argued that labour-market institutions should never be viewed in isolation, but should rather be seen as a reflection of a more fundamental set of power relations in the society. Labour markets are therefore marked with the features of the state that reproduces them. So for example, the militarized New Order Indonesian state has constructed labour-market institutions with a clearly designated role for the military. Claiming a dual function as guardians of order and promoters of social development, military leaders are elected into key positions in the official state trade union. (Lambert 1997) In contrast, the liberal democratic Australian State and the democratic culture that underpins it sit uneasily with the general direction of labour-market reforms. According to the 1985 report of the Hancock Committee, the almost century old system of collective bargaining rights reflected the fact that 'Australia has a history of support for individual and collective rights dating from the 19th Century. The community has, over the years, acknowledged and supported the right of people to organise, to associate freely, and to dissent....The role of trade unionism is accepted and endorsed within our society'. (*The Australian*, 30 January 1995)

Democratic values are indeed a powerful constraint. Thus the original draft laws were considerably softened in a number of key areas as the government was forced to negotiate the bill with the minority Democratic Party who succeeded in introducing changes when the bill was placed before the Senate. There were notable compromises in the areas of wage flexibility, the role of the AIRC and the trade-union role. Perhaps the most important concession was in allowing a 'no disadvantage test' to be applied to individual contracts known as Australian Workplace Agreements (AWAs). The government had hoped for a system where these agreements, once signed, would take immediate effect without the requirement of independent checks. A dissatisfied worker would have to go to the civil courts to challenge compliance with minimum conditions. The concession granted was that AWAs have to be checked by an Employment Advocate to ensure that they do not disadvantage workers in comparison to their award conditions. If there is doubt in this regard, the AWA must be reviewed by the AIRC in private. The Commission has the power to recommend changes or to reject the AWA. However, the government succeeded in maintaining the exclusion of unions from the negotiation of AWAs, unless specifically authorized by workers. The measures are designed to pre-empt union recruiting since non-unionized workers will be fearful to make such a move.

Another government objective is the simplification of awards down to 20 allowable conditions, thus achieving greater flexibility. Since the passage of the Act, a key AIRC ruling downgraded the status and the role of award regulation when it rejected an 11 per cent pay claim of the transport workers arguing that the Commission had 'to follow the designs of the Workplace Relations Act'. (*The Australian*, 16 May 1997) The decision means that awards assume a minimum safety net status only. The AIRC has until July 1998 to reduce awards down to the 20 conditions. In the interim, employer organizations and the union movement are locked in conflict over the nature of these changes. The peak employer organization, the Australian Chamber of Commerce and Industry (ACCI) propose that employers should be allowed to change award conditions through individual agreements with workers. Unions rejected this arguing that such a system would undermine award protection. The two groups hold contrasting views on which award provisions fall within the 20 allowable conditions.

These labour-market reforms reflect a fiercely contested, unresolved struggle for the soul of the nation. On the one side, the government is under intense pressure for further reform. Treasury warned that Australia had to reform 'at a faster pace than other countries'. (*The Australian*, 19 May 1997) Echoing the views of employer organizations, the Reserve Bank governor has argued that the Workplace Relations Act reforms 'had not gone far enough' and were 'less ambitious than those in the United Kingdom or New Zealand'. There was a need to 'speed labour market deregulation'. (*The Australian*, 16 May 1997) In response the Minister for Workplace Relations has promised 'a second wave of industrial reform' to be introduced at the next federal election. (*The Australian*, 27 July 1997) Whilst the pressures to further deregulate the labour market intensify, so too do the pressures emanating from those affected by the reforms. Recent studies reveal that Australia has become a tense, mistrustful, anxiety haunted society. Personal experience of downsizing and closures render the community's fears real and immediate. Deep pessimism and uncertainty stemming from the increasing numbers of companies moving their manufacturing base into Asia reflect the mood now dominating community and political life.[11] Even the government's own bureaucrats recognize that introducing further labour-market reforms will only serve to deepen the anxiety and the mounting anger against governments and political parties advocating the change. The Reserve Bank governor acknowledged that these reforms would be unpopular politically because they entailed 'reduced job security and the possibility of a new class of working poor emerging'. (*The Australian*, 16 May 1997) Whether or not this translates politically at future elections depends upon the degree to which the Labor Party continues to distance itself from labour market deregulation and other reforms that it had introduced.[12] However, notwithstanding particular political scenarios, possible electoral backlash against the reforms is a constraint on government, limiting the degree to which Australian labour markets can become a principal vehicle of competitive advantage.

The government recently conceded that labour-market reform alone would not establish Australia's international competitiveness. Other positive steps were needed. (*The Australian*, 14 July 1997) Indications are that the government is pinning its hopes on the possible introduction of Asian styled EPZs in Australia. In a move designed to counter the anger and fear generated by the closures and relocations the Industry Minister argued that EPZs that 'provide tax holidays' should be used to entice foreign investment and export activity. (*The Australian Financial Review*, 24 April 1997) This focus on EPZs heightened with closure of BHP Steel in Newcastle and the rumours of possible investment in Indonesia. When the Prime Minister visited Newcastle in July he stated that EPZs were being considered as part of the solution to the closure of BHP. In this we see how downward spiralling corporate tax rates are used as a competitive weapon. In this regard, a recent international tax survey is illuminating. The survey highlighted the way in which low Asian corporate tax rates are pressurizing OECD nations. The UK reduced its corporate rate to 31 per cent, which is well below the OECD and EU averages. The 15 member states of the OECD are presently considering a plan to introduce a code of conduct to end tax competition. (*The Australian Financial Review*, 11 July 1997)

In summary, this brief review of the rise of soft authoritarianism realized through individual contract unilateralism is but one aspect of Australia's hesitant, contradictory march to Asian styled employment relations. The analysis thus far has revealed that Australia's democratic institutions and culture have, to a degree, constrained this transition. Despite the new hostile environment, a national union movement of some two and a half million members remains a social force which employers and government are forced to negotiate with. National employers associations have goaded the government for its failure to secure the swift demise of trade unionism, characterizing conservative leaders as displaying weak leadership. These interventions have provoked the next stage in the industrial relations transition process: strategically planned, open warfare against union organization. Full scale planned attacks, the likes of which Australia has never seen before, have been launched against the mining and the maritime unions. These are Australia's strongest, most strategically placed unions. Defeat would rip the heart and muscle from the entire movement, leaving only the crippled corpse and battlefield memories of what were once one of the world's strongest labour movements.

War Declaration

War is defined as a state of open hostility, a conflict conducted by force, where ordinary law is suspended. In its determination to break union power swiftly rather than gradually through individual contracts, government and employers suspended the rules of democratic industrial relations. In so doing they adopted entirely new rules in their war game. This new form of intervention would test the strength of the trade-union movement and the power of Australia's democratic institutions, thereby providing some insight as to how far the society will embrace authoritarian labour regulation under the banner of global competitiveness.

The essential features of this conflict are now briefly reviewed. Concluding this chapter thus is pertinent to the general theme of this collection – globalization and labour relations, for, as was stated in the introduction, the outcome of these battles may define both the future of trade unionism and the character of global change into the new century. For as Roy Adams has commented, 'some industrial disputes rock the world'. (in *The Globe and Mail*, 30 April 1998) He noted the impact of the shipyard strike in Poland in 1980, the air traffic controllers strike in the US and the miners strike in the UK.

The shift to a warlike approach arose out of government and employers frustration with soft authoritarianism, which had only produced mixed results. The take up rate of individual contracts was uneven. A clear pattern had already emerged. Certain large mining multinationals are trying to impose the individual contract system, whilst leading manufacturing companies have maintained union-based arrangements, arguing that they will gain little advantage from the reforms.[13] Manufacturers assert that they would benefit more from a positive industry strategy that addresses the problems of import penetration and market access into Asia's tariff protected economies than in attempting to exclude trade unions.

Full-scale warfare is often preceded by skirmishes to assess the strength of the opposition. Hostilities against the MUA followed earlier attacks on the powerful Construction, Forestry, Mining and Energy Workers Union (CFMEU). Lengthy, bitterly fought disputes at Rio Tinto's Hunter Valley mine and at the US ARCO corporation's site in Central Queensland are indicative both of the corporate strategy of the mining multinationals and of union determination to resist the change. A five-week long strike was triggered at the Rio Tinto coal mine when the company tried to introduce AWAs to the 430 strong workforce with the intent of realizing more flexible work practices to get into the 20th century. (*The Australian*, 18 July 1997) These included freedom to use contractors, part-time, temporary or casual labour on any work as required; individual performance assessment; the right to allocate over-time at management's discretion, rather than through a union seniority list; and finally, the right to hire and fire on merit as decided by the company. The latter would replace recruitment from a union list of retrenched miners and retrenchment on a 'last on, first off' basis. The company offered a substantial $10,000 a year pay inducement as well as improvements in superannuation and medical benefits to any who volunteered for individual contracts. All but seven workers refused the contracts, insisting instead on a collective agreement. The stand off continues. At the Central Queensland mine, 250 workers have been on strike for 14 weeks after ARCO issued an ultimatum: sign individual contracts that would introduce the same set of conditions as sought by Rio Tinto, or face dismissal. The union has predicted that no one will take up the contracts because the union and the local communities were committed to the strike. The strike is costing the company $3 million a week. These attacks on unionized workplaces were merely a curtain raiser to the main play – the destruction of the MUA.

The Defining Struggle

The federal government prepared a game plan to break the MUA as meticulously as did Thatcher with the miners in the 1980s. In early 1997 a secret plan to de-unionize the Australian waterfront was prepared by government paid consultants. The attack was justified by arguing that the introduction of non-union labour was essential to Australia's international competitiveness. (*The Australian Financial Review*, 15 August 1997) The plan included an assessment of legal issues surrounding such action. The ACCI issued a users' guide listing legal remedies to hit the union when they reacted to this government initiative. Over the past year, the Prime Minister repeatedly vowed to break the MUA. The strategy to achieve this end is now outlined and the events surrounding its implementation are described.

Prelude: Activating a Covert War Plan

Secret documents reveal that plans were developed as early as March 1997 to train a non-union workforce to take over, following the engineering of mass dismissals. The document stated, 'Stevedores would need to activate well-prepared strategies to dismiss their workforce and replace them with another, quickly, in a way that limited the prospect, for example, of the commission (Australian Industrial Relations Commission) ordering reinstatement'.[14]

In early December 1997 the MUA discovered and exposed a secret operation to train new stevedores in Dubai, a free trade zone where foreign workers predominate and where trade unions are outlawed. The 70 trainees were from the Australian Defense Force. Two former Special Armed Services (SAS) commandos were placed in charge of the operation. The group was sent to Dubai to participate in an estimated $30 million project. When the scheme was exposed, the ITF threatened to blockade Dubai. The trade dependent Dubai government immediately caved in and cancelled the trainees' visas. The project was abandoned on 14 December. This military styled operation then moved to Melbourne. One of the SAS organizers of the aborted exercise explained to a meeting in Melbourne organized by a Commando Association that plans had been formulated to trigger a major waterfront dispute in April. Fynwest, a company established by the SAS leaders, entered into arrangements with a company that had been recently established by the National Farmers Federation (NFF) called P & C Stevedores Ltd. The latter had secured a $20 million 'war chest' from business donors. The companies were granted a two-year lease of Melbourne's Webb Dock from Patrick.

On the night of 28 January, Patrick cancelled the evening and midnight shift at Webb Dock. A battalion of security guards armed with riot gear, shields and batons obtained from the Victorian Prisons Department, were sent in to secure the wharf. Under orders from Patrick, they took control of the massive portainer cranes and locked out the MUA workforce. The Patrick Stevedore trainees included ex-army personnel and persons were brought in from New Zealand.

The MUA responded through strike action against Patrick in Melbourne and Sydney. Opportunity for such action presented itself when discussions began on a new enterprise agreement with Patrick. Having already committed itself to major action against the union in April, the company was in no mood to negotiate a new agreement. While the MUA sought to preserve existing award conditions, the company demanded the abandonment of overtime rates, annual leave and sick leave entitlements and a substantial change in the wage structure. The strikes, including a week-long stoppage at Sydney's Port Botany terminal, the country's second largest, had a significant impact. For example, 500 containers representing $15 million of cargo that included refrigerated meat, wool and milk powder was left stranded on Melbourne's docks as a result of a 48-hour strike at East Swanson dock. Patrick claimed it had lost $10 million since January 1997 and was close to bankruptcy as a result of the actions. This was a mere prelude to the main event – the dramatic firing of Patrick's entire workforce on the evening of 7 April.

Capital Strike

Around 11 pm on Tuesday, 7 April, Patrick effected a lock out of the unionized workforce. Almost simultaneously and under the cover of darkness, the company moved security guards, clad in black and holding German Shepherd dogs, capsicum spray and batons into all the major port terminals. The struggle for the future of trade unionism in Australia had begun.

As news of these events broke, the government stated that it was determined to achieve waterfront reform. A news commentator noted, 'Margaret Thatcher took on the coalminers and won; Ronald Reagan sacked air traffic controllers and won; and John Howard picked a fight with the warfies and...watch this space.' Howard, a great admirer of Thatcher and Reagan, would love to be bracketed with them in a pantheon of union busting heroes. (*The Australian*, 9 April 1998)

Howard's Industrial Relations Minister, Reith, hailed the action as 'a decisive turning point in the history of the waterfront'. (*The West Australian*, 8 April 1998)

Patrick director, Chris Corrigan stated, 'We will move forward with a new workforce which, like most Australians, wants to do a fair day's work for a fair day's pay. This initiative will improve dramatically Australia's international competitiveness and open the nation's gateways to the world's best practice'. (*The Australian*, 8 April 1998) A business analyst David Barnett enthused that the sacking of Patrick's unionized workforce and their replacement by one third of the number of contract workers 'was a great step forward for Australian manufacturers. Their costs will fall, and their prospects of becoming successful exporters will rise, after the removal of an economic burden which the whole nation carries'. (*The Australian Financial Review*, 9 April 1998)

Both the company and the government had long prepared for this moment. They were convinced that their strategy, which had never been used against trade unions in quite the same form, would achieve a swift outcome. There were four principal elements to this strategy: a capital strike, a propaganda war, redundancy and legal sanctions against local and international solidarity. While all these features were important features of the overall strategy, only the capital strike will be briefly elaborated since this element provides an insight into a new set of anti-union tactics, spawned by globalization ideology. This is pertinent to the book's central theme, the obvious question being, do such novel tactics present a possibility for emulation in other nations?

Barnett confidently asserted, 'It would seem that Patrick, Patrick Stevedores, the government and Australia cannot lose this fight, so well has the ground been prepared'. (*ibid*) This meticulous planning was nowhere more evident than in the restructuring of Patrick that was designed to effect a capital strike. In September 1997, some six months prior to the established D-Day, Patrick began a corporate restructure that would permit a capital strike against the union. On the 23 September, Patrick completed a complex inter-company transaction, which they believed would enable them to legally dismiss their entire workforce and contract a new one. To give effect to this they realized the restructure shown in Figure 10.1.

The establishment of this new complex web of holding companies and subsidiaries was designed to achieve the following effect. On 23 September, without the workforce recognizing the implication of the change, the employment of 2100 workers by Patrick Stevedore Holdings was transferred to four new subsidiaries, National Stevedore Tasmania, Patrick Stevedore No. 1, 2 and 3. These four subsidiaries were labour hire companies that employed workers and on-sold employment services to a company especially established to purchase those services, Patrick Stevedore Operations 2. This company was owned by Patrick Stevedore Holdings, which was in turn owned by Lang Corporation.

Figure 10.1

The Complex Web of Holding Companies and Subsidiaries of Patrick

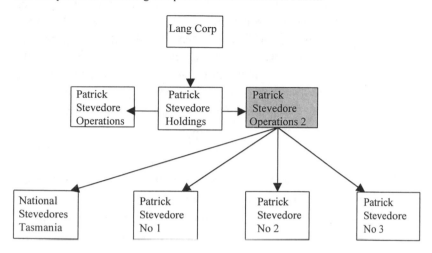

Prior to 23 September 1997, each of these subsidiaries owned assets and the business of the stevedoring operation at particular ports as well as employing the labour for that operation. On 23 September, the subsidiaries sold the assets and the business agreements to Patrick Stevedore Operations 2 under a Business Purchase Agreement (BPA). These labour hire companies were stripped of $300 million which was used in new share deals and the repayment of debt. Consequently, the labour hire companies had no assets. Under the BPA, Patrick Stevedore Operations 2 owed between $14 and $16 million to the subsidiaries. Each of the subsidiaries entered into a Labour Service Agreement (LSA) with Patrick Stevedore Operations. Clause 2.3(h) of each LSA stated 'The Contractor will ensure that the performance of the Services are not interfered with or delayed or hindered for any reason'. The LSA went on to state that should this provision be breached, a rectification notice will be issued to the Contractor. If the breach is not rectified within a 30-day period, the LSA can be immediately terminated.

Clearly, the LSA gave Patrick the power to strip the labour hire companies of their only remaining asset – labour. This would render the subsidiaries insolvent and as a consequence, allow Patrick to claim that the workforce had not been dismissed but had in fact been rendered redundant. Patrick believed that Australian Corporations law placed them in an unassailable position because holding companies are not necessarily liable for the debts or decisions of a subsidiary. Since the subsidiaries had no assets, creditors, including unpaid workers, would find it impossible to launch legal action to retrieve money or their jobs. When the entire workforce was locked out on the evening of the 7 April, Patrick claimed that they had not been dismissed but that the labour hire companies had become insolvent and had been placed under an administrator. On the 7th, Patrick entered into a new set of labour hire arrangements with the farmers' PCS Resources who agreed to provide 353 workers under three-month contracts. They also entered into a three-year maintenance contract with Genelect Engineering Services Pty Ltd.

In the long history of conflict between capital and labour, capital strikes are not uncommon. Capital has often withdrawn funds from businesses and in some instances entire industries in the face of worker demands and the need to drive the rate of profit higher. Globalization has facilitated the process of transfer between nations and regions. Patrick's action is, however, one of those rare instances where the providers of capital hope to immediately continue operating in the same locations, under the same name, but with a new, dramatically cheaper workforce. Financial analysts have calculated that as a result of the mass sackings, Patrick could reduce its wage bill by 62 per cent, cutting the unionized wage bill from $112 million a year to a mere $42 million for the contract workers. (*The Australian Financial Review*, 9 April 1998) This would enable a pre-tax profit rate on investment of 11 per cent, which the institutional investors argue is still not high enough. Company accounts reveal an increasing level of profit. Patrick made a profit of $10,911,000 for the 1995 financial year. This doubled in 1996 to come in at $20,431,000. However, the problem for Patrick is their massive debt leverage, which is an underlying pressure on the company to attain high rates of return on investment. Once Patrick took the action the share price of Lang Corporation surged by 15 per cent to a record high of $2.19.

This strategy raises the following question that is highly pertinent to the general theme of the book: have globalization policies of financial and economic deregulation not, to some degree, transformed the nature of capital itself? Of course, there is an awareness of the ways in which these policies have created a highly mobile capital that has accelerated the internationalization of corporations. This has enhanced the power of companies to act against trade unions through capital movements from nations where strong unions exist to nations where unions are repressed. The current dispute reveals ways in which globalization ideology has empowered companies to take more direct action. Patrick did not have to enter into a chase around the globe for union-free ports where they could try to achieve higher profit rates. They could use corporate law in Australia to challenge union rights. This radical strategy was a product of the changed nature of capital itself. Patrick expresses this most clearly. The company is an example of the 'new, elusive and less predictable capital' driven by the large investment funds in 'the big end of town', commented Mark Westfield. (in *The Australian Financial Review*, 9 April 1998) This is not a traditional stevedoring company, prepared to give and take, but essentially live with the union. Rather, the company represented 'the fast money of the 1980s and 1990s when financial engineering designed to empower relatively small investments with massive leverage dazzled the marketplace of the day. Corrigan and Scanlon bought Patrick in 1993 with one aim only: to reduce the number of stevedores and then to make money out of the business'. (*ibid*) High gearing meant a high indebtedness to the banks and other financial institutions. These represent a capital impatient for swiftly secured high returns. As evidenced by the substantial increase in Patrick's share price immediately following the mass sackings, these institutions are impatient with social institutions such as trade unions that may constrain the quick money path in some way. This aggressive, short-term focus that is so hostile to trade unionism, is a product of globalization policy.

The other principal elements of the strategy against the union also enhance understanding of the tensions between globalization policies and the sustenance of democratic rights within nations. The Australian government and Patrick launched an intensive propaganda war against the MUA that essentially demonized dock workers as overpaid, lazy people who are unproductive and are therefore costing the nation dearly. Using liberal economic discourse, both claimed that this situation had arisen because of the monopoly control of the MUA. There is not the space in this chapter to enter into the complexities of waterfront productivity. However, it is important to note that a global efficiency discourse centred on notions of international benchmarks, always appears to claim a moral high ground, placing trade unions on the defensive. Efficiency is equated with flexibility, which is equated with union-free workplaces. Unions are presented as a barrier to these outcomes. In reality unions are a barrier to massive cuts in wages and conditions (a 62 per cent reduction in the case of Patrick) which is the real flexibility agenda.

The government and Patrick also believed that they could win the day by buying out the unionized workforce. The government offered to directly finance redundancies in the hope that the unionized workforce would quickly accept the cash. In its initial announcement the government stated that it was advancing $250 million for redundancies and that workers would receive up to $250,000 each. However, the MUA quickly revealed that this was a distortion. The actual redundancies being offered were in the region of $70,000. The government also warned that any international solidarity action would be met by the full force of the new industrial laws that imposed huge penalties against parties involved in organizing trade boycotts. They launched immediate High Court action against the ITF in London.

Trial of Strength

The government and Patrick were of the view that with the forces that their combined power represented, their pre-emptive strike would achieve a swift and clean transition to a new industrial order on Australia's waterfront. Confidence resided in the notion that trade unions were essentially a spent force. There might be a last gasp but this was not likely to derail the bold, decisive action taken.

In this regard, the government and Patrick seriously miscalculated in three fundamental areas. Firstly, they miscalculated the resilience and the wider popular appeal of trade unionism in Australia. This is not to say that a majority of Australians supported the MUA. In reality, the action against the MUA created deep divisions with the population. However, when the maritime union organized pickets at every Patrick terminal across Australia, union members received widespread community support. The mass picketing prevented the movement of any containers in or out of Patrick's terminals for over a month. The company had succeeded in bringing non-union labour in, but they could not succeed in conducting normal trade. As was the case in Eastern Europe in the late 1980s, the events again revealed the potential of a people's power movement in the face of even the most determined strategy. There were numerous moments when the police concentrated in numbers in a determined effort to break the pickets and force a pathway for the heavy-duty trucks. With few exceptions they failed simply because the vast numbers of people on the line far outweighed police resources. Forcibly breaking up lines involving thousands of people and bundling them into police vehicles appeared to be something neither the government nor the police had the political will to carry through. Many ordinary citizens who joined the lines, had never done so before. They were simply people who were outraged by the attack on a democratic institution that, if successful, would change the face of Australian society.

Secondly, they miscalculated the international trade-union reaction to the events and the power of their secondary boycott laws to prevent international solidarity action. They sought to muzzle the ITF through successfully taking out a High Court injunction in London against the ITF organizing international boycott action. However, the government lost an appeal against the ruling. Unions as far afield as South Africa, Japan and the United States put plans in place to boycott any Australian shipping loaded with non-union labour. Australian produce was also a target. A special national shop steward council of maritime workers in South Africa under the banner of the Congress of South African Trade Unions (COSATU) decided on an indefinite boycott of all shipping and all Australian goods. Five hundred protesters from the International Longshore and Warehouse Union prevented the Columbus Matson from being unloaded when it docked in Los Angeles on the 9 May. Contrary to government expectations, Australian law appears to have little force when applied internationally.

Thirdly, they miscalculated legally. Section 298K(1) of the Workplace Relations Act protects the right of workers to belong to a union. The MUA succeeded in gaining an injunction against Patrick, which requires the company to reinstate the sacked workers until the outcome of a court case brought by the union claiming unlawful sackings. Despite appeals taking the original Federal Court decision to a Full Bench and then to the High Court, the reinstatement ruling held with the judges contending that there was an arguable case of unlawful conspiracy.

As a result of the court orders, the administrator of the Patrick labour hire companies has been forced to remove the Patrick Stevedore workers and re-employ the unionized workforce. However, despite the court victory, the MUA is still in a tenuous position, given the fact that the labour hire companies have been stripped of their assets. The government and Patrick have warned that unless the MUA agree to significant changes the labour hire companies will go into liquidation. They are demanding that the MUA accept non-union labour onto the docks and the right of stevedore companies to outsource work. They are also demanding radical changes in award conditions and a 66 per cent cut in the workforce. Reith has warned that 'it is crunch time for the union' which has to decide 'whether or not these companies head towards liquidation or whether they'll sensibly agree to a set of reforms'.

The MUA retorted that they would refuse to respond 'with a gun at our heads'. (*The West Australian*, 12 May 1998)

Conclusion: Globalization and the Future of Trade Unionism

This chapter has analysed the historic industrial relations transition in Australia. The democratic system where the state watched over the welfare and prosperity of workers is being transformed into a more authoritarian system where workers expect little except a tanning from market forces. The conflict on the Australian waterfront captures the contradictions of this transition. Government and influential employers seek a swift, clean transition. However, as the dock dispute reveals, Australia's democratic institutions and traditions are constraining a full-blown transition. In particular, the Australian trade-union movement has demonstrated its resilience in the face of the best planned most co-ordinated attack ever waged against Australian trade unions. Conservative analysts had predicted that the unions would crumble before these powerful forces and that any reaction to the mass sackings would merely be a last gasp.

One can conclude from the analysis that present globalization policies undermine democratic institutions and culture in general and industrial relations in particular. Discourse and practice allow little space for strong, independent trade unions, capable of challenging the logic of unfettered global market forces. For as Michel Camdessus, the head of the IMF warned when he visited Australia in the midst of the waterfront dispute, 'labour market practices cannot be insulated from market conditions'. (*The Australian*, 6 May 1998) Market authoritarianism is transmitted through corporations that have internationalized as they use practices in countries such as China as a benchmark to assess practices embodied within democratic industrial relations systems.

Clearly the relationship between trade unionism and the current policies and practices of globalization is a problematic one. European unions are shielded from these pressures to a degree as a result of the cultural depth of social democracy and the sheer economic size and global power of the EU. The demise of Australian trade unionism would nevertheless further isolate the EU as one of the few remaining instances where collective rights of association are in any way protected. Australia is a relatively small player on the global stage. However, its union movement is internationally significant. The movement's demise would undoubtedly be a set back to trade unionism generally. Equally, if the present storms are ridden out successfully, images of a fight for democratic rights in the workplace, strongly supported by the community and international unionism may well prove to be a model for a global renewal of trade unionism.

This renewal of trade unionism provides just a glimmer of hope that the logic of neo-liberal globalization is beginning to be seriously challenged. The challenge that is emerging is certainly not confined to the intense battles being waged on the Australian waterfront. The newly emergent unions in Asia are on stage, acting to undermine the logic of lean production which is the essence of the present form of global restructuring. (Moody 1997) In January 1997 the Korean Confederation of Trade Unions (KCTU) launched a nation-wide general strike against the state's attempts to undermine employment. On 27 May 1998, the KCTU launched a two-day general strike and threatened further general strikes in June unless the government repealed the Mass Dismissal Law and the Temporary Employment Agency Law. The two laws were introduced in February 1998 as the government used the economic crisis as an opportunity to assert that labour-market flexibility and the capacity of companies to downsize was essential to South Korea's international competitiveness and capacity to recover economically. The general strike had as its central demand the repeal of these laws. The imposition of the latter law reveals a strategy that is remarkably similar to the one pursued by Patrick and the government in Australia. The KCTU leadership argued that the Temporary Employment Agency Law which permits the establishment of labour hire companies 'has opened the door to a widespread replacement of regular full-time workers with temporary workers'.[15] As was the strategy with Patrick, this opens the way for the replacement of full-time, unionized workers with non-union, contract workers. Kim Moon Seok, a Hyundai Union leader warned, 'We will fight against the company's unilateral layoffs to the end'. (*Australian Financial Review*, 27 May 1998)

Indonesia's 'May Revolution' led by students resulted in Suharto's resignation. (*Far Eastern Economic Review*, 28 May 1998) Significantly, one of the first reform acts of the newly installed President Habibie was to free the internationally recognized leader of one of the main independent union movements in Indonesia, the Indonesian Prosperity Union (SBSI) which had its illegal status dropped. The country's new Labour Minister stated that Indonesia would, for the first time, ratify ILO Conventions on freedom of association. Unionists have already announced the formation of the Indonesian Workers Party. One can predict that the long suppressed independent unions are likely to re-emerge with a flourish. This will impact not only on the democracy struggle in Indonesia but also on the dynamic of globalization itself.

We are therefore witnessing in these intense struggles the birth of forces that may well develop the capacity to challenge the lean sculptured globalization that has so undermined independent unionism since the late 1970s. For as Moody (1997, p. 3) has argued, unionism became transformed during this period into 'global business unionism' which came to support corporate restructuring in the cause of global competitiveness. He argued that when unions support 'massive downsizing in the name of competitiveness it is a dead end for workers and their unions'. (Moody 1997, p. 2) Perhaps the present intense struggles in Australia, Indonesia and South Korea are indeed indicative of a break with these decades of the backward march of labour, where unions had simply become the bearers of bad news to their own members and through their complicity in restructuring, to workers in general. These struggles capture the mood of 'tense, mistrustful, anxiety-haunted societies' where globalization has produced deep insecurity, as Hobsbawm observed. (*The Guardian Weekly*, 30 June 1996) The new struggles are signalling a new path, new militant response that produces hope that a sense of security and predictability in working life can be reclaimed. Certainly the sense of people power that has been forged on the streets of Jakarta, the docklands across Australia and in the large conglomerates of South Korea, is willing that transformed future. Success in this new venture cannot be predicted at this early stage. What can be said, however, is that this renewal reveals a trade unionism that is far from being the spent force that conservatives have predicted. Deep international linkages now exist between these union movements. A new internationalism is being forged as each comes to the aid of the other in the midst of these ferocious battles.[16]

Notes

1. Debates on the Multi-lateral Agreement on Investment are one indicator of this transition stage between internationalization and globalization.
2. Formed in May 1925, the ACFTU had grown out of the intense anti-colonial struggles that followed the nationalists 1911 defeat of the Qing dynasty. The establishment of the Kuomintang party (KMT) and the Chinese Communist party (CCP) during this period foreshadowed a split in the unions. Following the KMT attack on communist unions from 1927, the CPP prioritized peasant struggle and

tended to neglect union work in the urban centres. Consequently, when the CPP came to power in 1949, the ACFTU was not in a strong bargaining position.

3. Between 1950 and the reforms of 1979, this subordination was highly contested. Arguments for a more autonomous role for unions expressed during the 1956 Hundred Flowers Campaign were quickly crushed by the 'anti-rightist' purge that followed. The silencing of the ACFTU during the Cultural Revolution was followed by its reinstatement under Deng as having a key role in the four modernizations. For an excellent summary history see Asia Labour Monitor (1988).

4. Apo Leong's article 'Labour Rights in the Pearl River Delta' (1997) reported that a migrant worker was locked up in a dog cage with two Alsation dogs for five hours when he was allegedly found stealing some toys from a Taiwanese joint-venture in Shenzen. Reported in *Apple Daily* (Chinese), Hong Kong, 16 September 1995. In another reported incident, three young migrant workers were forced to kneel in front of all employees in a hat factory wearing cardboard signs saying 'I am a thief' and were beaten for allegedly stealing some leather shoe bottoms and making themselves shoes. In reaction, 190 of the company's 600 workers resigned in protest. Reported in *South China Morning Post*, Hong Kong, 6 December 1996.

5. *Search and Destroy: Hunting Down free trade unions in China*, ICFTU, April 1997. The report provides evidence of the forms of brutal repression taken against those who attempt to foster independent unionism in China. This includes physical abuse combined with the placement of these unionists in prison sections reserved for inmates carrying infectious diseases, primarily tuberculosis and hepatitis; the denial of access to proper medical care even when they have contracted diseases and the harassment of family and relatives of unionists. The report points out that these practices contravene the UN Convention against Torture and other Cruel, Inhuman or Degrading Treatment or Punishment that has been ratified by China. See also the *US 1996 Human Rights Report* on China, Bureau of Democracy, Human Rights, and Labor, 30 January 1997.

6. GEW, the joint-venture in Shenzhen was not unionized. The company employed 1300 women workers whose average age was 18. GEW paid 700 Yuen for the work permit of each. This was deducted from the worker's wage over the first 12 months of employment. Should a worker be dismissed during this period for misconduct or because they were not sufficiently productive, they were required to repay the balance. Field research, May 1993.

7. These arguments are embodied within the Business Council of Australia's, *Enterprise Bargaining: A Better Way of Working*, which focused and set the terms of the labour-market deregulation debate. Politically, these ideas were expressed in the 1993 Liberal Party document, Jobsback.

8. *The West Australian*, 8 August 1997. The article commented on a survey of 4500 workers on workplace stress conducted by the ACTU which found that 36 per cent were stressed by company restructuring and 29 per cent worked long and unpredictable hours. Chamber of Commerce and Industry of Western Australia spokesperson on health and safety made the comment on the positive value of stress.

9. Under the new Western Australian laws, union access to workplaces was severely restricted, a complex system of secret ballots for strikes introduced and industrial action circumscribed through a loose definition of essential services. Contravention of these restrictions can result in specified fines and common law action.

10. The Coalition government was forced to compromise in a number of areas due to pressure from a minority political party, The Australian Democrats who controlled the Senate. Lower House bills have to be approved in the Senate after they have been passed in the Assembly. However, whilst the compromises limited wage flexibility through retaining Award rates as benchmarks, the government achieved its primary goal of creating a labour-market system that promoted individual employment contracts over collective bargaining.

11. Metal Trades Industry Association Report, Make or Break: Seven Steps to make Australia rich again, August 1997. The conclusions of the report are based on two surveys. The first surveyed 200 Australian and overseas executives. The second surveyed community attitudes and confidence levels.

12. The Labor Party has vigorously opposed the Workplace Relations Act and more recently they have rejected the form of labour-market deregulation that they themselves introduced – enterprise bargaining. They are also calling for a slowdown in tariff reductions.

13. This conclusion is drawn from current research I am engaged in that explores the restructuring of Australian manufacturing and its relocation into Asia. All companies surveyed have avoided confronting unions on the issue of individual contracts. All are positive about the constructive role that Australian trade unions have played in workplace change.

14. From the MUA document, *War on the Waterfront*, p. 7, published on the 8 April 1998. Also available on the internet: http://mua.tcp.net.au/Pages/war.html

15. KCTU communique, 25 May 1998, entitled, *Stage is set for a Historic Encounter: KCTU calls for Negotiations and a General Strike*.

16. Linkages between unions in the region that have been forged over the past decade are now receiving widespread international support from the established international trade-union movement through the ICFTU and through the various International Trade Secretariats. The linkages are leading to an inexorable shift from global business unionism to global social movement unionism. The main characteristics of this new internationalism that is regionally initiated, may be summarized thus. 'Regional Linkages': The union initiative seeks to link workers across a region where the differences in regulation and production regimes are extreme. The singular aim of such a linkage is the acceleration of the growth of independent unionism in nations where democratic organizing rights are denied. Linkages have therefore been made with unions in Asia that are emerging outside of the system of authoritarian regulation. 'Militant Internationalism': The internationalism that has emerged out of these linkages has exploited the vulnerability created by globalization. Economic integration has increased the level of trade and communications dependency of nations. Boycott pressure can be applied to the extent that unions are well organized in these sectors. This action worked successfully in 1995 when the Western Australian government was forced to withdraw new anti-union laws as a result of militant union action in Australia combined with the threat of shipping and airline boycotts. These pressures

worked again in 1997 and 1998 when the Australian government attempted to introduce non-union labour on the Australian waterfront. 'Global social movement unionism': Engagement in international action has resulted in moves to create a genuinely global unionism. The international trigger can be pulled quickly only if union leaders (officials, organizers, delegates) and members in these strategic sectors have the possibility of internalizing a deep and sophisticated internationalist culture. What is meant by this is that leadership and membership come to understand working-class issues in other nations as well as they understand their own struggles. This is an organizational question that unions in the region believe can be resolved through a rotating exchange of delegate level leaders. These exchanges would result in an inculturation process as the persons involved would lead educational seminars on the issues that their own movement faced. Cultural symbols in the form of posters, banners, stickers would be exchanged. This is essential preparation to ensure that the grass roots is well prepared ahead of the crises for it is ordinary workers who, in the final instance, have to implement boycott decisions. Boycott action has been successful where attention has been paid to the development of an international class culture. Such moves at union integration are an important first step towards the creation of global unionism which reflects a deeper, organic sectoral linkage of national union movements across the key regions of the new global economy. Global unionism assumes a social movement character because the radical step of boycott action cannot be taken unless the affected union is already engaged in national action. As the recent maritime strike in Australia illustrates, such action assumes a social movement character as sectors of the community join with the union movement in the defence of working class rights. 'A new working class politics': This alternative organizational form, which has already come into existence, will only consolidate if it is accompanied by a new class politics that will challenge the neo-liberal globalization model which unions have adopted. This would involve a renewal of the sense of class interests in the globalization process and commitment to the politics of resisting the logic of global lean production. Unions linked into the regional initiative all identify themselves as socialist. The challenge is to translate this politics into defined stages the first of which is the rebuilding of political movements to represent working-class interests and unions with the capacity of pushing back the frontier of control in the workplace.

References

Chan, A. (1997), 'Labour Rights are Human Rights: Chinese Workers under "Market Socialism", unpublished.

Davis, E. and R. Lansbury (1993), *International and Comparative Industrial Relations*, Sydney: Allen and Unwin.

Gao, M. (1997), 'Migrant Workers from Rural China: Their Conditions and Some Social Implications for Economic Development in South China', in D. Schak (ed.), *Entrepreneurship, Economic Growth and Social*

Change: The Transformation of Southern China, Brisbane: Griffith University, Centre for the Study of Australia-Asia Relations.

Garnaut, R. (1987), *Australian Protectionism*, Sydney: Allen and Unwin.

Greenfield, G. and A. Leong (1997), 'Workers Under China's Communist Capitalism', *Socialist Register*, London: Merlin Press.

Gruen, F.H. (1985), 'How Bad is Australia's Economic Performance and Why?', Discussion Paper No. 127, Center for Economic Policy Research, Australian National University.

Hirst, P. and G. Thompson (1996), *Globalization in Question*, Cambridge: Polity Press.

Hong Kong Trade Union Education Centre (1990), *A Moment of Truth: Workers' Participation in China's 1989 Democracy Movement and the Emergence of Independent Unions*, Hong Kong: Hong Kong Trade Union Education Centre.

Howard, P. and R. Howard (1995), 'The Campaign to Eliminate Job Security in China', *Journal of Contemporary Asia*, **25** (3), 338-55.

Hyman, R. (1989), *The Political Economy of Industrial Relations*, Basingstoke: Macmillan.

Kelly, P. (1992), *The End of Uncertainty: The Story of the 1980s*, Sydney: Allen and Unwin.

Lambert, R. (1997), *State and Labour in New Order Indonesia*, Perth: University of Western Australia Press.

Leong, A. (1997), 'Labour Rights in the Pearl River Delta', in J. Porges (ed.), *At What Price? Workers in China*, Hong Kong: Asia Monitor Resource Centre.

Marx, K. (1976), *Capital: A Critique of Political Economy*, 1, Penguin Books.

Moody, K. (1997), *Workers in a Lean World*, London: Verso.

Pusey, M (1991), *Economic Rationalism in Canberra: A Nation Building State Changes its Mind*, New York: Cambridge University Press.

Rickard, J. (1984), *H.B. Higgins*, Sydney: Allen and Unwin.

Solinger, D. (1997), 'Employment Channels and Job Categories Among the "Floating Population"', in G. O'Leary (ed.), *Adjusting to Capitalism: Chinese Workers and their State*, Armonk, New York: M.E. Sharpe.

Strange, S. (1996), *The Retreat of the State: The Diffusion of Power in the World Economy*, Cambridge: Cambridge University Press.

Ward, R. (1958), *The Australian Legend*, Melbourne: Oxford University Press.

Wing-yue, L. (1988), *Smashing the Iron Rice Pot: Workers and Unions in China's Market Socialism*, Hong Kong: Asia Monitor Resource Centre.

Zysman, J. (1996), 'The Myth of a Global Economy: Enduring National Foundations and Emerging Regional Realities', *New Political Economy*, **1** (2), 157-84.

Index

ABB, 66
Accornero, A., 111
accountability, 68–70, 72
activism, 111–12
Adam, B., 141
Adams, R., 232
Addison, J.T., 123
adjustment, 12–14
advanced countries, 53–4
   impact of globalization, 17–18
      on wages and welfare provision,
      48–52
   supra-national regulation, 23–4
   Third World competition and jobs in,
      42–4
Agfa, 172
Airline Flight Database, 175
Akzo Nobel, 16–17
Albert, M., 18
All China Federation of Trade Unions
   (ACFTU), 222–3, 224
Allen, V.L., 195
Altvater, E., 17, 25, 26, 102
AND International Publishers, 172–3
Anderson, B., 94
Angell, I., 78
Anglo-Saxon capitalism, 18, 20
arbitrary conglomerates, 170
arbitration and awards system, 218–19,
   230
ARCO, 233
Asia, 214–15, 216–17, 225–7
   see also under individual countries
assistant geologists, 200, 201
association, freedom of, 216–17
AT&T, 172
Attali, J., 57, 64–5
attitudinal climate survey, 203–4
Australia, 26–7, 30–1, 212–48
   Conciliation and Arbitration Act, 218
   conflict, 212–13, 232–42
      capital strike, 235–40
      covert war plan, 233–4
      declaration of war, 232–3
      defining struggle, 233–4
      endgame, 212–14

      trial of strength, 240–2
   democratic industrial relations
      system, 218–19
   Federal Act, 228
   home appliances industry, 225–7
   labour relations reform, 227–32
   Trade Practices Act, 228
   Workplace Relations Act, 212, 227,
      230, 241
Australian Chamber of Commerce and
   Industry (ACCI), 230, 233–4
Australian Defense Force, 234
Australian Industrial Relations
   Commission (AIRC), 228, 229,
   230
Australian Workplace Agreements
   (AWAs), 229, 233
Austria, 50
authoritarianism, 216–17
   China, 219–24
   global impact, 225–7
   soft in Australia, 227–32
automobile industry, 71
autonomy, 87, 88
   relative, 64–6, 69–70
awards, 218–19, 230

Bach, H., 26
Bairoch, P., 37–8
Bamforth, K.W., 195
Bank of International Settlements, 47
Barnett, D., 236
Bechterman, G., 14–15, 24
Beck, U., 142, 148
Beukema, L., 17, 147, 152, 154
BHP, 218–19, 231
Black and Decker, 225
Blomström, M., 44–5
bonded labour system, 222
book publishing, 177
Bourdieu, P., 14
Bourguinat, H., 60
boycotts, 241
Boyer, R., 3, 8, 22, 60, 79, 102, 129
   'pure' market functioning, 89
Bretton Woods system, 46, 47